THE
GREAT
MONEY
BUBBLE

THE
GREAT MONEY BUBBLE

Protect Yourself from the
Coming Inflation Storm

DAVID A. STOCKMAN

Humanix Books
www.humanixbooks.com

Humanix Books

The Great Money Bubble
Copyright © 2022 by David A. Stockman
All rights reserved

Humanix Books, P.O. Box 20989, West Palm Beach, FL 33416, USA
www.humanixbooks.com | info@humanixbooks.com

Humanix Books is a division of Humanix Publishing, LLC. Its trademark,
consisting of the words "Humanix Books," is registered in the Patent and
Trademark Office and in other countries.

Disclaimer: The information presented in this book is meant to be used for
general resource purposes only; it is not intended as specific financial advice
for any individual and should not substitute financial advice from a finance
professional.

ISBN: 9-781-63006-219-4 (Hardcover)
ISBN: 9-781-63006-220-0 (E-book)

Printed in the United States of America
10 9 8 7 6 5 4 3 2 1

Contents

Chapter 1

Washington's Infernal Inflation Machine

Inflation has always been about more than bothersome high prices, such as a three-dollar cup of coffee or a four-dollar gallon of gasoline. And nowadays, it also encompasses far more than the simplistic idea that inflation reflects too much money chasing too few goods.

Under today's policy regime, in fact, inflation is global, virulent, and ubiquitous. That's because it's the toxic spawn of unhinged central bankers who have flooded the financial system with trillions of fiat credits snatched from thin digital air in a manner that contradicts and defies every textbook written before 1995.

This bacchanalia of central bank credit and liquidity is economically and socially ruinous. It showers windfalls on the rich while penalizing workers, savers, retirees, small businesses, and most of Main Street economic life, even as it fosters rampant fiscal profligacy in Washington and egregiously speculative excesses on Wall Street.

How did we get here? It starts with the late economist Milton Friedman, the originator of the common "too much money, too few goods" view of inflation's origin. His anti-gold, pro–Federal Reserve monetary philosophy—one followed by his myopic disciple Ben Bernanke, the former Fed chair—makes Friedman one of the great villains among the macroeconomic thinkers of modern times. Nevertheless, his famous rule of money supply growth does shine a powerful spotlight on the infernal inflation machine that has arisen on the banks of the Potomac.

More than a half century ago, Friedman contended that as a matter of common sense, high-powered money—represented by the Federal Reserve's balance sheet—should grow no faster than the economy itself. If the money multiplier remained constant, therefore, the broader money supply would also be constrained to a fixed growth rate of around 3 percent so as not to validate inflationary GDP gains above the real growth capacity of the economy.

Let's consider how that idea worked out in practice as measured by the Fed's balance sheet—which, like any bank (and any business or household), has assets and liabilities. The assets are U.S. Treasury securities and government-guaranteed mortgage debt. Its liabilities are U.S. currency in circulation and dollars held in reserve at the Fed by ordinary banks.

On the eve of the Lehman Brothers meltdown, in September 2008, the Fed's balance sheet stood at $925 billion. It had taken nearly 94 years to get there from the day the bank first opened for business, in late 1914. In a sense, that roughly $10 billion per year average growth of the Fed's balance sheet reflected the orthodox central bankers' version of the Ohio State football team offense: three yards and a cloud of dust, relentlessly moving the monetary football slowly down the field.

So at Milton Friedman's rule of thumb of 3 percent growth per year from its September 2008 level, the Fed's balance sheet today should stand at $1.3 trillion. Alas, it's actually pushing $8.8 trillion and expanding at a $1.44 trillion annual rate, at least until further notice from the wannabe monetary politburo that today rules all finance and economics from the Fed's headquarters in the Eccles building in Washington.

The wellspring of today's virulent inflation is the $7 trillion excess above Friedman's rule that has been piled high on the Fed's balance sheet. That's modern inflation in its protean form. It's the monetary fuel of what I call Washington's infernal inflation machine.

Debt Tsunami

Well-nigh all of today's economic ills arise from this bloated balance sheet. These include slowing real GDP growth, hollowed-out domestic industry, stagnant real wages, rising wealth maldistribution, runaway government debt, massive speculation and financial bubbles, a nation of indentured debt serfs, and most recently, surging prices for goods and services.

Because it is so monumentally and so ahistorically outsized, this tsunami of Federal Reserve credit has literally flooded into every nook and cranny of the financial system and the Main Street economy itself, seeking outlets just as air under pressure seeks release. Consequently, inflationary upwellings occur far and wide, well beyond the narrow boundaries of inflation as most people understand it—rising prices for goods and services we see reflected in the consumer price index (CPI).

This kind of rampant central bank monetary inflation is something wholly new, and it has spread throughout the entire global economy. As a result, the traditional economic models and vocabulary are not fit for purpose when it comes to explaining it or assessing the financial maelstrom this kind of inflation portends. That's what this book is all about.

Most especially, this new and rampant form of inflation means that the historical focus on goods and services prices is woefully deficient. When it comes to today's rogue central banking regime, the rising price of *assets*—seen in the skyrocketing cost of housing, soaring debt, fantastic stock and bond bubbles, and speculative enterprise generally—is far more relevant and far more dangerous.

There is a powerful reason, in fact, as to why monetary inflation has first manifested itself in soaring asset prices and rising debt rather than in consumer price increases, as Friedman would have predicted. In essence, the Fed's monetary inflation project was globalized by foreign central banks following in its footsteps. That led inexorably to a race to the monetary bottom, making the tools of traditional economists obsolete.

One such common tool is the Phillips curve, the notion that when the labor force and production capacity of a country are fully utilized, demand outruns supply and inflation takes off. Scratch a central banker or Wall Street economist these days, and this "overflowing macroeconomic bathtub" story is what they will tell you.

In short, prices are held to be rising because farms, factories, and services can't keep up with how much people want to buy. They have also insisted in recent years, somehow with a straight face, that any absence of accelerating consumer inflation proves there is still plenty of room in the tub for more "stimulus" from the easy-money central bankers.

Yet the Phillips curve as the fulcrum point of modern central banking always was and remains a thoroughly pernicious idea. As a Reagan supply-sider, I rejected it, even as it applied back in the day to the United States as a stand-alone superpower economy.

The reason is straightforward. In a properly functioning free market blessed with sound money, rising wages and rising prices attract more wealth-producing investment and labor, thereby balancing supply and demand rather than inflating the general price level. As we rightly insisted then, more work and higher output don't cause inflation, otherwise expressed as a depreciation in the value of money. Central bankers and politicians do.

The truth of this axiom became even more pertinent when economic life went truly global in the 1990s with the simultaneous rise of China's vast export sector and new technologies that enabled efficient global supply chains. As we amplify throughout these pages, those trends had the effect of causing domestic goods production to be steadily offshored in pursuit of ever-lower production costs. The secondary effect of the exportation of production was a *deflationary* inflow back to the United States of cheap, imported goods. That trend temporarily held down the officially measured inflation rate in the form of the CPI, what most people perceive as inflation.

The twin developments of cheap foreign production and newly efficient global supply chains meant, of course, that the domestic Phillips curve model was irrelevant. Excess domestic demand simply leaked out into the vast global supply base. Fooling around thereafter with crude U.S. macroeconomic markers—such as the U-3 unemployment rate, which measures only people looking for jobs, not everyone out of work or on short hours, and the personal consumption expenditures (PCE) deflator, which allows Fed politicians to ignore real inflation by looking at the effects of people buying cheaper or fewer things as prices rise—eventually became downright laughable, both as a matter of analysis and especially as a set of rigid, almost religious central bank policy targets.

Misunderstanding Keynes

Nevertheless, after Alan Greenspan became the Fed chairman in 1987, the Fed kept running its printing presses at faster and faster rates in pursuit of the supposedly sacrosanct policy goals of full employment and price stability. The Fed's inflation-adjusted balance sheet, which from 1952 to 1987 had crept higher by just 0.82 percent per year, went into overdrive under Greenspan and his heirs and assigns, rising by 8.12 percent per year—even after discounting all the inflation that the Fed itself had created.

But to understand the significance of this tenfold increase in the annual growth rate of the Fed's real balance sheet, we must take a big step back in the economics history books. The planking for today's rampant monetary growth was laid by British economist John Maynard Keynes, whose fundamental error was the idea that market capitalism tends toward repeated recessionary lulls that can only be remedied by "demand stimulus" delivered by governments and their central banks.

Yet rather than delivering the nirvana of full employment accompanied by just the "right" amount of inflation, as Keynes and his modern-day disciples advocated, the Fed's unhinged money pumping had another effect: it drastically inflated the price of assets—stocks, real estate, and so on—relative to the actual income growth. Real wages have been flat for years, but anyone lucky enough to own stock or property is, at least on paper, far richer.

And that fact is both crucial and never, ever acknowledged by the central bankers and their Wall Street megaphones. The ratio of household assets to personal income, excluding government transfer payments, has literally exploded during the last 35 years, rising from its longtime average of 5.75 times to 9.60 times in 2020. Obviously, we are not dealing with small numbers here. The soaring household asset-to-income ratio totals an extra $60 trillion in asset value!

That $60 trillion is the difference between the pre- and post-Greenspan eras of central banking. Under the reasonably sound money regime that preceded Greenspan, household asset holdings today would stand at $89 trillion. By contrast, today's actual level of $149 trillion is the clear result of egregious central bank money printing. As such, it bears no relationship whatsoever to the evolution of the underlying Main Street economy of the past three decades.

This $60 trillion difference is not a sign of relentlessly rising prosperity, as the permabulls of Wall Street loudly proclaim. It's actually the opposite: it is a clear sign of insidious, unsustainable inflation like never before imagined, even as it is obstinately ignored or denied by the central bankers who caused it to happen. In this book, you will learn exactly how we got here as well as what you need to do as an investor to avoid the worst of the calamity that inevitably will follow.

A Crucial Shift

It's important to understand how three decades of rogue central banking have brought us to the current impasse. Like the case of a frog in water being slowly brought to a boil, the mainstream economics narrative of Keynes and Friedman, along with the reigning Fed gospel as proclaimed by Greenspan and Bernanke (and their successors so far), has become so accepted that the transformation of the relationship between income and asset valuations has been totally hidden from ordinary Americans. By accident or design, nevertheless, it happened.

Remember that 1985 was not some kind of economic dark age but the culmination of more than a century of unprecedented economic growth and concurrent gains in middle-class living standards, a shift in wealth never before imagined anywhere in the world. Between 1954 and 1985, the inflation-adjusted median family income in 2019 dollars rose from $34,700 to $63,000—an increase of 82 percent. During the next 31 years, by contrast, it rose by just 22 percent.

At the pinnacle of that pre-1985 prosperity, household assets, including stocks, bonds, real estate, bank accounts, life insurance, and other such assets, totaled $17.9 trillion. That total thus represented 5.75 times that year's $3.1 trillion in personal income earned from all sources, excluding transfer payments such as Social Security benefits.

That specific asset-to-income ratio was par for the course during the preceding century of undeniably rising prosperity. For instance, the ratio of assets to income averaged 5.8 times during the heyday of American industrial prosperity from 1959 to 1970. It diminished only slightly to an average of 5.6 times during the high-inflation period from 1970 to 1985.

Given that history, there was absolutely no economic reason for this crucial ratio—a kind of price-to-earnings ratio (PE) multiple for the entire U.S. economy—to rise. In fact, in the decades after 1985, all the factors that would support a higher asset-to-income ratio increasingly ran in the wrong direction. As we will document in this book, the country's true economic growth rate dropped by nearly half, productivity growth weakened materially, and the household savings rate fell drastically.

If anything, household asset growth should have slowed relative to income gains. Instead, once Greenspan got the printing presses fired up—first to bail out Wall Street in 1987 and thereafter to remain the toast of the town in Washington—the ratio of asset values to personal income took off.

It reached 6.7 times by 1997, after Greenspan famously warned about "irrational exuberance" in stock valuations, then promptly forgot about it. The ratio rose further to about 8.2 times on the eve of the housing crash in 2007. Under Greenspan's successors Bernanke, Yellen, and Powell, the ratio has continued to move skyward as the elemental source of that asset inflation, the Fed's balance sheet, has mushroomed.

We can say with virtual certainty that no Fed boss has ever looked at the chart that follows. The dotted line represents the actual production side of the Main Street economy as well as can be estimated. It includes everything earned in the process of production and investment: wages, salaries, bonuses, realized capital gains, dividends, interest, and proprietors' profits. The only thing excluded is transfer payments, which are not earned and do not represent economic production.

On this basis, household incomes grew by 4.6 percent per year over that 35-year span (1986–2021) or by just half that rate when you strain out the loss of purchasing power to CPI. Astoundingly, household assets over the same period erupted, rising to $149 trillion from $18 trillion.

That's a $131 trillion gain, of which fully $60 trillion (45 percent) represents not the growth of household incomes but an increase in the valuations of the assets they own. By any other name, that's stunningly virulent inflation.

Real Income vs. Total Assets, 1945–2021

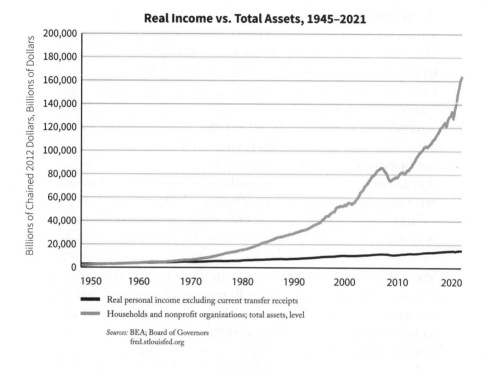

- ▬ Real personal income excluding current transfer receipts
- ▬ Households and nonprofit organizations; total assets, level

Sources: BEA; Board of Governors
fred.stlouisfed.org

In short, blinded by an obsolete Keynesian economic model and a veritable religious obsession with its "dual mandate" of steady inflation and full employment, the Fed has been on the wrong track for nearly 35 years. American capitalism's unequaled record of distributed prosperity is now listing badly in the face of gale-force monetary inflation ignited by the Fed itself.

Government's Heavy Hand

As a congressman from Michigan in the late 1970s, I voted with relish against these "dual mandates." I didn't think it was the role of politicians to second-guess economic data—GDP, housing starts, employment levels, business investment, and retail sales—that resulted from the interactions of millions of workers, employers, entrepreneurs, consumers, savers, investors, and speculators on the free market. Decades later, I still don't.

Indeed, the idea that market-driven GDP should find its own natural level without a heavy-handed assist from the government was then and remains today the opposite of the reigning orthodoxy. Rather than vibrant, free, productive capitalism, that orthodoxy sees the U.S. economy as a self-contained, hermetically sealed system that is always badly malfunctioning and forever falling short of its potential, thereby requiring constant external stimulus from Washington via its fiscal and central banking branches.

Owing to this crude, mechanistic Keynesian model, central bankers maintain, mistakenly, that the level of slack or tightness in national labor and product markets must be diligently monitored via the putatively scientific telemetry reflected in the U-3 unemployment level and the consumer inflation rate. Using readings expressed to the second decimal place, Washington officialdom believes it can calibrate the fiscal and monetary flow such that the resulting stimulus causes the economic bathtub to be filled precisely to the brim but never over.

That wasn't remotely true even a half century ago when the U.S. economy was more inward looking, but it's utterly preposterous today. That's because the domestic U.S. economy is self-evidently wide open to the overpowering influences of global trade, capital flows, and the relative labor and production costs everywhere on the planet, all at once.

The 1978 Humphrey-Hawkins Act made full employment an official government goal, taking the country inexorably down the path of inflation-seeking Keynesianism. Meanwhile, real goods imports in 1975 totaled $241 billion (in 2012 constant dollars), accounting for 4.1 percent of GDP. By 2020, real goods imports totaled $3.03 trillion and accounted for 16.1 percent of GDP, 12.5 times more than 1975.

That massive change makes all the difference in the world. It's the smoking gun that makes a mockery of today's officious but clueless central bankers. The radical fourfold increase in the import share of GDP means that a surge of excess demand in the domestic economy today cannot "fill the macroeconomic bathtub of GDP" to the brim, as our foggy-minded Keynesian central bankers presume. Nor does it send the inflation gauges climbing to 2 percent and beyond, per the hoary Phillips curve theory, which mistakenly presumes that all national economies are somehow closed systems.

Instead, excess domestic demand races across U.S. borders and into the maws of the global economy faster than green grass passing through a goose. That's exactly what happened to a disproportionate amount of $6 trillion in stimulus spending, all the free stuff and bailouts that were injected into the U.S. economy in response to the Covid lockdown. The state-owned Chinese firms that got the business laughed all the way to the bank.

The result is that traditional monetary and fiscal stimulus in the United States ends up being expressed mainly as increased jobs and production in China and other low-cost producers, and until recently the price effect in the United States has remained essentially deflationary. That's because the marginal supply of industrial and consumer purchases reflects the low labor-cost "China price" for goods, the "India price" for technology-enabled services, and the "Mexico price" for final assembly of factory-made output such as cars and air conditioners.

Given these realities, the stupidest thing imaginable is a central bank that is rigidly and fetishistically committed to domestic employment and inflation targets such as 3.5 percent unemployment and 2 percent inflation. The very idea of it is profoundly wrongheaded and thoroughly destructive, as I will demonstrate later in this book.

Nevertheless, in America today, an activist Federal Reserve reigns supreme with virtually no dissent from the political world, Wall Street, or corporate America. And the reason is straightforward. All the interested parties like it that way. In fact, they love it to death.

The Fed cannot possibly—not in a million years—hit and sustain its domestic full employment and inflation targets in a globalized economy. But it can try, try, and try some more, pumping endless liquidity, cheap debt, and raging financial asset inflation into the canyons of Wall Street as it does so.

That's Washington's infernal inflation machine at work. The politicians (and Wall Street) love it because the system they built effectively euthanized the so-called bond vigilantes, the last remaining obstacle to heedless spending, thereby freeing them to indulge without limit.

Chapter 2

Cheap Money, Broken Politics

The $29 trillion in public debt we now carry as a nation does not represent a breakdown of fiscal discipline on both ends of Pennsylvania Avenue so much as it captures the perfidious influence of bad money in the realm of political governance. The carrying cost of the federal debt has gotten so dirt cheap—it's actually negative after inflation—that politicians no longer care about the public debt. Nor do they fear the possibility that large, persistent fiscal deficits will drive up interest rates and crowd out household and business borrowers.

It wasn't always that way. Even after the giant Reagan deficits in the 1980s, public debt remained under 50 percent of GDP. A bipartisan consensus held that it should be contained at the ratio or preferably rolled back, which produced large deficit reduction enactments under both George H. W. Bush and Bill Clinton.

Yet the bipartisan consensus proved to be no match for the palliative of low interest rates. That was especially the case after the GOP was taken over by deficit-don't-matter demagogues such as Newt Gingrich and Dick Cheney.

The year 2000 was an inflection point. Once Greenspan launched the Fed into drastic interest rate repression to reverse the dot-com crash, it was Katie-bar-the-door time. Public debt grew from $5.7 trillion and 55.6 percent of GDP after the modest budget surpluses of the later Clinton years, to $10.7 trillion and 67.4 percent of GDP under George W.

Bush, and then to $19.9 trillion and 104 percent of GDP under Barack Obama. Then the self-described "king of debt," Donald Trump, earned his nickname and then some, taking public debt to $27.7 trillion and 125 percent of GDP—beyond even the World War II peak—in just four years. Finally, there followed in the Oval Office a real Democrat spender and trillions more of public debt to be carried by future generations.

Needless to say, this eruption of the public debt is inflation every bit as much as rising consumer prices because it is the wholly artificial product of reckless central bank credit expansion. In effect, by causing the carrying cost of those towering debts to be radically and falsely underpriced, the Fed made it extremely easy for the current generation of politicians to bury future taxpayers in unpayable debt.

Federal Debt and Share of GDP

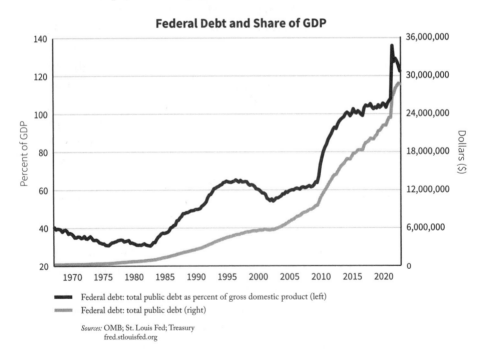

Federal debt: total public debt as percent of gross domestic product (left)
Federal debt: total public debt (right)

Sources: OMB; St. Louis Fed; Treasury
fred.stlouisfed.org

Of course, Wall Street also loves the Fed's rampant monetary inflation. Money market rates at zero are the mother's milk of carry-trade speculators. Ultracheap debt enables the endless leveraged arbitrage of risk assets. The end result of aggressive money pumping is a "Fed put" under the stock market index averages, the belief that the Federal Reserve will support the stock market in all circumstances. So everybody gets a trophy. No one is carried out on their shield. There are now tens of thousands of millionaires and billionaires who have been arbitrarily and undeservedly gifted wealth by central bank–generated asset inflation.

Corporate America itself is especially hooked on massive central bank money pumping. It enables out-of-this-world financial engineering designed specifically to goose share prices, activity that only magnifies the value of executive compensation in the form of stock options.

Accordingly, since 2000 there have been upward of $25 trillion in stock buybacks and economically pointless and usually way overpriced M&A deals. These diversions of cash flows and balance sheet capacities cause wealth to be redistributed to the stock-owning classes at the top of the economic ladder at the expense of productive investments in plant, equipment, technology, and human resources in the Main Street economy.

It all adds up to a rotten regime of inflationary money and to a lame rationalization that is even worse—namely, the specious claim of today's central bankers that the legislative mandates for stable prices and maximum employment of the Humphrey-Hawkins Act make them do it, whether it's prudent, effective, and rational or not.

That's a lie. The Fed could do the right thing and urge Congress to repeal Humphrey-Hawkins on the grounds that its goals are impossible to reliably quantify and operationalize. And, more importantly, that the goals of any such legislation are far beyond the power of a national central bank to deliver—even as the first among unequals—in a deeply and dynamically interconnected global economic and financial system.

Short of that, the Fed could easily and honestly punt. That is, it could define price stability as generally low inflation tending toward zero and full employment as that level of labor utilization that results when the free market is least obstructed and burdened by the fiscal, regulatory, and tax intrusions of the state.

Exporting Inflation

Such broader, more generalized formulations would not require in the slightest the spurious quantitative "goals" and the resulting madcap money printing of recent decades. They would not cause the entire price-signaling system of capitalism's most important nexus—free capital markets—to be deliberately and systematically distorted by the inherently deficient groupthink of the 12 mortals who compose the Federal Open Market Committee (FOMC), which sets U.S. interest rate targets.

In short, owing to breakthroughs in information technology, efficient global transportation networks, intricate globe-spanning supply chains, and endless cheap capital fostered by worldwide central bank financial repression, the idea of the Phillips curve occurring in just one country is dead as a doornail.

Thus there is no national economic bathtub of GDP for the Fed to pump up to the brim, thereby ringing the bell on its goals of full employment and 2 percent inflation. Just the opposite. The Fed's money pumping in today's highly integrated, open global economy instead causes inflationary demand to be exported to the rest of the world, where it is absorbed by low-wage, low-cost producers. Simultaneously, a deflationary supply of cheap goods from China and other low-wage nations is imported to feed ravenous levels of American household consumption.

Accordingly, the Fed's so-called mandates of managed inflation and full employment are unnecessary, obsolete, and profoundly counterproductive. Rather, they have become a convenient cover for Washington's infernal inflation machine, a hellish default to runaway borrowing and spending in the public sector and reckless borrowing and speculating in the financial markets.

The consequences are not benign. Upward of $86 trillion in total debt—combined household, business, financial, and government borrowings—now represents the highest leverage rate against national income in U.S. history. Debt at this level guarantees that growth of the Main Street economy and American living standards will grind to a halt while dead ahead loom a fiscal apocalypse and the thundering collapse of the greatest financial market bubbles in history.

To make things crystal clear, here is our progression since World War II:

- At the time of Nixon's cancelation of the dollar's anchor to gold, total U.S. debt stood at $1.65 trillion and represented 151 percent of GDP, an implicit national leverage ratio that had prevailed with only minor deviation for the entire previous century of robust economic growth.
- Even as late as Alan Greenspan's arrival at the Fed in mid-1987, total public and private debt stood at $10.2 trillion and 219 percent of GDP.
- By the eve of the housing bust in 2007, these figures had soared to $52.6 trillion in total debt and 358 percent of GDP.
- Following the year of the pandemic lockdowns and the Fed's $4 trillion balance sheet eruption, total debt stood at $85.9 trillion and 370 percent of GDP as of September 2021.

That's debt inflation like never before imagined. And like all inflation, its effects have not been benign. On the one hand, real GDP growth since 1951 makes a mockery of the Fed's justification for turning on the afterburners on its digital printing presses. As monetary policy has evolved in an increasingly destructive direction, moreover, the trend rate of real GDP growth has unmistakably deteriorated. Witness the following:

- postwar "golden" era, 1951–70: 3.72 percent per year
- initial fiat money era, 1970–87: 3.24 percent per year
- Greenspan money-pumping era, 1987–2007: 3.08 percent per year
- postcrisis fiat credit explosion, 2007–20: 1.28 percent per year

You read that right. Real GDP growth has slowed to barely one-third its golden-era rate despite the evolution of Fed policy toward increasingly massive money printing (i.e., balance sheet growth) on a continuous basis. At the same time, financial asset inflation has been off to the races. After Greenspan cranked up the printing press—at the time of Black Monday, the October 1987 stock market meltdown—the market value of corporate equities compared to nominal GDP changed dramatically. Equity valuation rose by 19.6 times to $64.5 trillion from $3.3 trillion, while nominal GDP rose to $21.5 trillion from $4.8 trillion, or by 4.4 times.

Guns and Butter

The fact is, there is no reason since 1987 that corporate equity should have grown much faster than nominal GDP. The profit content of GDP has not significantly grown from its historic levels. Pretax corporate profits averaged just 10.8 percent of GDP between 2000 and 2020, a figure only slightly higher than the 10.3 percent average between 1955 and 1970.

In fact, the value of corporate equity should never have risen much above 80 percent of GDP and certainly not above the one-time peak at 100 percent touched temporarily during LBJ's short-lived "guns and butter" boom ending in 1968. In dollar terms, even at the 1968 peak ratio, corporate equity would be worth $22 trillion today, not the $65 trillion level actually posted in the fourth quarter of 2020, which comes to 320 percent of GDP.

The yawning difference is caused by financial asset inflation, the product of soaring PE multiples unjustified by the economic facts on the ground. The difference of $43 trillion is the elephant in the room that, unaccountably, the Fed claims does not even constitute inflation and for which it has no responsibility in any event.

Corporate equity has not been the only financial asset that has been subject to massive, cumulative inflation. During the same half-century period, the market value of household real estate has soared from 100 percent of GDP to a peak of 185 percent prior to the 2008 financial crisis. It remains at 165 percent of GDP today. There is no reason for the disconnect except that in August 1971, President Nixon severed the final link between the dollar and gold, thereby freeing central bankers to commence the great asset inflation binge that still rages on.

Needless to say, financial asset inflation is not an equal opportunity gift down the economic ladder. Asset windfalls accrue to those who have the assets. Between the fourth quarter of 1989 and the first quarter of 2021, financial asset holdings evolved as follows:

- top 1 percent: +$32.5 trillion or a gain of 812 percent
- bottom 50 percent: +$1.7 trillion or a gain of 325 percent

Moreover, not only did the lower classes not get much out of rampant asset inflation; they got the lion's share of the debt. That baleful reality is captured in the net worth statistics published by the Fed itself. Between 1989 and the first quarter of 2021, net worth changed as follows:

- top 1 percent: net worth of $4.78 trillion rose to $41.52 trillion (8.7 times)
- bottom 50 percent: net worth of $763 billion rose to $2.62 trillion (3.4 times)

And that's all you need to know about Washington's infernal inflation machine. When Greenspan kicked off the age of Keynesian money pumping, the top 1 percent held about $4 trillion more net worth than the bottom 50 percent of households. Today that differential has grown to a staggering $39 trillion.

This fact is the big hidden truth. The accumulation of central bank–fostered financial asset inflation has been so fantastic for so long that the top 1 percent no longer have any compunction about swinging for the fences. If Bitcoin or Tesla goes bust, their second and third homes and private jets are not likely to be impacted.

That means the wealth-holding classes increasingly are all in on the speculative mania fostered by the central banks. Rather than a bulwark of financial prudence, stability, and blue-chip bonds, as was the case once upon a time, the very wealthy, their family offices, and their favored hedge funds are transforming the Fed's lunatic infusions of liquidity and fiat credit into a ticking financial time bomb the likes of which the world has never seen.

The Inflation Deniers

As I've shown in the previous pages, there is an extra $60 trillion in household assets hanging around the U.S. economy, and that didn't happen by the economic equivalent of immaculate conception. It's the product of the Fed's unhinged money-printing spree over the last three decades and amounts to the gross inflation of financial assets.

To reprise, when Alan Greenspan first cranked up the Fed's printing presses in the fall of 1987, its balance sheet stood at $200 billion. It had taken 73 years to get there, dating from the Fed's creation. Now just 34 years later, that balance sheet is 43 times bigger and stands at $8.8 trillion. And it has been growing at a rate of $120 billion per month until recently.

So why do our groupthink-addled Keynesian central bankers insist that inflation does not apply to financial assets—stocks, bonds, "blank check" special purpose acquisition companies (SPACs), nonfungible tokens (NFTs), crypto, housing—but only to the price of goods and services? One must also ask why 2 percent consumer price inflation is such a good thing that central banks must pull out all stops to achieve it and apply the shortest possible measuring stick to it, thereby providing an excuse for even more money printing.

With respect to the exclusion of financial asset inflation, the answer is obvious: We have rampant asset inflation, so by definition, it does not count. Otherwise, the central bankers would have been forced to shut down their red-hot printing presses and abandon their current glory as supposed masters of the financial universe long ago.

But like all power-seeking bureaucrats, that's the last thing they are about to do, even if it means willfully closing their eyes to the financial inflation screaming from the headlines. Consider, for instance, the sudden and absurd run-up in the price of cryptocurrencies since the fall of 2020. The theoretical appeal of nongovernment money aside, what else would you call a one-year rise of 400 percent, 525 percent, and 1,500 percent for Bitcoin, Litecoin, and Ethereum, respectively?

Of course, the money printers would say that no one has to eat, wear, or drive cryptos, so the speculators and the masters of the universe on Wall Street are entitled to their fun. It's none of the Fed's business!

But actually, it is. That's because, in today's world, periodically crashing financial markets are the primary cause of recessions, as was the case in both 2001 and 2008. Purportedly, prevention of exactly these kinds of collapses is the central bank's main job. But it's more than that. Soaring financial asset inflation massively distorts economic activity and ultimately undermines job growth and GDP. These are matters right at the heart of the Fed's self-proclaimed mandate.

Buyback Bonanza

Just since the year 2000, for instance, corporate stock buybacks have totaled about $10 trillion, and there have been another $15 trillion in M&A deals. The overwhelming share of the latter was done because they could be financed with cheap debt, not because these deals generated productivity and added value. Meanwhile, stock buybacks tap cash flows and balance sheet capacity that might otherwise be allocated to investments in productive Main Street assets, such as plants, equipment, technology, R&D, and labor force enhancement.

Indeed, until the official adoption of 2 percent inflation targeting in 2012, though informally followed during the Bernanke-Greenspan years in the decade prior, the occupants of the Fed's home, the Eccles building, understood that as a practical matter, inflation distorts decision making by managers, workers, and investors alike. This was especially true during the years of Fed chairmen William McChesney Martin (1952–70), Arthur Burns (1970–78), and Paul Volcker (1979–87).

Back then, containing inflation was viewed as essential to maximizing Main Street job growth and prosperity in general. The emphasis always and everywhere was pressing inflation lower from above, not today's absurd central bank policy of pushing it higher from below.

Financial asset inflation didn't get a pass. Central bankers and most everyone else knew inflation was bad in all its forms and manifestations and that the inflation control valve was the central bank's legal monopoly on the production of high-powered money and fiat credit.

It also was understood that in a world not afflicted by central bank printing press money, production came first. Income, spending, saving, investing, and the accumulation of financial assets followed.

In this supply-side-driven world, inflation is inherently contained in the arena of goods and services because spending derived from income cannot outrun supply, the source of that income. By the same token, asset price inflation also is contained because honest price discovery inherently checks speculation. And artificially cheap debt fostered by a central bank is not available to subsidize unproductive money dealing and financialization.

Back then, all inflation—of goods, services, and assets—was viewed as bad. Central bankers had not yet matriculated to the higher calling of becoming the financial version of medieval theologians concerned with the monetary equivalent of the number of angels that can stand on the head of a pin. In practical terms, they didn't parse the running inflation rate to the nearest tenth of a percent, such as 1.9 percent versus 2.1 percent. And they looked at a variety of inflation indicators—commodity indices, various forms of the consumer and producer price indices, and an array of asset prices—not a single, anointed metric: the dubious measure called the "core PCE deflator," which badly underweights housing and medical costs and, among other defects, says that when soaring steak prices lead consumers to eat more chicken, forced food substitution cancels out inflation.

Nor did Martin, Burns, et al. even consider the flakiest Fed belief of today: that if consumers have the good fortune to experience a respite from the relentless decline in the purchasing power of their money, the Fed should respond by forcing underlying inflation to run hot so that it will average 2 percent over an "extended" period of time, the duration of which they refuse to even specify.

Before Greenspan

The implications of the old-fashioned adult view of inflation are profound. Central bankers wanted as little inflation as possible over the broad range of its manifestations on both Main Street and Wall Street. They wouldn't have dreamed of fueling the rise of inflationary excesses seen now, the meme stocks goosed up by online mobs, the crypto-crazy speculators and stock market buy-the-dippers, and the buy-and-hold, stocks-grow-to-the-sky crowd.

Prior to Greenspan, the proinflation nonsense we see now at the Fed and other central banks would never have happened. Period. And the reason is not hard to grasp. The inflation target back then was qualitative and commonsensical: accept as little inflation as you can.

Accordingly, no Fed chief before, say, 1998 would have viewed the economy as "lacking inflation" and concluded that the Fed needed to keep its foot on the printing press accelerator to the tune of $120 billion per month in order to achieve some kind of inflation target.

No one back in the day would have monetized U.S. Treasury and mortgage debt securities at the current $1.44 trillion annual rate owing to "too little inflation." Traditional central bankers, in fact, would have said 2 percent inflation year in and year out is too high!

Consider what happens when you average two possible measures of the general price level—the 16 percent trimmed mean CPI, often called underlying inflation, and the core PCE deflator. It's not "lowflation" by any means. In fact, the average annual change of the 16 percent trimmed mean CPI and the core PCE deflator is as follows:

- 2000–2020: 1.92 percent
- 2012–20: 1.82 percent
- 2019–20: 1.92 percent

So what in the hell kind of shortfall is 1.92 percent annual inflation over a 21-year period? In truth, it's actually much too high for people on fixed incomes, savers, and workers who compete in the global labor market and don't get automatic cost-of-living increases.

Nevertheless, the monetary theologians at the Fed and their acolytes on Wall Street insist on ignoring the 16 percent trimmed mean CPI, which averaged 2.13 percent over the 21-year period, in favor of the Fed's preferred measure, the core PCE deflator, which averaged 1.71 percent over the same period. Put another way, by my reckoning, the Fed has flooded the financial markets with upward of $7 trillion in new fiat credits since 2006 mainly because of a meaningless statistical shortfall in inflation measures, one that amounts to just 40 basis points per year.

That's madness, but it also gets us to the profoundly deleterious but unspoken corollary of the Fed's obsession with creating inflation. To wit, the true inflation generated by the Fed impacts everything—goods, services, assets, wages, and production costs generally. The Fed unaccountably assumes that it all comes out in the wash. If not annually, at least over time, the goodness that purportedly comes from the magic of 2 percent inflation is assumed to accrue to workers, managers, investors, rich, and poor proportionately. Everybody gets a trophy.

Except, no, they do not. Not even remotely.

To the contrary, Fed-fueled inflation is the greatest discriminator imaginable. Among other ills, it bestows unspeakable windfalls on the top 1 percent and top 10 percent, who own most of the tradable and inflatable financial assets, while crushing ordinary savers who need to keep funds in risk-free bank accounts or short-term Treasury bills.

More importantly, it literally depletes the real earnings of workers who must compete with low-wage workers abroad and, increasingly, robots funded by ultracheap capital. The Fed's one-size-fits-all inflation goal of 2 percent does not "fit all" because today's dynamic global economy means prices, wages, and costs do not march higher in lockstep to the beat of the Fed's drummer.

For want of doubt, consider one of the most important items not included in the Fed's crabbed definition of inflation—residential housing prices.

Comparing Apples to Apples

The chart below cuts through all the statistical chaff and Keynesian misdirection by simply computing the number of hours of work required from the average worker to buy a median-priced home in the United States. It happens to span the half century since Richard Nixon pulled the plug on sound money in August 1971 and started us down the road to today's insidious central banker doctrine that inflation is somehow good for us.

**Median Home Sales Price Divided by
Average Hourly Earnings, 1970–2020**

Median sales price of houses sold in the United States / average hourly earnings of production and nonsupervisory employees, total private

Sources: Census; HUD; BLS
fred.stlouisfed.org

By converting worker hours to worker years, I have factored in the steady deterioration in the U.S. jobs mix toward a higher proportion of part-time and generally lower-paying jobs. The average production worker clocked 36.7 hours per week and 1,908 hours per year in 1971. Those numbers have dropped to 34.2 hours per week and 1,778 per year at present.

Accordingly, the computations are as follows:

	Second Quarter, 1971	Fourth Quarter, 2020
Median home price	$25,800	$358,700
Average hourly wage	$3.60	$24.97
Hours worked to buy	7,160	14,365
Annual hours worked	1,908	1,778
Years worked to buy	3.75	8.08

The idea that inflation is good for you and housing asset price inflation doesn't count has appeal in the academic puzzle palace we know as the Fed. But among workers who now need to put in 8.08 years on the job to buy a home they could purchase with the sound money of 1971 for just 3.75 years of work—not so much!

Owing to Ben Bernanke's inflation-targeting folly, the Fed adopted an official goal of seeking a targeted level of inflation in January 2012. There wasn't a shred of empirical evidence or a theoretical basis for the resulting 2 percent annual target except for what amounts to a "just in case" notion peddled by unreconstructed Keynesians still in thrall to the myth that deflation caused the Great Depression.

Later in this book, I address the fact that commodity, industrial, and consumer prices are not the only channels in which central bank–fueled inflation manifests itself. But even so narrowly construed, the best year-over-year measure of general consumer inflation we have is the aforementioned 16 percent trimmed mean CPI. And it points to no inflation shortfall problem whatsoever.

In fact, since Bernanke's 2 percent inflation target was adopted in January 2012, the index has risen at a 2.07 percent compound rate per year. For the year ended in June 2021, the increase was actually 2.9 percent. If those outcomes are not close enough for government work, pray tell, what would be?

To be sure, the trimmed mean CPI has oscillated above and below the 2 percent target based on commodity, credit, trade, and other cyclical fluctuations. But given the way this particular index is constructed—throwing out the 8 percent highest and 8 percent lowest price changes in the CPI basket each month, which are always different components—there simply is no case for the "lowflation" boogeyman so feared by the Fed and obsessed over by Wall Street.

That's because the trimmed mean CPI is not biased by the various outliers—up or down—in the short run. In the long run, then, it naturally reflects the full basket of items that compose the CPI. That makes it far superior to other shortcuts to monthly index stabilization, such as ignoring the cost of food and energy, the "core" measure of CPI that pretends that these essential elements of the cost of living don't matter.

Even then, the CPI basket of prices itself undermeasures inflation owing to its so-called hedonic adjustments for "quality" and to devices such as the previously mentioned substitution effects.

Chapter 3

Chicken versus Steak

For instance, imagine that the ratio of steak to chicken purchases across the economy is 50/50. Half of that particular slice of the family food budget is spent on one variety of protein and half on the other. If the price of the steak rises by 20 percent and the chicken by 2 percent, this two-component example index would rise by an average of the two, or 11 percent. That's the true price inflation.

Now imagine that owing to the surging cost of steak, the steak-to-chicken ratio shifts to 20/80. We spend 20 cents of the food dollar on steak and 80 cents on chicken, since it's cheaper. The two-component index would rise by just 5.6 percent under Bureau of Labor Statistics (BLS) methodology. But now we're measuring a decline in living standards, not price inflation.

Needless to say, impacted consumers know when their living standard is being eroded due to rising prices. People realize they're buying chicken because steak is too expensive. Honest students of the nettlesome problem of constructing a general price level index understand as well. That's because the above adjustment factors turn the CPI into a cost-of-living index (COLI), not an apples-to-apples index of change in the general price level.

Moreover, we know from direct conversations with Alan Greenspan back in the 1980s that his reasons for initiating the aforementioned flaw in the CPI calculation were far from scientific.

Behind the scenes, Greenspan fancied himself the GOP's economic consigliere. He wanted to find some clever way to reduce the cost of living adjustments in Social Security and the other federal entitlements without forcing cowardly GOP legislators to walk the plank of entitlement reform. As budget director under President Ronald Reagan, I was all ears, since we knew the votes weren't there.

So Greenspan doubled down after he became Fed chairman in 1987. He devoutly wished to be lionized as the man who vanquished the rampant inflation of the era, and what better way to accomplish that than by sawing off the inflation measuring stick?

In fact, the Boskin Commission of the 1990s was headed by another Republican economist, Michael Boskin, who also wanted to reduce the budget expense of cost-of-living adjustments (COLAs) on the sly. The commission eventually issued a report that sanctioned this transformation of the CPI into a COLI rather than a price index. It also introduced the even more insidious idea "hedonic adjustment."

In plain English, a hedonic adjustment amounts to a bureaucrat's judgment of how much the quality of a product has changed—think about a cell phone you bought in 2005 versus one you have today—and a "wet finger in the air" estimate about how much the sticker price in the stores should be reduced for purposes of BLS inflation estimates.

Does the BLS really have the ability to track thousands of consumer-end items to quantify changes in product quality for either an alleged benefit, such as safety airbags in cars, or detriment, such as suspiciously smaller candy bars or junk appliances made in China? And when it comes to the services components of the CPI basket, such as babysitters, yoga instructors, or hospital care, how do you accurately define the product to begin with, let alone track changes in quality, when so many services are bundled, paid for by third-party insurance, or simply imputed (a fancy economics word for "guessed at") by the BLS?

As to the matter of imputation—which shockingly covers upward of one-third of the CPI—that's especially sketchy. For instance, take the case of home ownership, which according to both the BLS and common observation, is a very large item in the consumer's market basket. In fact, it is currently given a 24.263 percent weight in the overall official inflation index.

A Price Mirage

But the skunk in the woodpile is that this one-quarter component of the index, your home, isn't directly measured, even though the level of transparency in housing prices is among the highest of all consumer goods. Instead, the Census Bureau, on behalf of the BLS, periodically asks several thousand consumers who own their own homes what they would rent their abode for should they choose to become a landlord and live in a tent in the meanwhile. This is the basis for the so-called owners' equivalent rent (OER) component of the CPI.

So the monthly changes in more than 24 percent of the CPI are anchored to nothing more than wild-ass guesses of telephone respondents who undoubtedly think the question is nuts in the first place. However they make their guesses for the Census Bureau interviewers, the result has been a large, systematic shortfall in the actual cost of home ownership: since the year 2000, for instance, the S&P/Case-Shiller index of home prices, which is based on the resale prices of a common set of properties over time, has risen at a 4.14 percent annualized rate compared to OER, which has risen at just 2.62 percent.

We are talking here about a 20-year period, not just a few months. What that means is that as the market price of residential properties rises robustly over time, the true economic cost of the shelter services embedded in property ownership rises proportionately. In May 2021, the Case-Shiller index rose by 17 percent over the previous 12 months, the biggest annualized jump since August 2004. That's what the whole OER rigmarole is about and suggests why the BLS stopped using direct housing prices. To wit, reported OER since January 2000 has risen at just 63 percent of the rise in the true market price of housing.

Moreover, due to the longer-term housing boom-and-bust cycle of recent years, the gap between the two has become even larger. The Fed adopted inflation targeting in January 2012. Since then, the Case-Shiller index is up by 6.24 percent per year while the OER is up by only 2.84 percent—just 45 percent of the actual home price gains.

Nor is this the half of it. Even the Boskin Commission's remolded CPI reported too much inflation for Bernanke's tastes, so when inflation targeting became official policy in 2012, the Fed adopted the PCE deflator as its inflation index, thereby causing the measuring stick to be sawed off still more.

As suggested previously, the PCE deflator isn't even a price index. It is a device that the Bureau of Economic Analysis (BEA) uses to adjust reported personal consumption expenditures. For instance, if consumers buy more digital gadgets as technology prices are falling, or fewer medical services as those prices are rising, the PCE deflator interprets those choices as "lower inflation."

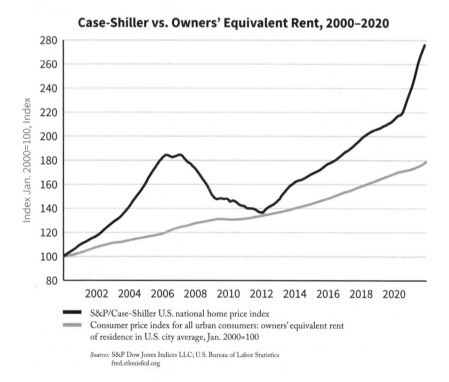

Case-Shiller vs. Owners' Equivalent Rent, 2000–2020

■ S&P/Case-Shiller U.S. national home price index
▬ Consumer price index for all urban consumers: owners' equivalent rent of residence in U.S. city average, Jan. 2000=100

Sources: S&P Dow Jones Indices LLC; U.S. Bureau of Labor Statistics
fred.stlouisfed.org

What the PCE deflator measures is thus not the inflation of a fixed-market basket of goods and services but a continuously shape-shifting mix of household spending. To add insult to injury, 30 percent of the prices used to compute the PCE deflator are not even in the CPI! That's because they represent the price of intermediate goods purchased by businesses for use in production and government goods, which often are delivered at subsidized prices or entirely for free. Consequently, these goods are "priced" by the government statistical bureaus based on best guesses. You really can't make this up. A goodly part of the Fed's preferred inflation yardstick consists of invisible prices for government services that BLS bureaucrats assume to be low and steady.

"Missing" Inflation

So when you get down to it, here is what you actually have in the Fed's official inflation measuring stick. The PCE deflator's weightings consist of the following:

- 53 percent hedonically adjusted prices from the CPI market basket
- 17 percent homeowners' guesses about the fictional rental value of their own homes
- 30 percent BLS guesses about the cost of government goods and intermediate business purchases

Not surprisingly, the Fed's sawed-off measuring stick has fallen increasingly behind the more accurate and serviceable trimmed mean CPI. Therein lies the vaunted "inflation shortfall"—inflation we're supposedly missing and that the Fed must create—and it's as phony as a $3 bill.

Since January 1, 2012, the PCE deflator has risen by 1.73 percent annually while 16 percent trimmed mean CPI rose 2.07 percent. It would be fair to say that the 34 annual basis points difference between these two inflation measures has been worth tens of trillions of dollars to the speculators and gamblers who flourished during their romp in the Fed-fueled casino that has been Wall Street since at least January 2012.

Since the fourth quarter of 2007, the Fed's balance sheet has expanded by 807 percent compared to the 46 percent gain in nominal GDP. And the overwhelming reason offered by the Fed heads for this relentless assault on the principles of sound money is a monetary version of "Look ma, no hands!"

That is to say, there is no inflation when you measure it incorrectly and then compare it to the arbitrary 2 percent benchmark conjured up by Ben Bernanke rather than to a commonsensical standard of zero inflation. This is surely one of the biggest big lies of all time, yet when it's repeated often enough by the monetary demigods in the Eccles building—to the applause of Wall Street speculators and government spenders alike—it becomes gospel.

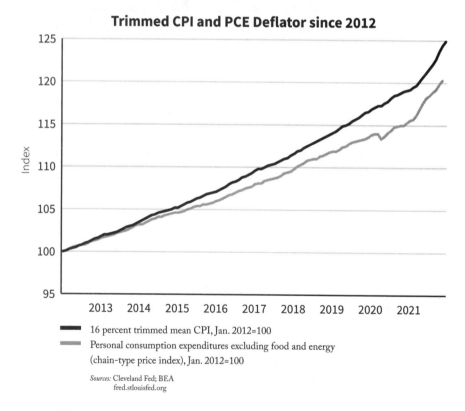

Trimmed CPI and PCE Deflator since 2012

16 percent trimmed mean CPI, Jan. 2012=100

Personal consumption expenditures excluding food and energy
(chain-type price index), Jan. 2012=100

Sources: Cleveland Fed; BEA
fred.stlouisfed.org

For instance, in what was supposed to be a think piece about the inflation outlook in the *Wall Street Journal*, one of the Fed's more servile fanboys, Greg Ip, wrote about how "lowflation" remains a stubborn challenge. In an article published March 1, 2021, Ip wrote, "Inflation is near a decade low and well below the 2 percent level the Federal Reserve targets as ideal. The usual conditions for rising inflation—tight job markets and public expectations of rising prices—are glaringly absent."

What a load of horse pucky! Of course, you can't blame this journalist entirely. He was just repeating what Fed chairman Jay Powell said at the time to the much-relieved congressional committee before which Powell was testifying. To quote Powell himself, "The kind of troubling inflation that people like me grew up with seems far away and unlikely."

When it comes to a reasonably accurate measure of inflation, there is no "decade low" anywhere in sight—even one that understates overall price level changes. Yet since the precrisis peak in the fourth quarter of 2007, the Fed's balance sheet has grown 16 times faster than national income (measured as GDP), mainly in pursuit of the fantastical goal of 2 percent inflation.

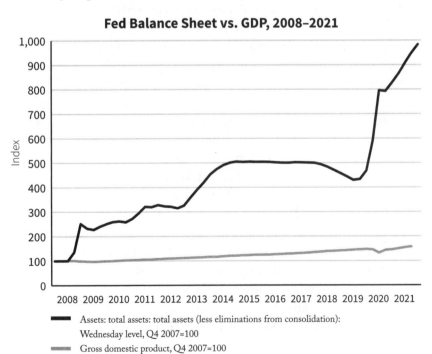

Fed Balance Sheet vs. GDP, 2008–2021

Index

Assets: total assets: total assets (less eliminations from consolidation): Wednesday level, Q4 2007=100

Gross domestic product, Q4 2007=100

Sources: Board of Governors; BEA
fred.stlouisfed.org

Massive Inflation

So where did all the inflation implied by this yawning gap actually go?

Simply, it went into the most fantastic stock bubble in human history and a resulting distortion in the distribution of national wealth that is not only unconscionable but, more crucially, threatens to unleash redistribute-the-wealth political forces like at no time since FDR.

Of course, the solution is to go to the root of the matter. Namely, we should put an end to the insane central bank campaign against a nonexistent deflationary threat. At length, a collapsing casino will take care of the wealth maldistribution matter all on its own.

Do the foolish people who inhabit the Eccles building ever wonder about the vast disproportion between their ritualistically cited goals and the insidious impact of the "accommodative" policies that they deploy to purportedly further those goals? The plain fact is that 0.05 percent to 0.15 percent money market rates (the Fed fund's current target band) in even a 2 percent inflation environment are a carry-trade speculator's dream, to say nothing of the 3 percent to 5 percent inflation rate that prevails today. Central bank bond buying with credit snatched from thin air at a staggering $1.44 trillion annual rate is a recipe for massive inflation of financial asset prices, rampant speculation, and malinvestment throughout the warp and woof of the entire financial system.

Since giant financial bubbles always lead to sorrow, loss, waste, and economic setback in the end, what could possibly be so important about these so-called employment and inflation goals as to justify the massive fueling of these certain adverse risks? Beyond that, there is also the screaming injustice of the process, which showers Wall Street insiders with huge, unearned windfall gains in the run-up to the top, then hammers retail investors who always get suckered in at the end to take the losses.

Of course, despite the Fed's ritual invocation of "statutory" mandates, Congress has never legislated a 2 percent inflation target or the shape-shifting metric of full employment that has ranged between 5 percent and 3.5 percent on the U-3 unemployment measure over recent decades.

These both were invented over the years based on the Keynesian "bathtub" model of the U.S. economy. This model falsely claims that aggregate demand is the regulator of economic growth and employment and that falsifying interest rates, bond prices, yield curves, and the values of other financial assets derived from them can raise aggregate demand to full employment and 2 percent inflation.

Stated differently, if you flood the GDP bathtub with credit-financed aggregate demand with just the right dexterity and duration, the PCE deflator and U-3 unemployment meters on the brim will eventually flash "done!"

That's the theory, and it's actually about as stupid and primitive as it sounds.

Still, at the present moment, even the Keynesian true believers domiciled in the Eccles building can't really believe that today's radical monetary policies are justified by their supposed full-employment goal. That's because, self-evidently, the unacceptably high U-3 unemployment rate cited by Jay Powell in his recent testimonies has absolutely nothing to do with a shortfall of demand that purportedly can be remedied by central bank money pumping and interest rate repression. To the contrary, the current unemployment rate and related output shortfalls are about as pure a supply-side phenomenon as has ever transpired. The government shut down businesses during the pandemic by legal orders and compounded the crime by instilling massive, unjustified fears of social congregation in bars, restaurants, movies, gyms, and malls among the consuming public. Remove this government assault on the supply side and the U-3 unemployment rate—whatever its merit, which isn't much—will head right back to where it was prepandemic. No demand stimulus needed!

Time Warp

The proof is in the pudding. Unlike during every other recession in the past, real personal income, which is a good proxy for aggregate demand, actually soared by nearly 5 percent during 2020. Owing to the massive increase in transfer payments provided by multiple bailouts, this huge gain was actually higher than during every expansion year since 2000, and it towers over the comparable recession year figures for the last 50 years. The consumer had enough spending power to satisfy the most rabid Keynesian model. They just didn't have sufficient legal and safe outlets to release it.

Change in Real Personal Income during Recession Years, 1973–2020

- 1974: –0.58 percent
- 1980: +0.71 percent
- 1982: –1.53 percent
- 1991: +0.13 percent
- 2002: +0.37 percent
- 2009: –2.99 percent
- 2020: +4.91 percent

In effect, the Covid recession and the accompanying bailouts have smoked out the money printers. Their real obsession is hitting their 2 percent inflation target and mechanically filling up the bathtub of GDP—even if aggregate demand has nothing to do with the shortfall. They have imbued these objectives with essentially magical properties.

Thus the Keynesian model of the economy is stuck in a 1930s time warp. As indicated, John Maynard Keynes believed that capitalism had a death wish, causing it to lapse toward underperformance, recession, and depression absent the helping hand of the enlightened state.

The shorthand for that tendency toward cyclical collapse is macroeconomic deflation. It was, ironically, Keynes's latter-day critic, Professor Milton Friedman, who squared the circle and passed on the resulting erroneous deflationist model to who became his single most dangerous apostle, Ben Bernanke, as I amplify more fully in the coming chapters.

There is no evidence whatsoever that a 2 percent inflation target is better for growth and jobs than the prior de facto target of zero. Its real virtue is just arithmetic; it gave the central bankers a 200 basis point margin of error to keep the economy from slipping into the dreaded deflation zone.

There is no other way to explain the Fed's obsession with achieving a strict 2 percent inflation rate to the second decimal point and its new scheme of "averaging" 2 percent over time. Certainly, the alternative idea that a loosely defined "little bit" of inflation helps grease the economy's wheels of expansion could not justify the claim that an actual reading of 1.73 percent on the PCE deflator over the last nine years is not close enough for government work, nor that it somehow constitutes a drastic, intolerable shortfall.

At the end of the day, the Fed's mechanistic 2 percent inflation target—which has led to the massive counterfeiting of the dollar and egregious financial bubbles—is simply a proxy for its misbegotten war on deflation and the founding myths of the 1930s. Back then, as in most credit-fueled booms, the vast expansion of lending during the Great War and the roaring '20s left banks stuffed with bad loans that could no longer be rolled over when the music abruptly stopped in October 1929.

In the aftermath of the crash, upward of $20 billion in bank loans were liquidated, including billions of write-offs due to business failures and foreclosures. Nearly half of the credit contraction was attributable to $9 billion in stock market margin loans called in when the stock market bubble collapsed in 1929. Loan balances for working capital also fell sharply in the face of falling production.

This was the passive consequence of the bursting industrial and export sector bubble, not something caused by the Fed's failure to supply sufficient bank reserves. In short, the liquidation of bank loans was almost exclusively the result of bubbles being punctured in the real economy, not stinginess at the central bank. In fact, there has never been any wide-scale evidence that outstanding bank loans declined from 1930 to 1933 on account of banks calling performing loans or denying credit to solvent potential borrowers.

Yet unless those things happened, there is simply no case that monetary stringency caused the Great Depression. As I show later, Friedman and his followers, including Bernanke, simply came up with an academic dodge—a falling money multiplier—to explain away these obvious facts. Today that canard hangs over the financial system like the sword of Damocles. Fighting the wrong war against deflation, the Fed has pumped upward of $8 trillion in fiat credit into the financial system since the turn of the century. That fact has levitated the financial markets into the nosebleed section.

Chapter 4

A Collapse of
Epic Proportions

At the end of the day, the inflation deniers in the Eccles building have set up the financial system for a collapse of epic proportions. And they have done so notwithstanding the fact that the compound growth of the inflation rate, represented by trimmed mean CPI, since they adopted inflation targeting, in January 2012, was actually 2.07 percent.

If it were only a cowering fear of Wall Street's entitled bullies and billionaires, that would be bad enough. But the Fed heads are so intellectually self-deluded that they can't even bring themselves to call a spade a spade. Housing price inflation has roared at and beyond the insanity of 2004–7. In the April 2021 minutes of the Fed meeting, they came up with this tepid observation: "A number of participants commented on valuation pressures being somewhat elevated in the housing market." You think?

For the latest available month, the Federal Housing Finance Agency's index, based on more than 6 million repeat sales of the same single-family homes, rose at 15.7 percent year-over-year. That's the highest annual gain ever recorded, including during the peak of the Greenspan housing bubble of 10.7 percent year-over-year in September 2005. In other words, these folks have their heads buried deep in the sand of their own groupthink and simply can't see the inflationary cyclone they have released on both Wall Street and Main Street.

A veritable housing price explosion is happening on the highways and byways all across America, especially in the exurbs, towns, and countrysides where city folk have stampeded during the pandemic. As the *Wall Street Journal* reported recently, bidding wars are happening from coast to coast and have begun even in burned-out Rust Belt towns of Allentown and Bethlehem, Pennsylvania:

> The median listed price for a house jumped 24 percent in January from a year earlier in the metropolitan area surrounding Allentown, the Rust-Belt city whose decline was memorialized in a 1982 Billy Joel song, according to data from Realtor.com. It was the same in such spots as Martin, Tenn., a small city 150 miles from Nashville, where the median asking price went up 159 percent over the same period; in Kendallville, Ind., about 30 miles outside Fort Wayne, it climbed 56 percent.
>
> The average price for a house in the Allentown metro area, which includes Bethlehem, was about $225,000 a year ago. . . . It has since shot past $270,000 in a market so hot that open houses trigger traffic jams, and properties sell in 48 hours.

One of the drivers of this frenzy is big Wall Street hedge funds and private equity shops flush with massive amounts of the Fed's ultracheap debt. As the savvy veteran real estate analyst John Burns noted, cited by the *Wall Street Journal*, "The cash flows are better in the Tulsas and Allentowns of the world for those seeking to rent out properties. In the fourth quarter of 2020, nearly a fifth of homes sold in the Allentown area were bought by investors, according to Mr. Burns's data."

With the exception of a few urban markets, such as Manhattan and San Francisco, there is a chronic shortage of inventory. Heavy sales volumes are causing prices to rise wildly in excess of income growth. In Bethlehem, for instance, the monthly number of homes for sale has fallen by 65 percent from normal levels, causing buyers to bid with their eyes closed, per the *Wall Street Journal*: "Buyers feel pressure to make snap decisions, and some forgo routine home inspections for fear of losing to another bidder. 'If you're a buyer, this is the most frustrating time,' said Jonathan Campbell, vice president of DLP Realty in Bethlehem. The local market, he said, is outpacing the mid-2000s housing boom."

Other reasons for the supply scarcity include the government's pandemic-driven mortgage forbearance program, which has sharply reduced an important normal source of incremental supply: foreclosure sales, especially on the lower end of the market. Second, there is a dearth of trade-up sellers because supply and price are even more prohibitive higher up the value ladder. In other words, owing to Covid lockdown dislocations and the population reset to areas outside the big cities, there was already going to be a heated residential housing market.

Add to the bonfire the Fed's hideously low interest rates generally and the sheer lunacy of buying $40 billion in housing mortgage paper per month, driving interest rates even lower, and the Fed has accomplished that which was inconceivable during the fraught times right after the 2007–9 housing crash—namely, it has rekindled an even more out-of-control housing boom than Alan Greenspan accomplished a decade-and-a-half before.

Housing Surge

Now roaring home price inflation will at least in part work its way into the CPI and PCE deflator in the months and years just ahead. Based on an estimate of the spillover effect of housing asset inflation to shelter costs, Goldman Sachs projects that CPI shelter inflation is likely to surge to 3.8 percent year-over-year by the end of 2022 and exceed 4 percent in 2023, a higher rate than at any point in the prior economic cycle.

And that gets us to the final point about the Fed's relentless inflation denialism—the manner in which both the government agencies and the Fed manipulate inflation data.

As mentioned previously, so-called hedonic adjustments for improved quality and functionality were introduced into the CPI in the late 1990s per the recommendations of the Boskin Commission. What these adjustments do, of course, is take the sticker price that consumers actually pay and adjust it downward—sometimes substantially so—to reflect bureaucratic guesses as to the value of faster computer speeds or safety features such as airbags in cars.

One of the biggest of these hedonic adjustments is in auto prices. During the period between 1971 and 1997, new auto prices rose about 6.2 percent per year. Upon the introduction of hedonic adjustment to car prices, however, inflation just plain stopped dead in the water. Somehow, the annual increase over the last 23 years was just 0.1 percent. No wonder the Fed can never find enough inflation. The green eye-shades at the Bureau of Labor Statistics have essentially defined it out of existence.

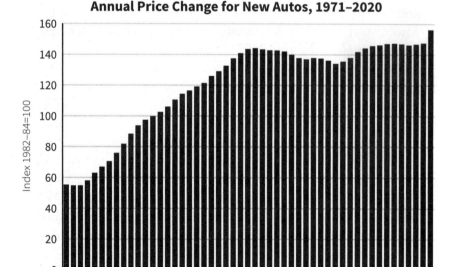

Annual Price Change for New Autos, 1971–2020

Index 1982–84=100

■ Consumer price index for all urban consumers: new vehicles in U.S. city average
gross domestic product, Q4 2007=100

Sources: U.S. Bureau of Labor Statistics
fred.stlouisfed.org

But not in the real world, where more than 100 million middle-class households struggle to make ends meet. Here is the sticker price data for the iconic Ford Mustang coupe over the last 50 years:

	1971 Mustang	1997 Mustang	2020 Mustang
Sticker price	$3,006	$15,355	$39,880
Hours worked to purchase	835 ($3.60/hr)	1,228 ($12.50/hr)	1,597 ($24.97/hr)
Worker hours per year	1,908	1,800	1,778
Months to purchase	5.3	8.2	10.8

By 2020, it cost 10.8 months of work at the average wage to buy the Mustang. That's 32 percent more than it did before hedonics were incorporated into the CPI, even though the government claims that the price essentially stopped rising 23 years ago.

Our Fifteen-Cent Dollar

There is no way to comprehend the virulent, widespread inflation that has overcome the American economy without understanding the financial turning point of modern times—Richard Nixon's scrapping of the dollar's last link to gold at Camp David in August 1971.

The resulting devastating hit to the purchasing power of the dollar speaks for itself. The dollar of August 1971 is worth just 15 cents today. That won't buy you a paper cup, let alone the coffee to fill it.

And no, this isn't just the impact of the 1970s double-digit inflation some may remember. By 1980, the dollar still was worth half of its pre–Camp David value. Since then, it has never stopped eroding—the direct result of the explicit, proinflation policy of the Federal Reserve.

Nor is this a matter of a no-harm, no-foul regime in which we all inflate together in lockstep fashion. To the contrary, with the passage of time, some wages, prices, and costs have ended up way ahead of inflation, but others have fallen behind, sometimes drastically so. Way ahead are financial assets held by the wealthy; falling behind is exemplified by the severe erosion of the purchasing power of savers, fixed-income retirees, and wage earners who must now compete in the global market for goods and services.

With respect to those left behind in the Fed's proinflation parade, take the case of hourly manufacturing wages. Notwithstanding a quadrupling of real GDP over the past 50 years, the inflation-adjusted manufacturing wage rate today is actually 6 percent lower than it was a half century ago, in 1971.

As we have seen, compared to a half century ago, it now takes more than twice as many work years—8.08 versus 3.80—for an average wage earner to buy the median family home today.

The radically disproportionate and profoundly inequitable impact of the Fed's proinflation policy over the decades is just one of its many ill effects, however. As I illustrate here, misbegotten monetary policy also has caused a vast offshoring of America's industrial economy to China and other low-wage competitors. That offshoring process has undermined middle-income prosperity and overall economic growth. Simultaneously, Fed policy has channeled vast amounts of resources from the Main Street economy into Wall Street gambling dens, further undermining productive investment and real growth.

To be sure, the prosperous times before Nixon's perfidy were not all rainbows and unicorns. Despite its theoretical attractions, the regime we had before 1971, the Bretton Woods gold-exchange standard, turned out to be operationally flawed because it ended a powerful disciplinary feature that had made the pre-1914 gold standard a historic success.

Nixon and Gold

First, some history. Under the pre-1914 gold coin standard, holders of U.S. dollars and checking deposits in dollars could redeem them for gold at the fixed rate of $20.67 per ounce. As a result, inflationary government policies invited a flight to gold. That fact acted as an abrupt check on monetary depreciation.

Under the post–World War II Bretton Woods system, however, private citizens were prohibited from doing business in gold. Convertibility was only possible between national governments and their central banks. Washington soon learned that as the free world's largest military superpower and bulwark against Soviet expansionism—real and imagined—the U.S. government had wide latitude to discourage demands on the Treasury for gold. Washington could force its allies to accumulate paper dollar reserves, whether they wanted to or not.

At length, however, the U.S. government overplayed its hand. Under Lyndon Johnson's inflationary "guns and butter" spending policies there occurred an unstable and unsustainable buildup of dollar claims abroad. Those claims could have been redeemed for gold as promised under Bretton Woods only at the price of a deep U.S. recession. In turn, that would have denied Nixon his desperately sought landslide reelection in 1972, or likely any victory at all. So Tricky Dick pulled the plug on gold, and the rest is history.

Bad history. One misstep at a time, the abandonment of gold has led to the 15-cent dollar and the hideous financial asset inflation of the present era. That woebegone journey finally has culminated in the current clown car of Washington central bankers who insist on creating $120 billion in fraudulent credit per month to "create" inflation. And until the very 11th hour with monthly inflation figures soaring, they had no plan to desist until the labor market and the economy were "healed," whatever that meant.

After all, why does the Main Street economy need help from the Fed when everyday prices and wages are now soaring owing to a shortage of workers, computer chips, cars, and imports of every type? And why do financial markets need more liquidity and cheap speculator credit when they are already flying, carefree, into la-la land?

Still, the pre-1971 economic history proves beyond a shadow of a doubt that you don't need a proinflation central bank to enable economic growth and rising prosperity, as the present-day Fed and its Wall Street acolytes insist. And it also reminds us that there is not some innate tendency for a currency to relentlessly depreciate.

Consider the purchasing power of the dollar over the 25 years from 1921 to mid-1946. That period encompassed the roaring '20s boom, the Great Depression bust, and the near-doubling of the U.S. economy's size during World War II. Yet the purchasing power of the dollar in 1946 was the same as in 1921, at which point the worst of the World War I inflation had been wrung out during the postwar recession.

Despite having zero net inflation over that quarter-century period, at the recommencement of peacetime in 1946, real GDP stood 207 percent higher than in June 1921. In today's economic vernacular, that computes to an outcome that is tantamount to economic nirvana—4.6 percent annual growth of GDP with zero inflation.

Moreover, quibbling about 1930s-era deflation and the command- and price-controlled war economy through the end of 1945 doesn't deny the truth that growth and inflation are not joined at the hip as our Keynesian central bankers now incessantly proclaim. That's because the even better comparison is of the period between the second quarter of 1921 and the third quarter of 1929—bookends encompassing the period between the conversion to peacetime after the Great War and the collapse of Wall Street in October 1929.

A Sound Dollar

During that golden age of prosperity, the price level as measured by the CPI actually fell by 2 percent, even as real GDP expanded by 62.5 percent. That translates to a 6.1 percent annual real GDP growth rate and a gentle 0.25 percent annual decline (deflation!) in the price level. There was no Phillips curve trade-off between growth and inflation whatsoever. And while the diminutive Fed of that era made some major mistakes—principally, its attempt to prop up the British pound and French franc after the mid-1920s, a move that fostered the stock and bond market booms and then crashed at the end of the decade—it never even remotely fretted about too little inflation. And that is because of a sound U.S. dollar that retained purchasing power!

Indeed, the sound dollar depicted by the dotted line below was the primary mission of our central bank while the booming economy was achieved by a free market with no "stimulus" help at all from the Fed. By the lights of today's Keynesians, the balanced-budget policies of the era's great Treasury secretary, Andrew Mellon, were supposedly contractionary.

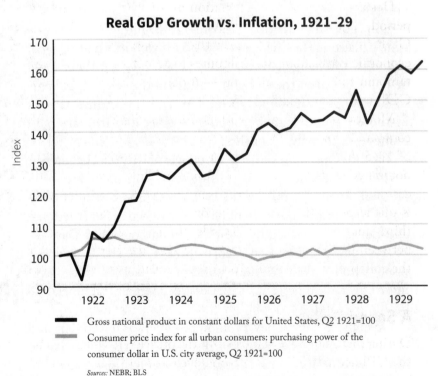

Real GDP Growth vs. Inflation, 1921–29

Gross national product in constant dollars for United States, Q2 1921=100

Consumer price index for all urban consumers: purchasing power of the consumer dollar in U.S. city average, Q2 1921=100

Sources: NEBR; BLS
fred.stlouisfed.org

As I detail later on, the entire 2 percent inflation regime was built on erroneous pre-World War II scholarship by Milton Friedman and his myopic disciple Ben Bernanke. Except they studied the Depression years after 1929 while ignoring entirely the crucial preceding 15-year period, during which the Fed opened for business in November 1914 and was promptly drafted to finance America's ill-fated entry into World War I.

The effect of massive money printing to finance the war was a 51 percent depreciation of the dollar's purchasing power by the crest of postwar inflation in June 1920. After the war, of course, the allied governments did commit themselves to the task of recouping that lost purchasing power but with only middling success, especially in Europe, thanks to the newfound power of organized labor and socialist policies.

Still, governments had good reason to purge roaring wartime inflation. They had sold war bonds to both their investor class and to average citizens alike, promising that they would be redeemed after the end of hostilities at the prewar gold parities. Strange as it sounds to modern ears, governments back in those days took their promises—especially in matters of money—extremely seriously.

The attempt to resume gold convertibility at the prewar parity of $4.85 per pound sterling was Winston Churchill's allegedly infamous mistake in 1925. But that's Keynesian history reinforced by the antigold monetary theories of Friedman and Bernanke. In fact, by the time the famous "100 Days" of FDR's New Deal was enacted in June 1933, the U.S. dollar was well on its way to the restoration of its 1914 value, having recovered 60 percent of the loss recorded at the June 1920 bottom.

Of course, fiat money promoters—such as Friedman and Bernanke—blamed exactly this restoration of the dollar's value in the early 1930s for the Great Depression. They referred to this positive development, of course, by the pejorative term "deflation" and held that it resulted from the fact that currency and deposits (the M1 money supply) in the banking system contracted sharply during the four years after the October 1929 crash.

As a matter of fact, commercial bank deposits did shrink by 26 percent between the precrash baseline in the second quarter of 1929 and the fourth quarter 1933 bottom, falling to $33.5 billion from $45.5 billion. But that wasn't because the Fed was too stingy with reserves and currency. Its balance sheet actually expanded robustly during the same four-year period, ground zero of the Great Depression, rising by 8.3 percent per annum from $4.72 billion to $6.50 billion.

Misunderstanding History

What happened in the banking system, therefore, had not been instigated by the 8.3 percent per annum growth rate of the Fed's balance sheet. Rather, what occurred was the sweeping liquidation of the bad loans made during the boom times of the Great War, when the United States became the world's arsenal and its granary, and the 1920s, when Wall Street had lent massive amounts to the rest of the world to finance America's booming exports (the equivalent of more than $1.5 trillion at today's economic scale). These bad debts also included a reckless level of margin lending accumulated in the run-up to the stock market crash.

By definition, when loans and other assets are liquidated, the deposit footings of banks also shrink. But bank deposits do not drive lending and GDP; they reflect it. In fact, purging bad credits adds to economic efficiency and growth by permitting labor and capital resources to be reoriented toward more productive ends.

In any event, this is how the "more inflation" mantra under Bernanke and his successors originated way back in the 1930s—not in the actual history of the Great Depression but in Friedman's woefully erroneous take on its causes. Specifically, he claimed that the sound money gold standard had shackled the Fed, preventing it from engaging in the kind of money-pumping spree that Bernanke inflicted on the nation decades later in 2008 and 2009.

In summary, the "deflation" that Friedman decried was not caused by Fed actions from 1929 to 1933. Instead, it represented the necessary work of a free market healing itself. The shrinkage of the bloated banking system and overextended credit, which essentially peaked in 1929, was really nothing more than a belated and old-fashioned purge of monetary inflation that had originated in the financing of the Great War, a process that the world at that time well understood and had experienced following previous conflicts dating back centuries.

In short, the years 1929 to 1933 did not prove that capitalism had some kind of deflationary death wish or that gold-backed money inherently causes economic contraction, such that it can only be cured by central bankers astutely managing a fiat money supply. These facts refute the hoary "just in case" or margin-of-error notion that is the analytical underpinning of Bernanke's insidious 2 percent inflation target, one to which we remain tethered to this day. Free market capitalism does not slip into an irreversible deflationary spiral on its own, and we don't need central bankers to target a 2 percent or better rise in the general price level so that inflation doesn't run so close to a supposed zero percent edge and risk slipping into a deflationary abyss.

There is no abyss! That's just a convenient fiction of Keynesian central bankers.

Of course, eventually, the New Deal put the kibosh on sound money altogether. FDR devalued the dollar by 59 percent in early 1934, reducing the gold conversion point from its historic $20.67 per ounce to $35 per ounce and requiring all holders of gold and gold certificates to surrender them in return for unbacked U.S. Treasury bonds. But by then, the "natural" part of the Great Depression—the purge of World War I and roaring '20s excesses—was over. In fact, industrial production bottomed in the second quarter of 1932 and began a normal rebound thereafter, one that finally brought national output back to its 1929 precrash level by the second quarter of 1935.

But this wasn't the doing of FDR's wacky smorgasbord of interventions and spending on three-letter recovery efforts, such as the National Recovery Administration (NRA), the Agricultural Adjustment Act (AAA), the Public Works Administration (PWA), and countless more. Rather, the New Deal retarded a natural recovery for more than two years, from mid-1933 to mid-1935, owing to the imposition of a statist straitjacket on Main Street economic life. By 1935, even FDR abandoned the idea, shifting to the more procompetition Second New Deal.

The Fed was again drafted into the service of war finance during World War II, when the Treasury bill and bond rates were pegged at 0.38 percent and 2.5 percent, respectively. But after the so-called Treasury Accord in 1951, the Fed was freed from these pegs, and William McChesney Martin, who had fashioned the accord at the Treasury, became Fed chairman.

Taking Away the Punch Bowl

During the next 11 years, through 1962, the planking was laid for noninflationary postwar prosperity by the Martin-run Fed. Over that period, real GDP expanded by 44.2 percent, a healthy 3.3 percent per year. In an everlasting rebuke to today's manic money printers, this happened while the Fed's balance sheet was nearly stationary, creeping up by just 0.2 percent annual growth over the period.

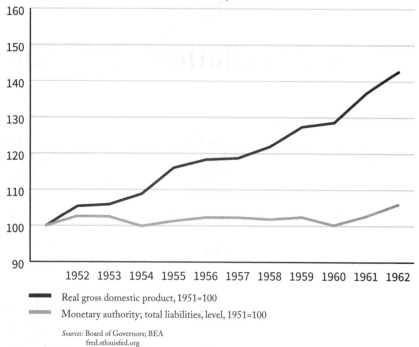

Real GDP Growth vs. Fed Balance Sheet Growth, 1951–62

Real gross domestic product, 1951=100

Monetary authority; total liabilities, level, 1951=100

Sources: Board of Governors; BEA
fred.stlouisfed.org

Martin, of course, famously proclaimed that the job of the Fed is to take away the punch bowl just as the party was getting started. That discipline may well have contributed to three short recessions over the period. But the proof is in the pudding. The real growth rate over the entire period—recessions and all—averaged more than twice the paltry 1.5 percent rate that the Fed money pumpers have generated since the precrisis peak in the final quarter of 2007.

Chapter 5

Your Grandfather's Inflation

During the next eight years, through the Camp David event in August 1971, the tide began to change dramatically. Lyndon Johnson wanted his "guns and butter" and the Harvard Keynesian economists brought into the White House in 1961 were not about to let sound money and William McChesney Martin get in the way.

At one point in December 1965, as spending for the Vietnam War and the Great Society were exploding, LBJ famously brought Martin down to his ranch in Texas for a dose of the "treatment." That is, a blistering admonition—delivered by a 6-foot-4 Johnson hulking over Martin, who was pinned up against a wall—in favor of a fiscal extravaganza to be financed by the Fed.

Unfortunately, Martin largely complied. The results speak for themselves. In contrast to the first 11 years of Martin's tenure, the Fed's balance sheet exploded over the next eight years, rising by 6.2 percent per year. That fueled the first installment of an inflationary boom. Real GDP did grow by 4.2 percent per year, but consumer inflation, which had been largely dormant during the 1950s after the Korean War ended, surged to 3.5 percent per year.

This outbreak of rising prices is what finally put the Bretton Woods gold-backed dollar on the rocks, paving the way for Nixon's perfidy at Camp David. The manner in which it unfolded is straightforward: the Fed monetized part of LBJ's big deficits after 1965, causing a domestic boom and a huge influx of imports on the "butter" side of the ledger. The "guns" side resulted in an accelerated outflow of dollars to fund foreign military operations and Washington's far-flung network of foreign economic and military aid.

The resulting numbers are crystal clear. Between 1960 and 1965, the U.S. surplus on goods and services of $26 billion nearly offset the payment outflows for guns and empire building, which totaled $26.3 billion over the same six-year period. In 1965, however, the Vietnam War sharply escalated and Great Society spending at home also began to surge, so this tolerable balance ended. During the seven years between 1966 and 1972, domestic imports soared and the cumulative surplus on goods and services shrank to just $1.4 billion. Meanwhile, the outflow for empire-building surged to $46.2 billion.

This $45 billion gap resulted in an enormous buildup after 1965 of dollars abroad, an imbalance not effectively offset by America's paper surplus on investment income because most of that was unrealized and not repatriated. As a consequence, the pressure for dollar redemptions in gold became enormous, a movement led by Gaullist France. At length, it also led Treasury Secretary and Texas easy-money man John Connally to famously tell America's allies that the dollar was "our currency and your problem."

The real problem, in fact, was the upcoming 1972 election, which Nixon was not about to lose. So Nixon did the dirty deed, but it was LBJ and a generation of big-spending cold warriors who laid the groundwork and intimidated the Fed into cranking up the printing presses, bringing the final end to sound money.

What followed was a nightmare—the next decade saw soaring inflation, a deep recession in 1975, and lagging economic growth after Nixon's election-year boom. The breakdown started with the Fed, which pumped up its balance sheet by 8 percent per year from mid-1971 to the end of 1979, when the hapless Jimmy Carter finally brought in Paul Volcker to quell the inflationary storm. And a storm it was, as evidenced by an average 8.3 percent annual rise in prices (CPI) during the nine years ending in the fourth quarter of 1980.

The inflationary breakout was far worse at the double peaks of the fourth quarter of 1974, when the year-on-year CPI increase printed at 12.1 percent, and the first quarter of 1980, when the year-on-year rise soared to 14.6 percent. At the same time, real GDP and household income growth slowed sharply over the decade. Economic growth slowed to just 2.8 percent per year after the Nixon boom ended in the second quarter of 1973.

Roaring inflation and slowing growth—dubbed "stagflation" by the press—devastated the average American family. During the nearly two decades from 1954 to 1973, real median family income rose from $34,700 to $62,150, a sparkling 3.1 percent annual increase. In contrast, over the next 10 years through 1983, family income actually shrank by 0.32 percent per year!

The crucial takeaway is that owing to the lack of an international pressure-relief valve of cheap imports, the Fed's inflationary policies passed directly through the Main Street economy like green grass passing through a goose. The 8 percent growth rate of its balance sheet led to 8.3 percent average inflation, along with weakening real GDP growth and falling real family incomes.

The Volcker Interregnum

As it happened, Volcker rode to the rescue. He was appointed Fed chairman in August 1979. The essence of his accomplishment was that he refused to accommodate either Jimmy Carter's roaring inflation or Ronald Reagan's erupting fiscal deficits. Instead, he hit the brakes on the runaway balance sheet growth at the Fed, slowing it to just 5 percent per year.

That choice unavoidably triggered the deep recession of 1981 and 1982, but it's important to wave away the mists of time and recall the stunning drop in the CPI inflation rate that accompanied the shift to determined restraint at the central bank. From a peak year-on-year rate of 14.6 percent in the first quarter of 1980, CPI plunged steadily until it hit bottom at 1.2 percent year-on-year in the fourth quarter of 1986.

The virtual ski slope downward in the inflation rate is all the more remarkable considering that the consensus at the time was that inflation was so deeply embedded in the national wage-cost-price structure that it could be reduced only in tiny baby steps over an extended period of time and would never again fall to the pre-1965 level of 1 percent to 2 percent per year.

Unfortunately, the Volcker interregnum was the last hurrah for sound money. But its true significance has been lost in and obscured by urban legends manufactured since then by self-serving partisans in Washington and on Wall Street. Future generations of Republicans took the 1980s experience to mean that deficits don't matter much and aren't inflationary and that unfinanced tax cuts caused the so-called "Morning in America" boom of the later Reagan years. In so doing, they essentially abandoned the GOP's historic role as the guardian of sound money and fiscal rectitude in American democracy.

Likewise, Wall Street soon embraced the abandonment of Volcker's stern financial discipline in favor of Alan Greenspan's "wealth effects" policies. The latter held that virtually unlimited inflation of financial assets was fine so long as consumer-level inflation—as measured by an increasingly shortened yardstick—remained "disinflationary." The latter was defined informally at first as 2 percent to 3 percent per year under Greenspan and then made official with the adoption of Bernanke's 2 percent inflation-targeting policy in January 2012.

These urban legends had calamitous effects on capitalist prosperity in America. They are the foundation on which Washington's infernal inflation machine has evolved from the novel to the ridiculous and, now, to the sublime.

Above all else, these misbegotten propositions fail to recognize that at some point in the 1990s, the economic and financial world was turned upside down by what is surely a freak occurrence in world history: China's "red capitalism." In one fell swoop, as it were, the Fed's flood of dollars into the global economy enabled China to drain its rice paddies of hundreds of millions of poor peasants, turning them into industrial workers and fueling the greatest malinvestment spree in history with a gargantuan amount of debt and cheap capital, which I will illustrate in the next section.

The result was a deflationary wave of export mercantilism that profoundly changed the environment in which the post-1971 fiat money central bankers at the Fed and their developed-world counterparts operate. Accordingly, the inflation we experienced prior to the mid-1990s can be described as "your grandfather's inflation." On the surface, it's the old-fashioned Friedmanite story of too much money chasing too few goods, but what is truly relevant is the unstated predicate underlying these central bank–fueled inflationary bursts.

To wit, throughout most of this period (1965–90), the United States was the planet's low-cost producer of industrial goods at volume. When domestic production capacity and labor got fully absorbed domestically, there was no reserve production base abroad to supply incremental U.S. demand at current or lower prices.

In that context, the Fed's money printing fueled artificial and excess demand via rapid credit expansion. In turn, that led to rising prices and a cascade of self-fueling price-wage-cost spirals in the domestic economy. It was those spirals that Volcker's austerity vanquished with considerable speed.

But after the mid-1990s, the effect of the Fed's monetary stimulus found a sharply different outlet. On the margin, excess U.S. demand flowed to the shiny new low-cost export factories of China, precipitating what amounted to a "red tide" of global deflation. In that context, America's Fed-inflated wages, costs, and prices were suddenly at a profound competitive disadvantage on world markets, meaning that the twin bursts of 1970s commodity and consumer inflation had not been a free lunch after all.

Accordingly, it needed to be purged (deflated), not accommodated and exacerbated by central bank policy. Of course, the very opposite happened. Greenspan is the everlasting villain of the set piece that followed. He invented the ruse he called "disinflation" and thereby blocked a deflationary purge that would have been the inherent result of maintaining sound money in the 1990s.

Offshoring America

The result was the eventual offshoring of America's industrial economy. That drastically reduced sustainable economic growth and Main Street prosperity, but it also ushered in a period of imported deflation from China and its supply base. In turn, the effects of the Fed's inflationary money printing were channeled from the Main Street economy of goods and services to the Wall Street casino of soaring financial asset prices and speculative enterprise.

Needless to say, that channeling of the Fed's money pumping from Main Street to Wall Street gave rise to two very big lies—namely, that the Friedman formula about "too much money chasing too few goods" is obsolete, giving the central bank free rein to print money at will; and that the resultant soaring paper wealth being generated in asset markets was real, sustainable, and a sign of resurgent capitalist prosperity.

Neither of these propositions is remotely true, of course, but they were the basis upon which the small group of unelected economists, bankers, and apparatchiks who operate the nation's central bank were enthroned as financial demigods. In completely and insouciantly abrogating the laws of sound money, these suddenly all-powerful central bankers made it the profound self-interest of Washington politicians and Wall Street operators alike to give them a wide berth. That's because the initial impacts of cheap debt and soaring financial asset prices were a previously unknown ease in financing government deficits and unspeakable financial windfalls for traders and speculators.

But there truly is no free lunch. Nor do rampant debt creation and speculative wagering generate sustainable and equitable wealth. Unfortunately, however, the costs of such profligacy can be deferred and largely hidden for extended periods of time. And that's exactly what happened during the "great inflation sabbatical" of 1995–2019.

The Great Inflation Sabbatical

So let's turn back to the fundamentals and examine how the goods-and-services inflation of the 1970s mutated into the raging financial inflation of the last several decades.

The eruption of labor and other domestic production costs during the 1970s left the U.S. economy badly exposed to an attack by low-cost foreign suppliers. China's nascent export machine seemed to spring into existence fully formed after the mid-1990s. Nevertheless, the first quarter century of fiat money in the United States (1971–95) amounted to an all-out war on America's working class and its industrial base.

That's because the red-hot inflation of the 1970s and the simmering level of "disinflation" under Greenspan's early years at the Fed's helm fueled a terrible explosion of labor costs in the United States. Between the first quarter of 1972 and the first quarter of 1995, domestic unit labor costs—expressed as wage increases minus productivity gains—soared by 178 percent on a cumulative basis.

That amounted to a relentless 4.5 percent per-year growth in the cost of producing goods over a 23-year period, even as China's leader, Deng Xiaoping, was herding his peasant laborers by the tens of millions into shiny new export factories in Guangdong Province and elsewhere in China's vast interior. In combination, this was a screaming incentive for American purveyors of goods to move their factories to or source their production from China. Today's great technocolossus, Apple, is living proof of that.

At the same time, all that drastic inflation of U.S. wage rates and production costs didn't do a damn thing for American workers. The inflation-adjusted average hourly wage actually fell by 17 percent during roughly the same 23-year period. It is truly hard to think of a more pernicious policy than that depicted by the nasty "X" pattern of falling real wages and soaring unit labor costs in the chart below. To be clear, this was not the work of capitalism, free trade, greedy corporate executives at home, or even nefarious Chinese Communist trade-policy manipulators in Beijing.

To the contrary, the heads of American industrial workers were handed to China on a platter by the Federal Reserve. The Fed first inflated the U.S. economy during the 1970s, and then under Greenspan, it blocked the deflationary purge of excess domestic production costs that could have kept industrial jobs in America and protected the real wages of American workers.

Real Hourly Wages vs. Unit Labor Costs, 1972–95

■ Average hourly earnings of production and nonsupervisory employees, total private, Jan. 1972=100 /
consumer price index for all urban customers: all items in U.S. city average, Jan. 1972=100 (left)

▬ Nonfarm business sector: unit labor costs for all employed persons, Q1 1972=100 (right)

Sources: U.S. Bureau of Labor Statistics
fred.stlouisfed.org

Thus between June 1987 and early 2000, Greenspan and his colleagues foolishly expanded the Fed's balance sheet to nearly $610 billion from $270 billion, when it should not have been expanded at all. That kept domestic inflation very much alive, thereby blocking a desperately needed rollback of the 180 percent increase in the domestic price level (CPI) that had occurred between June 1971 and June 1987.

In fact, the CPI rose another 3.3 percent per year, or 80 percent in total, between Greenspan's arrival at the Fed in August 1987 and the dot-com bubble peak in March 2000. All told, the domestic price level in March 2000 stood 322 percent above its mid-1971 level. That's the breathtaking scale of the monetary debauchment that central bankers generated during the first 29 years of fiat money. Once they discovered they could produce dollar liabilities at will without the inconvenience of either citizens or even foreign governments demanding to redeem them in gold, the Fed literally trashed the purchasing power of America's money while Greenspan claimed that he was heroically bringing inflation to heel.

Worse still, the Keynesian economists who advise the Fed argued that this 322 percent rise in the general price level over that three-decade period was locked in. That followed from their hoary old catechism about "sticky" wages and therefore the inability of modern capitalist economies to adjust the price level downward once it gets out of line.

The implicit theory, apparently, is that once you make the mistake of inflating there is no turning back and that in some magical way the Fed must compensate for the loss of domestic competitiveness on world markets by the expedient of doubling down on "stimulus" to the domestic economy.

The latter is absurd and the former isn't true. Notwithstanding a relentless effort by the unshackled Fed to "stimulate" the economy and inflation—as measured by its balance sheet growth to $610 billion from $90 billion over nearly 30 years—the real wages of American workers still fell by 17 percent between 1971 and 2000.

The only shred of truth in the "sticky" wages and prices argument pertains to wage rates set by quasi-monopoly unions in the heavy industrial sectors such as steel, autos, chemicals, and textiles during the decades immediately after World War II. But by the time of Greenspan's stint at the helm of the Fed, the industrial unions were broken. Following the 1980s, for example, several million units per year of new auto production capacity were built in the United States, but all of it was in right-to-work states such as Tennessee, Alabama, Kentucky, South Carolina, and Texas.

The deflationary Fed policy that Greenspan should have run would have mainly accelerated the flight of industrial production to lower-cost right-to-work (and Republican-led) states at home, had the old-line industrial unions refused to cut their inflated and unsustainable nominal wage rates and benefits. That kind of anti-inflationary domestic adjustment would have been far preferable to the actual flight of America's industrial base to the state-controlled and -subsidized factories in China.

Moreover, the Greenspan Fed's proinflation error ultimately extended far beyond the domestic shoreline. What it actually did was flood the world with excess dollars, thereby exporting both inflationary demand and America's industrial economy in the process.

Of course, under the honest currency float (i.e., free market) that Friedman assured Nixon would be the result of trashing the Bretton Woods agreement, the massive offshoring of U.S. production to China would have had very different consequences than what actually happened. The flood of Chinese exports to the United States and other developed economies would have generated not only the huge Chinese trade surpluses that did materialize but a sharply rising yuan as well.

In turn, that would have thrown a wrench into China's overnight rise as an industrial powerhouse between 1995 and 2007. That's because the yuan price of exports to the United

States would have translated into far higher dollar costs, thereby reducing the attractiveness of sourcing in China relative to domestic suppliers.

Red Capitalists

Except that there never was a "clean float" after the Smithsonian Agreement, the successor to Bretton Woods, collapsed in 1973. Foreign central banks, at the behest of their governments, intervened in foreign exchange markets heavily in order to keep their own exchange rates down and thereby benefit their export industries. This kind of dirty-float mercantilism became the norm in Asia, led by Japan, South Korea, Taiwan, and others.

The newly arrived red capitalists of Beijing, therefore, simply adopted the Asian export model with a vengeance. In response to Greenspan's flood of dollars and the buildup of their own initial trade surpluses, China repegged its exchange rate at about 8.30 yuan per U.S. dollar in November 1993 and kept it there, unwaveringly flat as a board, through 2005. In the interim, of course, this incredibly dirty float required China's central bank to scoop up dollars by the trillions in order to keep the yuan exchange rate pinned tightly to its peg.

The proof is unequivocally in the pudding. China's foreign-exchange reserves soared to $1.7 trillion by 2008 from $150 billion in 1995 and ultimately to a peak of $4.1 trillion in 2014. The reciprocal effect of those soaring reserves was the hollowed-out industrial economy of the United States and split-screen domestic inflation trends—the falling cost of goods amid a rising cost of services—which accompanied it.

Moreover, all this scooping up of excess dollars by the People's Bank of China (PBOC) had a corollary effect that was even more profound. As the PBOC's balance sheet mushroomed with U.S. Treasury bonds and other dollar "assets," the liability side exploded too. That is, as the PBOC bought dollars, it supplied yuan into the domestic financial system, thereby creating easy money at home like never before.

This massive outpouring into the Chinese economy of high-powered central bank credit was crucial. The thing that China's peasant masses and their rulers needed to escape the Middle Kingdom's vast, relatively inert subsistence economy was access to modern tools and production technology and cheap, abundant capital that could finance state-of-the-art factories and production infrastructure. And that crucial ingredient the Greenspan Fed handed to them on a silver platter in the form of vast dollar reserves to back their prodigious production of cheap yuan.

Without these huge-dollar foreign-exchange reserves, China's fantastic money pumping would have led to a domestic inflationary blowoff long ago, just like any unbacked monetary expansion has always generated, going back to Weimar Germany. Like the latter, the rise of red capitalism would have been stopped short by soaring imported inflation owing to a weakening foreign exchange rate. The world's new so-called factory floor would have been submerged in imports of unaffordable raw material and intermediate components.

Foolishly, Greenspan and company spared them the trouble by flooding the world with surplus dollars. One step removed, the currency-pegging PBOC transformed those unwanted dollars into onshore yuan, and soon China's banking system and domestic credit system were off to the races. And I do mean races. China's total nonfinancial debt—household, business, and government—rose to $3.9 trillion by 2006 from $500 billion in 1995 and then exploded to $22.9 trillion by 2014 and $42.5 trillion in 2020. That's an 85-fold gain in the course of just 25 years, and there is nothing remotely like it in recorded history.

To be sure, Keynesian economists in the United States have done their best to obscure the Fed's culpability for the burned-out industrial zones dotting "flyover America" from coast to coast. Along with their nonchalance about China's mountainous internal debt (about $50 trillion, counting financial debt), a much-repeated canard among Washington policymakers is the claim that China's ultradirty float mainly reflected the buildup of foreign-exchange reserves to protect it from a "currency crisis."

But that's self-serving humbug. In a floating exchange rate world of fiat currencies, there can't be any currency "crisis" and there is no need for currency "reserves." According to Friedman, the price mechanism would clear the exchange markets just like it does the markets for fresh apples or crude oil. Instead of periodic foreign-exchange crises and the need to defend a fixed foreign-exchange peg, there would be just a fluctuating foreign-exchange price, conceivably even one that fluctuates drastically.

Therefore, the very idea of foreign-exchange "reserves" is a vestigial throwback, ironically, to the world of sound money, where gold or gold-convertible currencies such as the U.S. dollar functioned as settlement assets between national economies. Alas, under a regime of floating fiat money—free or dirty—there are no balance-of-payments "settlements." Economies adjust to one another based on variable foreign exchange rates rather than reserve asset flows. The latter only become relevant under dirty floats, where so-called reserve assets are used to alter market outcomes in the defense of a pegged foreign-exchange price.

Smoking Gun

To be sure, anti-China hawks and protectionists have always blamed the evildoers in Beijing for this kind of manipulated dirty float. In China's case, it was so dirty that it led to an astounding $4.1 trillion in excess reserves on the PBOC's balance sheet. In a mechanical sense, that was the smoking gun that proved China was guilty of gross currency manipulation.

Except that it isn't a one-way street. China was earning all those excess dollars in large part because the Fed was printing them. Under professor Friedman's free-market float, the consequence would have been a sharply falling dollar foreign-exchange rate against the Chinese yuan.

Beijing was not about to tolerate that because it would have interfered with their quest to stay in power by turning China into the world's factory floor. So the Communist leadership simply reprinted in yuan what the Fed first printed in dollars, sequestering their vast accumulation of greenbacks on the balance sheet of the PBOC and other state agencies.

What it all amounted to was a destructive inflationary symbiosis. The Fed exported inflation to China and other low-cost venues, thereby justifying its massive interest rate repression at home on the grounds that domestic inflation was too low. In turn, the debt-happy politicians of Washington and the speculators of Wall Street found this bad-money regime to be a dream come true.

At the end of the day, Washington's infernal inflation machine at the Fed effectively midwifed the freak of economic history known as the Chinese "miracle" of red capitalism. China's debt-entombed economy is not a miracle; it's better described as a Ponzi scheme, an utterly artificial, malinvestment-ridden growth machine that survives only by dint of ever larger injections of debt to fund investments that are not economic and more often than not do not even generate positive cash flow.

The growth of China's money supply after 1995 is staggering. Facilitated by Greenspan's money pumping, the PBOC's injections into the domestic banking system enabled China's money supply (M1) to rise by 340 percent by 2005, 1,280 percent by 2013, and a staggering 2,200 percent by 2018. That computes to nearly 15 percent annually for 23 years running!

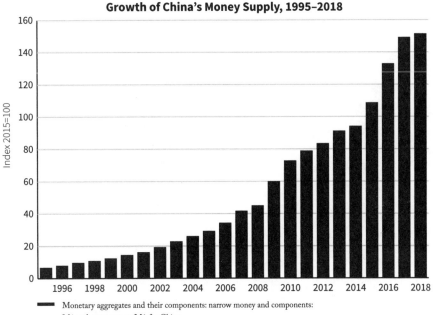

Growth of China's Money Supply, 1995–2018

Monetary aggregates and their components: narrow money and components:
M1 and components: M1 for China

Sources: Organization for Economic Co-operation and Development
fred.stlouisfed.org

It also explains how China's industrial economy emerged full-grown as an economic man-child. Taking on $50 trillion in debt turned its rice paddies and a peasant workforce into a $15 trillion industrial economy virtually overnight. Between 1995 and 2020, China's nominal GDP grew by 1,900 percent, nearly 13 percent per year. By way of comparison, the U.S. economy grew by 177 percent or just 4.2 percent per year during the same period.

Chapter 6

Post-1995 Split Screen Inflation

The turning point was 1995, the fulcrum that triggered a vast offshoring of the U.S. industrial economy and a gale-force flow of deflationary goods back to the U.S. economy, at least when you examine the trend of U.S. durable goods production versus consumption.

In 1972, the United States produced $206 billion worth of consumer durable goods (in 2012 dollars) and consumed $171 billion. The country thus was still a small net exporter of consumer goods. By 1995, however, the export surplus had disappeared, with production at $353 billion, reflecting a 2.3 percent per-year growth rate during the 23 interim years, while consumption was $447 billion, reflecting a growth rate of 4.3 percent per year in real terms.

After 1995, the world turned upside down. Thanks to the Chinese export juggernaut, U.S. consumers feasted on cheap durable goods. Real durables consumption reached $2.41 trillion at annualized rates in the first quarter of 2021, implying a 6.7 percent annualized growth rate during the interim 26 years. That nearly $2 trillion gain in U.S. durables consumption was the very embodiment of the deflationary inflow from China and East Asia.

Of course, no such thing happened on the domestic production side. Domestic production of consumer durables rose to $455 billion in constant 2012 dollars during the third quarter of 1999, and it still stood at virtually the same level, $461 billion, in the first quarter of 2021. Over the entire 26-year period, the growth rate of domestic production amounts to just 1 percent per year. Stated differently, after 1995, U.S. consumers spent on durable goods like there was no tomorrow, with outlays rising by 20 times more than the domestic production gain of just $108 billion.

Among other things, that helped to push the U.S. balance of trade on goods deep into the drink. Before 1971, small-trade surpluses hugged close to the zero line, as befits a stable, sustainable economy. Then during the first quarter century of fiat money through 1995, the trade deficit rose slowly as low-cost, mainly Asian producers emerged. Thereafter, however, the bottom dropped out. By 2020, in fact, the annual trade deficit on goods had reached $1 trillion.

U.S. Trade Balance on Goods, 1947–2021

Current receipts from the rest of the world: exports of goods—current payments to the rest of the world: imports of goods

Sources: U.S. Bureau of Economic Analysis
fred.stlouisfed.org

Free traders would have you believe that this is just nature taking its course and Adam Smith's comparative advantage at work. Nothing to sweat. Well, no, that's complete hogwash.

It is in fact the perverse result of the Fed's rampant money printing over the 34 years since Greenspan's arrival. It's proof positive that bad money contaminates economic evolution and the otherwise perfectly constructive process of free international trade.

The result is the inverse of your grandfather's inflation. The post-1995 period was a time of rampant inflation at the sources of its global origin—the printing presses of the Fed. Over the course of a long interregnum, the Fed's goods-and-services inflation was exported and much of the most productive part of the Main Street economy as well. But that is now coming to an end.

As to what is the most productive sector of the U.S. economy, the data couldn't be more clear. After peaking at 25.2 million jobs in 1979, employment in the high-pay, high-productivity goods-producing sector of the economy—manufacturing, utilities, mining, and energy production—contracted sharply. The goods-producing payroll count is down by 5 million jobs and the index of aggregate hours for that core segment of the labor market is lower by 23 percent. Moreover, experiencing a nearly one-quarter shrinkage of employment didn't do anything to help those workers who managed to hold on to jobs in the goods-producing economy either. In fact, the average wage today is $26.45 compared to $26.15 per hour in the first quarter of 1979, adjusted for purchasing power.

That's right. Nearly 42 years later, workers in the most productive sector of the U.S. economy have exactly 30 cents per hour extra to show for it. Needless to say, that's a screaming indictment in its own right of central bank policy in the era of fiat money. But what is even more jarring is the manner in which the loss of much of America's industrial economy over recent decades underpinned the Fed's big lie about "lowflation."

Here is the smoking gun: since the 1995 pivot point, the U.S. inflation rate as measured by the Fed's preferred PCE deflator has been an utterly split-screen affair. The deflator for services, largely domestically produced, has risen by 2.52 percent per year. A 1995 dollar, therefore, buys 52 cents' worth of services from domestic suppliers today.

By contrast, the PCE deflator for durable goods has *declined* by 1.83 percent per year, meaning that the same 1995 dollar would today buy $1.61 worth of goods, mostly from China, Vietnam, Mexico, and other low-cost suppliers. "Lowflation" is a statistical artifice and a pernicious lie. Accordingly, the overall PCE deflator—which has risen by just 1.78 percent per year since 1995—is a statistical fluke. It posted slightly below the magic 2 percent target only due to the gale of deflation accompanying a tsunami of cheap Chinese goods, which itself is the fetid fruit of the Fed's recklessly inflationary policies.

The True China Cost

The 2 percent inflation target is a ruse. On the portion of the general price level that the Fed can actually impact—domestically produced services—the target has been exceeded nearly every year for the last three decades. Needless to say, trends that are unsustainable tend to stop. And as I will show in the following pages, that's exactly what is now coming down the pike as the "great inflation sabbatical" of 1995 to 2019 comes to an end, owing to rising prices and costs in the China-based global supply chain.

Let's review. What we face now are a 15-cent dollar, thanks to policies promoted by the Fed since 1972; roaring financial asset inflation reaching a dangerously unstable level; and once-low domestic goods-and-services inflation now fixing to erupt higher.

Despite it all, both Washington and Wall Street snooze on, foolishly believing that the Fed's Greenspan-led $8 trillion money-printing fraud since August 1987 has paved the hard road of economic life with easy-money gold.

It has not. Not in the slightest.

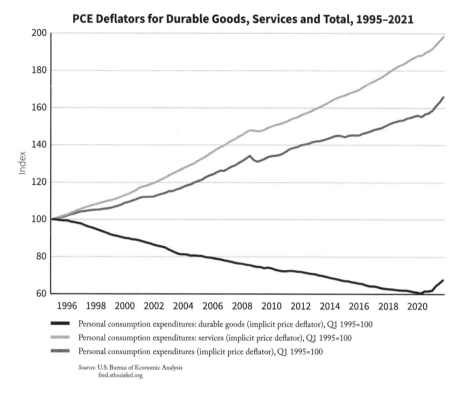

PCE Deflators for Durable Goods, Services and Total, 1995–2021

▬▬ Personal consumption expenditures: durable goods (implicit price deflator), Q1 1995=100
▦▦ Personal consumption expenditures: services (implicit price deflator), Q1 1995=100
▬▬ Personal consumption expenditures (implicit price deflator), Q1 1995=100

Sources: U.S. Bureau of Economic Analysis
fred.stlouisfed.org

The Great Inflation Sabbatical Is Over

You don't need a PhD in economics to know that the American economy changed drastically after the mid-1990s, and not for the better. You can actually see it with your naked eye in the data.

The short version of the story is that once the Fed-fueled tech boom of the 1990s ran out of gas with the dot-com bust in the spring of 2000, industrial production in the United States flatlined. That was a dramatic change from prior history, and it meant that the rise of real median family income also slowed sharply, dropping from 1.8 percent per year between 1954 and 1999 to just 0.7 percent during the past two decades.

As a result, Main Street living standards faltered. High-productivity output and good-paying jobs in the industrial economy have pancaked since the turn of the century. Between

1972 and the second quarter of 2000, the constant-dollar gross value of domestically made products increased by 122 percent, or 2.5 percent per year. By contrast, during the 21 years ending in the second quarter of 2021, real output crept forward by just 0.22 percent per year. That is, before production got outsourced to China around the turn of the century, annual U.S. industrial output had grown 13 times faster.

So the question remains: Where did all that printed money go if not into higher domestic production and jobs, as per the chipper narrative of the central bankers and Wall Street?

After all, during the first period, between 1972 and 2000, the Fed's balance sheet grew by about $500 billion, or $18 billion per year. During the last 21 years, the Fed's balance sheet has soared by $7.6 trillion, or $362 billion per year. When a central bank injects 20 times more fiat credit into an economy each year, it has to go somewhere, right? But as the chart below makes clear, all of that new money after the year 2000 didn't stimulate a whole lot of domestic production—so where's the beef?

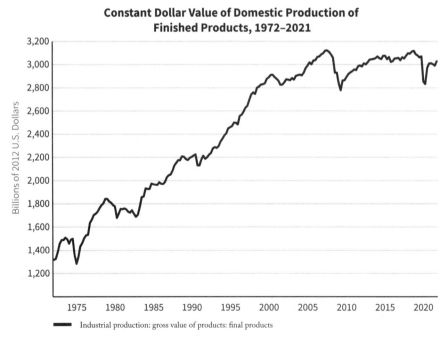

Constant Dollar Value of Domestic Production of Finished Products, 1972–2021

Industrial production: gross value of products: final products

Sources: Board of Governors of the Federal Reserve System (U.S.)
fred.stlouisfed.org

Actually, there is no mystery. Most of the fiat credit snatched from thin digital air by the Fed's open market desk never left the canyons of Wall Street, where it inflated financial assets of every type, size, shape, and duration. The leading edge of this tsunami of asset inflation, of course, was the Nasdaq-100 technology index for the simple reason that speculators can be easily persuaded by the hype surrounding growth stocks, new technologies, and so-called "disrupters."

Follow the Money

In essence, that's where the Fed-fueled inflation ended up—hiding in the stock market averages and in the consequently bloated 401(k) accounts of unknowing investors. And as we have seen, the telltale sign that rampant Fed-fueled inflation is lurking in America's decade-long stock market party lies in the disconnect between asset prices and income flows.

In a noninflationary world of sound money, it's axiomatic that stock prices represent the future cash flows of the companies issuing those shares. And it is also true that sooner or later, the growth rates of most companies bend toward the 2 percent to 3 percent long-run growth capacity of the Main Street economy.

That's true even of tech stocks in the Nasdaq-100, a proxy for growth stocks. For the most part, high-growth innovations and inventions represent displacement, not a true change in the underlying mathematics of the economy and corporate earnings. Consider the passing of the proverbial buggy whip by the likes of a gas pedal on an internal combustion engine vehicle. Once the shift from the old to the new technology is accomplished, which admittedly can take years, high-growth enterprises eventually become bound by actual GDP growth. That's because the apparent high growth rates of these replacement technologies, commonly pitched as "disrupters," mostly reflect the one-time migration of activity from the old to the new modalities, not an acceleration of end demand.

Thus Facebook has been a fast grower, but its revenues and profits are driven overwhelmingly by demand for advertising space, which actually grows slightly slower than overall GDP.

When the migration from billboards, newspapers, magazines, and TV is finally over, Facebook will become a 2 percent to 3 percent growth per year business. As proven over decades and decades, that's all the juice there is in the total advertising bucket. Facebook's founder, Mark Zuckerberg, knows this. It's why the company has rechristened itself as "Meta" and seeks now to build a completely new and somewhat fantastical business in virtual reality, the demand for which is unprovable.

The same is true of e-commerce. Amazon's sales have grown at 28 percent per year since the 2007 precrisis peak, whereas total retail sales have grown by just 2.8 percent per year—one-tenth that rate. But that huge gap represents displacement—the migration of sales from bricks and mortar to e-commerce.

Still, online commerce apparently will never entirely replace brick-and-mortar retail, nor does Amazon have a defensible, sustainable monopoly on e-commerce sales. At length, therefore, Amazon's growth rate, too, will bend to the 2 percent to 3 percent annual long-term retail trend, even if Amazon CEO Jeff Bezos colonizes the moon.

Indeed, the lion's share of Amazon's profit growth is owing not to e-commerce anyway but to its cloud computing business, called Amazon Web Services (AWS). But the migration to the cloud from stand-alone boxes is also a one-time event. That fact also implies single-digit growth rates for hot items like software as a service (SaaS) once the bulk of that migration is complete.

Nor is this a new story. The initially rapid but eventually unsustainable growth of hot restaurant chains, retail concepts, and services enterprises such as gyms has long reminded us that ultrahigh PE multiples are a fool's game. At length, virtually all high-growth companies are flanked by competitors with a better mousetrap and attacked frontally by the unavoidable iron law of low, single-digit GDP growth.

We treat these issues at greater length in the following pages, but the essential point here is that when hot sectors of the stock market get starkly separated from foundational GDP growth, speculators eventually get separated from their paper wealth as well.

A Flattish Future

To be sure, this inexorable triumph of the iron law of low, if steady, GDP growth may take a while to unfold—even decades—if the financial asset inflation in question is being incessantly fueled by egregious and persistent money pumping by the central bank. At length, however, sky-high PE multiples get smashed by the inertial forces of competition and flattish economic growth.

That's how we know when a persistently inflating asset bubble is nearing its end. The so-called tech bubble embodied in the Nasdaq-100 got its sea legs after 1995, at about the same time when much of America's industrial economy was exported to China. Indeed, when future historians tell the tale of the great tech stock boom and bust of the early 21st century, they will say that the boom began on August 9, 1995. That was the day shares of Netscape Communications, maker of the first widely adopted internet browsing software, more than doubled on its first day of public trading.

Naturally, Netscape's earnings did not grow to the sky, and its soaring PE multiple turned to dust. Its temporarily dominant share of the incipient browser market soon got vaporized by a competitor, Microsoft Internet Explorer. (Nor did Internet Explorer stay at the top of the heap, of course.) Netscape eventually was discontinued, and 13 years after its splashy IPO, technical support for all Netscape browsers and client products ended.

Netscape remains the poster boy for tech-stock disappointments. Neither companies nor whole business sectors have eternal life as high-growth engines. Yet that's exactly what is implied when asset values get radically divorced from their underlying foundation of income growth. In corporate finance terms, their long-run earnings rate gets capitalized way, way too high.

Drastic PE multiple inflation, in fact, is the dirty secret of the Fed's inflationary money-pumping scheme during the long interregnum of the great inflation sabbatical. Most of the massive liquidity pumped into the Wall Street dealer markets got absorbed in the run-up of stock and bond prices rather than in higher prices for goods and services. During the

26 years since January 1995, the inflation-adjusted index for the Nasdaq-100 has risen by 1,570 percent compared to the gain in real GDP of just 81 percent. Annualized, those are growth rates of 11.3 percent versus 2.3 percent, respectively.

It's difficult to exaggerate the importance of the yawning gap between the real price gain of the asset versus the increase in its underlying real income. It's the mark of the inflationary beast—the diabolical work of Washington's infernal inflation machine.

No set of companies as broad as the Nasdaq-100 can grow at a pace 19 times faster than GDP over a quarter century running. Yet unless the index was dramatically undervalued in 1995, which it wasn't, that is the implication. Of course, these companies did not grow 19 times faster than GDP, not even close. Instead, the Fed's tsunami of fiat credit has translated into soaring PE ratios on the back of a flood of printed money, which in turn explains much of the yawning gap between tepid income growth and soaring asset values.

Just in the last three years, for example, Nasdaq-100 earnings have grown to $386 per share from $278 per share. That's a modest 11.5 percent annual gain, yet the index itself has more than doubled during that period, rising to more than 15,000 from 7,000 points. Accordingly, the PE multiple of the index has risen from an already frisky 25.3 times for the June 2018 period (latest 12-month period) to 39 times based on earnings reported for the June 2021 period, the latest 12 months.

The Great Money Sump

The plain truth is this: at the top of the most extreme and sustained monetary stimulus ever recorded, a PE multiple at nearly four times the recent earnings growth rate of the Nasdaq-100 companies borders on lunacy. Not only is it evidence of an inflationary stock market boom waiting to crash, but more importantly, it explains how the Fed has printed massive amounts of fiat credits since 1995 without inflation itself, measured by CPI, taking flight too. The stock market became a great monetary sump that helped absorb the inflationary tide.

Of course, the Fed's house pets on Wall Street, the permabulls, claim that current sky-high PE multiples are logical and appropriate because interest rates are at all-time lows. As they see it, high PE ratios are merely the reciprocal of the superlow cost of money embedded in interest rates.

They aren't. The low interest rate canard is actually beyond stupid. That's because the PE ratio embodies the present value of earnings as far as the eye can see, while the interest rate at any given moment in time is whatever front-running carry traders are paying to hold debt securities on 95 percent overnight repo leverage, which essentially costs nothing thanks to the Fed's money market peg.

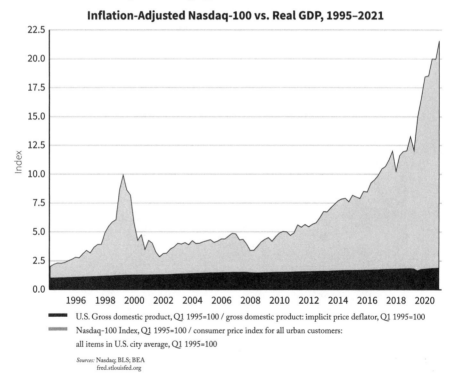

Inflation-Adjusted Nasdaq-100 vs. Real GDP, 1995–2021

U.S. Gross domestic product, Q1 1995=100 / gross domestic product: implicit price deflator, Q1 1995=100

Nasdaq-100 Index, Q1 1995=100 / consumer price index for all urban customers: all items in U.S. city average, Q1 1995=100

Sources: Nasdaq; BLS; BEA
fred.stlouisfed.org

If you want to treat PE multiples and bond yields on an apples-to-apples basis, the question is whether today's off-the-charts, –150 basis-point real yield on the 10-year Treasury is sustainable for time immemorial, or whether something like the real yields in place at the 1995 fulcrum point is more likely to be representative of the long-term bond yields and, therefore, capitalization rates (PE multiples) for stocks.

The question answers itself, of course, and the implications are crystal clear. At even a 250 basis-point real yield, the 10-year Treasury would today be yielding around 5 percent or more in nominal terms, not today's 1.50 percent.

It goes without saying, of course, that the Nasdaq-100 would not be trading at anything remotely close to 15,000 and 39 times earnings in an environment with an honest, sustainable bond yield of 5 percent. And it also means that when the Fed is finally forced to permit interest rates to normalize, the great stock market sump that has sequestered its tidal wave of inflationary money will collapse faster than the Mississippi levees fell during Hurricane Katrina.

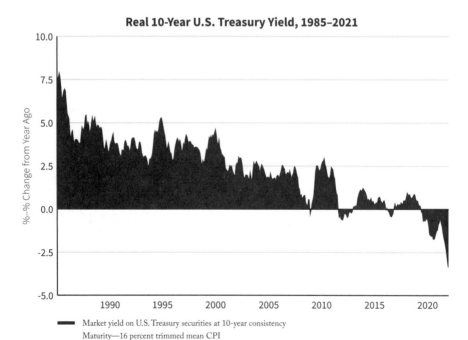

Real 10-Year U.S. Treasury Yield, 1985–2021

%–% Change from Year Ago

■ Market yield on U.S. Treasury securities at 10-year consistency
Maturity—16 percent trimmed mean CPI

Sources: Cleveland Fed; Board of Governors
fred.stlouisfed.org

The same can be said for the broader S&P 500. When it hit another all-time high at the end of July 2021, its latest 12-month reported earnings—the GAAP-compliant kind you must submit to the Securities and Exchange Commission (SEC) or go to jail—were estimated at $153.75 per share. The implied PE multiple, therefore, was nearly 29 times. That's flat-out off the charts.

Consider where PE multiples stood back in August 1995, when the Netscape breakout transpired. At that point, the S&P 500 index stood at 544, just 12 percent of the 4,419 level at the end of July. Also back then, in what is not at all ancient history, the latest 12-month earnings stood at $34.40 per share, implying a PE multiple of 15.8 times.

That made sense given the fact that the real yield on the 10-year Treasury at the time ranged between 200 and 300 basis points, par for the course in terms of both long-term history and economic logic. But as real yield was driven into the basement by the Fed over the next quarter century, PE multiples climbed steadily higher. By the peak of the precrisis stock market in October 2007, the PE multiples on the latest 12-month earnings had risen to 19.4 times. By the prepandemic peak in December 2019, it had pushed even higher—to 23.3 times.

Chapter 7

The $90 Trillion Bubble

The implication doesn't require a degree in corporate finance to grasp. Speculators on Wall Street and small-time traders at home may well repeat until the cows come home that PE multiples are appropriately high because interest rates are ultralow. But that's a self-hypnotic refrain. When the central banks are finally forced to throw in the towel on their "transitory inflation" baloney, nothing will stop the collapse of what amounts to a $90 trillion global stock market bubble.

The ordinary observer might well wonder how the above chart escapes the Fed's attention. After all, during the period since the Fed adopted formal inflation targeting, from 2012 to 2020, the average inflation-adjusted yield on the 10-year U.S. Treasury note has been just 0.19 percent. But that's absurd on its face. At no time in history have investors been willing to lock up their savings for 10 years for a return of just 19 basis points after inflation and virtually zero after taxes.

In fact, the average real yield from 1986 to 2006 was 3.47 percent per year. Since the U.S. economy didn't collapse with real rates at that level, it begs the question: What did the Fed think would be accomplished by pressing the real yield on the benchmark security of the entire financial system to just 1/20th of the level that prevailed during the solid economy recorded during this 21-year period? Certainly by now it should be self-evident that absurdly subeconomic interest rates at current levels have done nothing for average real GDP growth, which slowed to a crawl of 1.53 percent per year between the fourth quarter of 2007 and the second quarter of 2021.

Then again, goosing growth is not the actual reason the madmen at the Eccles building kept printing $120 billion per month of fraudulent credit until they were recently overwhelmed with goods-and-services inflation. Their real obsession was with "lowflation," which had reached a Moby-Dick level of fanaticism, blinding them to the facts on the ground.

On the one hand, they have resolutely ignored the soaring asset inflation their policies have fostered on the utterly silly grounds that asset prices are not in the PCE deflator and therefore fall outside the Fed's legislative mandate. Beyond that, the steady inflation of daily living costs also has been ignored by our paint-by-the-numbers central bankers. The fact is, the headline rate of consumer inflation was temporarily suppressed during the great inflation sabbatical by special factors that were beyond the Fed's remit. It's not remotely sustainable over the long haul.

A Monster Lurks Below

In the first place, years of deflation of durable goods—things such as washing machines and cars—are finally over and done. Global supply chains have been badly disrupted, and the Washington political consensus is following former President Donald Trump's lead in attempting to throw a moat around Chinese trade. Compared to the steady deflation of the CPI for durable goods between 1995 and 2019, durable goods inflation has now shot to the moon, rising by 14.6 percent in the year ending in June 2021.

You can't dismiss that steaming-hot number as a "base effect" owing to 2020's Covid disruptions, either. On a two-year basis, the CPI for durables is up by 6.6 percent per year, and on a three-year running basis by 4.6 percent. A key source of low overall inflation for years has thus gone AWOL.

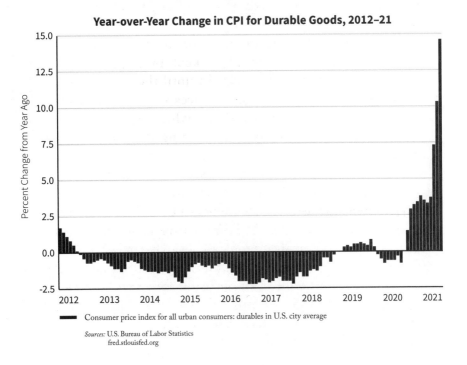

Year-over-Year Change in CPI for Durable Goods, 2012–21

■ Consumer price index for all urban consumers: durables in U.S. city average

Sources: U.S. Bureau of Labor Statistics
fred.stlouisfed.org

This development amounts to ripping off the Band-Aid, because lurking below the average inflation level all along have been nasty and persistent gains among other major components of the price basket. If the fools in the Eccles building were really as concerned about average Main Street Americans as they claim, they wouldn't have been bloviating about "lowflation" since nearly the turn of the century. Indeed, outside of energy, commodities, and durable goods, it is hard to find CPI components that haven't exceeded the Fed's vaunted 2 percent target.

Here is a representative list of the annual rate of increase that consumers have been facing for the past two decades, with only mild fluctuations around the averages for the 21-year period.

Average Annual Increase in CPI Components, January 2000–June 2021

- tobacco and smokes: 5.8 percent
- hospital care: 5.4 percent
- educational books and supplies: 4.4 percent
- tuition and child care: 4.2 percent
- medical care services: 3.7 percent
- cable and satellite TV: 3.3 percent
- household operations: 3.3 percent
- meat, poultry, fish, and eggs: 3 percent
- food and beverages away from home: 2.9 percent
- rent of residences: 2.7 percent
- transportation services: 2.6 percent
- movies, theaters, and concerts: 2.6 percent
- doctors and medical professionals: 2.6 percent
- electric utilities: 2.6 percent
- homeowners' equivalent rents: 2.6 percent
- gas utilities: 2.5 percent
- personal care services: 2.5 percent
- food at home: 2.1 percent

The truth is, the 2 percent to 4 percent annual increases for the items shown here are essentially steady-state outcomes. That the broader indices posted somewhat lower over that 21-year period—at 2.16 percent per year for the 16 percent trimmed mean CPI and 1.86 percent for the Fed-favorite PCE deflator—is essentially an aberration driven by cheap foreign-made imports and dubious inflation accounting by the Bureau of Labor Statistics (BLS).

In addition to the CPI durables component, which fell by 0.93 percent per year through February 2020 before rebounding sharply, you have some pretty implausible items that have been hedonically adjusted with a vengeance. For instance, the CPI component for new cars is up by just 0.6 percent per year since 1990, while the base price of the most popular car in

America for years running—the Toyota Camry LE—is up by three times more, at 1.8 percent per year.

The difference between the sticker price and the CPI, of course, is hedonics—purported quality improvements as guesstimated by the BLS. Remember, "hedonic adjustment" means the government discounts a rising cost because the product or service is demonstrably "better" than before—for example, today's supercapable smartphone versus the simpler "dumb" cellular phones of 20 years ago.

Due to hedonics, the CPI component for computers, peripherals, and related items was actually down by a whopping 11 percent per year during the 10 years between 2005 and 2015. In the related category of information technology, hardware, and services, that CPI subcomponent was down 5 percent per year over the same decade. Yes, there have been vast improvements in function, speed, and user convenience in these technological products, but the quantification of that change—essentially bureaucratic estimates about the subjective value gains we enjoy from better technology products—does not mitigate the actual result.

A recent careful study of the dollars-and-cents price trend for standard desktop computers by the website Statista makes this clear. It showed that over the same decade, the actual dollar charge to a consumer's bank account dropped by only one-third of the amount implied by the CPI for this category. That is, the pure price index was a lot less deflationary than reported by the BLS. Things got better, but they didn't actually get that much cheaper.

As a result of hedonic adjustments and imported deflation from cheap production abroad, the CPI headline figure thus appeared to be benign. That enabled the Fed to claim there wasn't enough inflation, even as it inflated financial asset prices fantastically.

Now, however, the deranged money pumpers have lost their anchor to the windward. Not only are durable goods prices rising rapidly after 25 years of relentless deflation, but the CPI for energy also has made a big reversal. Consider the 3.35 percent per year rise in energy costs since January 2000. By any common-sense definition of the term, a more than doubling of the price of a commodity over just two decades is inflation in spades.

But those huge gains came in two broad phases. The Fed has chosen to ignore the first phase while whining about the second in a totally context-free and misleading manner. During the eight years through the July 2008 blow-off top, the energy index was up by nearly 11 percent per year. Conveniently, since the Fed adopted inflation targeting in January 2012, the same data has declined by about 0.53 percent per year.

Needless to say, the Fed had very little to do with this 21-year cycle of extreme ups and downs on the global energy market. Yet it was not at all bashful about lamenting "lowflation" during the decade after the $150-per-barrel oil peak in 2008. The implication is that the oil price explosion was already baked into the index. The only thing that mattered for inflation targeting, therefore, was the subsequent arithmetic declines off the extreme July 2008 oil price peak—a trend that put heavy downward pressure on the overall inflation index.

No longer, of course. Now that energy prices are rising again—up 6.4 percent from the pre-Covid peak of January 2020—the Fed has shifted to a metric that reflects a cumulative multiyear average of 2 percent over an unstated duration. That supposedly explains away the fact that current overall inflation readings at 3 percent to 5 percent per year are way above target. But what it actually proves is that Bernanke's inflation-targeting policy construct has been bogus all along.

The fact is, the roaring energy inflation experienced during the first decade of this century is still largely embedded in the price level paid by consumers. In fact, as of June 2021, consumers were paying 103 percent more for energy than what they paid at the turn of the century, even as the median family income has risen by just 65 percent. Yet the monetary theologians domiciled at the Fed insist their inflation "goals" have not been met.

The problem, of course, is all the 2 percent to 4 percent per year increase items listed above are still going up by 2 percent to 4 percent. But now the anchors to the PCE deflator over the last decade—energy and durable goods—are rising at an aggressive pace as well. After nine years of either outright deflation or tiny annual increases, overall commodity prices excluding food are now up 15.6 percent on a year-over-year basis and by nearly 5 percent per year on a two-year, stacked basis.

Shrinkflation Is Back

In short, there is now no place for the consumer to hide, even as clever consumer goods marketers look for ways to obfuscate the pass-through of rising costs. In that regard, so-called "shrinkflation" is back with a vengeance. Products at the same price are getting smaller, lighter, and thinner to hide their actual rising cost.

As an example, a package of toilet paper rolls claims to be the same price for the dimensions and square footage of usable product, but careful observers might note that the cardboard core has gotten noticeably larger, meaning that the toilet paper's ply, or thickness, has been cut back considerably to compensate.

In fact, there is now an online group, on the website Reddit, dedicated to exposing the proverbial shrinking toilet paper problem of inflation. Here are just a few of their recent exhibits involving packaging and product changes for items being sold at the same price:

- Ziploc boxes of quart freezer bags that used to contain 54 bags now hold 50 bags.
- Keebler's Club crackers now come in boxes of 16 rather than 20 crackers.
- Doritos bags went from 9.75 ounces to 9.25 ounces.
- Tostitos bags went from 15 ounces to 13 ounces.
- Cheerios Family Size Honey Nut cereal went from 19.5 ounces to 18.8 ounces.
- Febreze air fresheners went from 9.7 to 8.8 ounces and from aluminum cans to plastic.
- Kirkland paper towel rolls went from 85 to 74 square feet.
- Spaghetti sauce in a jar has shrunk from 32 ounces to 24 ounces per jar.

- Cake mixes that were a pound are now down to 14.25 ounces in most cases.
- Thin-sliced cheeses have gotten thinner.
- Scott paper towel rolls shrunk from 43.6 square feet to 39.6 square feet.
- Clorox wet wipes went from 85 to 75 per pack.
- Kiwi brushes got a far smaller wooden handle.
- Kikkoman soy sauce went from 15 fluid ounces to 10 fluid ounces.
- Scotts Earthgro brown mulch bags got 25 percent smaller.

To be sure, I have no objection to clever packaging and marketing, nor do I think that consumers who don't pay attention to what they are getting for their hard-earned bucks need help from the nanny state when it comes to the kind of shrinkflation itemized here.

But I do seriously question whether the government has the capacity or competence to keep up with the constantly shape-shifting product offerings and value propositions that wash through the millions of products on retail and digital shelves throughout the nation. Maybe they do sometimes catch 16 versus 20 crackers in a box and adjust the price 25 percent higher, but what about thinner ply toilet paper and endless, similar product changes? There's not the chance of a snowball in a hot place that the BLS adjusts stated prices upward sufficiently for these more subtle forms of shrinkflation, including the loss of quality and product durability.

For instance, there is one big-time deflationary item in the CPI basket that anyone with kids or grandkids can spot a mile away—the total takeover of the children's toy market by Chinese manufacturers. During the period between 1978 and 1996, when toys were mostly made domestically, the CPI for toys rose by 3.1 percent per year. Since mid-1996, toy prices have plunged by a staggering 77 percent. That's 6.6 percent per-year deflation for a quarter century running.

Obviously, falling toy prices have helped keep the overall CPI down, but who in their right mind believes that the basket of toys being produced in China during 2021 is of even remotely the same quality as those supplied by American factories in 1978? The truth is, for every sticker price adjusted downward in the name of improved quality (a.k.a. "hedonic adjustment") such as airbags on autos, there has been an inverse decline in quality for other things we buy. Shrinkflation and Chinese-made junk have changed the product basket beyond recognition, and not for the better.

Stated differently, one of the great virtues of a dynamic, market-based capitalist economy is that it constantly innovates and evolves in ways that defy easy or accurate quantification. And that's true of the very idea of a general price index based on a market basket of goods and services. The challenges to item-weightings in the index and item measurements in the basket are well-nigh insuperable.

CPI for Toys, 1978–2021

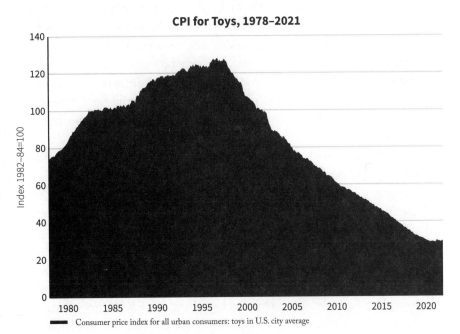

Consumer price index for all urban consumers: toys in U.S. city average

Sources: U.S. Bureau of Labor Statistics
fred.stlouisfed.org

That's why inflation targeting to the decimal point, the 2 percent target, is a mug's game that only a mathematician posing as an economist such as Ben Bernanke could have embraced. Given the simple fact that inflation can be only crudely and arbitrarily measured, the very idea that a central bank can have a rigidly fetishistic quantitative "goal" to be fanatically pursued come hell or high water is preposterous.

Long ago, a different generation and breed of central bankers—some of whom were actual bankers—knew that a key attribute of the sound money they were charged with overseeing was the stability of purchasing power over long periods of time. As we have seen, early Fed bankers produced a dollar that had no net change of value between 1921 and 1946. Their implicit inflation target, therefore, was something close to zero.

Even before the Fed's creation in 1914, zero inflation was essentially the order of the day. Between 1860 and 1900, for example, the inflation rate averaged just 0.25 percent per year. And that benign outcome was notwithstanding the huge inflationary effect of the Civil War, which was promptly squeezed out of the economy when hostilities and printing-press war finance ended. In 1841, wheat sold for 78 cents per bushel on the Chicago markets during the harvest season—a price that was still 80 cents per bushel by 1903 and barely 86 cents in August 1913, when Congress first began to debate the creation of the Fed.

In short, the traditional notion of long-term price stability and the modern Keynesian concept of fine-tuned inflation targeting are from opposite worlds. The former is strictly about the integrity of money, while the latter is merely an excuse for what amounts to monetary central planning and the coddling of the money dealers and financial speculators.

Ironically, however, the Fed's obsession with its inflation-targeting goals has led to the worst of all possible worlds—namely, roaring financial asset inflation, which is profoundly inequitable and destructive of capitalist prosperity, plus now, belatedly, goods-and-services inflation, which has come out of hiding from behind the China trade and Wall Street sump pump of financial asset speculation.

With respect to the China trade—including Donald Trump's anticonsumer tariffs and President Joe Biden's cabal of recycled war-party advisors spoiling for a fight with Beijing—the writing is clearly on the wall. During the long years of Fed wailing about lowflation after January 2012, persistently falling import prices were largely driven by China.

In fact, import prices fell by 1.6 percent per year between 2012 and the pre-Covid peak in January 2020. This was greeted negatively by the Fed because it pushed the overall inflation rate as measured by the PCE deflator marginally below its sacred inflation "goal." Yet the truth of the matter was nearly the opposite. In short, the United States imported deflation as it exported its industrial base to China. It was a bad bargain and in no way sustainable. Yet the Fed was so obsessed with inflation that it failed to recognize, beneath a purportedly deficient headline number, a handful of one-time "lowflation" trends destined to reverse themselves.

The data posted from 2012 to 2019 was a low-quality, low-inflation number, not the mythical macroeconomic deflation of Ben Bernanke's fevered imagination. Had our monetary politburo taken the trouble to examine the compositional elements of reported inflation since 2012, they never would have raged on about missing their 2 percent inflation target or had any excuse to prolong a zero interest rate policy (ZIRP) and quantitative easing (QE) long after the recovery from the Great Recession began.

Import prices are up 7.1 percent since January 2020 and have risen at an 8.8 percent annual rate since December 2020. They show no sign of reversing direction and for good reason: China has used up its surplus peasant labor, Vietnam has nearly done the same, and there are few other low-cost labor countries equipped to export cheap goods at high volumes.

In the idiom of the speculative world that the Fed has fostered on Wall Street, our central bank has been and remains long on cheap imports, durable goods and commodities, and tepid unit labor costs, without the slightest recognition that all of these "transitory" lowflation factors have reached their sell-by dates.

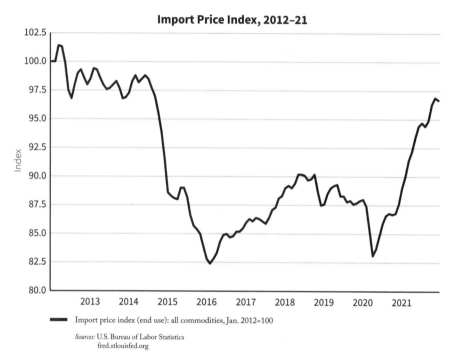

Import Price Index, 2012–21

■ Import price index (end use): all commodities, Jan. 2012=100

Sources: U.S. Bureau of Labor Statistics
fred.stlouisfed.org

In the midst of all this money pumping, the Keynesian fools have missed one subtlety after another while interpreting the incoming data they pretend to swear by. For instance, did it ever occur to them that one of the reasons wage costs appeared to be so well-behaved through 2019—and especially after pushed full-on inflation targeting starting in January 2012—is that they were both averaging down and exporting high-pay production?

As a result, the so-called jobs recovery after the Great Recession was overwhelmingly concentrated in the lowest-paying jobs in nonexporting sectors such as leisure and hospitality, education and health care, temporary employment, and other low-paying segments of the labor market. Accordingly, average weekly pay rose by just 2.5 percent per year between the first quarter of 2012 and the fourth quarter of 2019, in part because the labor force mix was steadily shifting to the low end of the wage scale. In fact, when you look at the wage data on an apples-to-apples basis, these benign trends disappear. Average weekly earnings in the leisure and hospitality sector, for instance, rose by 3.1 percent per year during that period, yet by the end of 2019, the weekly wage was still just 39 percent of the average manufacturing wage and only 35 percent of the average weekly wage for all goods-producing workers.

At the same time, owing to the immense pressure from the China price for tradable goods, weekly manufacturing wages in the United States rose by just 2 percent per year in nominal terms. Pay gains in the high-wage sectors thus were held down by imports while, owing to its increasing share of the employment mix, rising weekly pay in low-wage sectors actually held down the topline figure for overall pay gains.

These forces are now reversing. Owing to Washington's vast outpouring of stimulus payments, unemployment insurance toppers, moratoriums on rent and mortgage and student loan payments, and other free stuff, workers have dropped out of the labor market, causing wage rates in the leisure and hospitality sector to soar—up by more than 10 percent over the past year.

Meanwhile, the abatement of pressure from imports has resulted in a 50 percent gain in the rate of manufacturing wage increases. Compared to the 2 percent annual rate between the first quarter of 2012 and the fourth quarter of 2019, weekly wages in manufacturing are now up by 5.4 percent rate during the year ending in October 2021.

This means that the overall private sector weekly wage rate is off to the races. Pay surged at a 6.3 percent annual rate between the fourth quarter of 2019 and the second quarter of 2021, the highest rate of gain in the last 40 years. This step change in wage growth—to 6.3 percent from 2.5 percent—has had a knock-on effect on unit labor costs. Compared to the

1.7 percent average annualized increase recorded during 2016–19, unit labor costs in the total private sector have risen by an average of 4.8 percent per year during the last four quarters.

Fundamental economic forces reflect the Fed's relentless inflationary money pumping. The 7.9 percent annualized gain in unit labor cost in the third quarter of 2021 is now more than double the average 3.5 percent annual gain that was posted over the 36-year period between Nixon's Camp David perfidy in mid-1971 and the eve of the Fed's shift to all-out money pumping after the fourth quarter of 2007.

The historical record makes quite clear what happens after unit labor costs develop a head of steam. Between the second quarter of 1971 and inflation's peak in the fourth quarter of 1980, unit labor costs rose by 7.1 percent per year. CPI was not far behind and eventually rose at an 8.3 percent rate of increase during the same period.

For all intents and purposes, the great inflation sabbatical of 1995–2019 is over and done. Indeed, there is nothing at all "transitory" about the two major components of the Fed's vaunted PCE deflator. They are surging in tandem, meaning that the split-screen mix of falling goods and rising services that held down the PCE deflator over 2012–19 has ended.

Since the first quarter of 2020, the PCE deflator for durable goods has risen at a 5.6 percent annual rate, while the PCE deflator for services has remained steady at 3 percent per annum, just above the rate it has consistently posted over the past decade. Moreover, the short-term abatement in the sketchy owners' equivalent rent (OER) component of the services index is starting to accelerate as well, after a short swoon in 2020. During the two years prior to the pandemic lockdowns, OER was rising by 3.7 percent annually, or by about 50 basis points more than the home rental index.

By early 2021, however, OER had dropped below the home rental index to a year-over-year low of 1.8 percent in April. That held down the overall PCE deflator, where it accounts for about 14 percent of the weighting, but that brief dip is not remotely sustainable. Housing prices are soaring at 20 percent per year or more, so rental rates also are surging. For the third quarter 2021 period, for instance, the home rental rate rose at a 3.9 percent annualized rate and the OER by 3.7 percent annualized.

The same story holds true for the motor force of service inflation—medical care. That rose by 3.8 percent per year, year in and year out, between 2000 and its prepandemic peak in the fourth quarter of 2019. Due to the massive dislocations in the medical sector that went along with the pandemic, however, the medical inflation gain reported by the government has slowed to just 1 percent since the second quarter of 2020.

Of course, if you believe that's sustainable, well, I've got some proverbial Florida swampland to show you. The prior trend between the fourth quarter of 2017 and the fourth quarter of 2019 was actually 3.7 percent per year. The reason for the low reading since the second quarter of 2020 is simply that the initial shock of Covid to the medical system got priced in during the second quarter of 2020, when the medical services component of inflation surged at a 6 percent annualized rate.

The implication is bad news for consumers, of course, but for financial market speculators and millions of checked-out 401(k) investors, it's positively forbidding. In very short order the Fed will have no choice but to hit the monetary brakes—far sooner and far harder than is now priced in.

And that gets us to the coming lynching of what I call the FANGMAN (the conglomeration of shares in tech stocks Facebook, Apple, Netflix, Google, Microsoft, Amazon, and NVIDIA). These stocks have been at the core of the stock market sump, which has absorbed much of the Fed's relentless money pumping.

At the time that the Fed officially adopted inflation targeting, the combined market cap of the seven FANGMAN stocks stood at $1.16 trillion against the reported latest 12-months' net income, in June 2012, of $75 billion. During the subsequent nine years, the combined net income of the FANGMAN shares rose to $275 billion, representing a 15.5 percent annualized growth rate.

But here's the thing. Back in mid-2012, the PE multiple of the FANGMAN already was 17.7 times. That has now surged to 39 times for no reason other than the Fed's flood of liquidity, which has encouraged Wall Street speculators and retail investors alike to embrace the "low interest rates justify super-high PEs" canard and jump onto the bandwagon of growth at any price.

As a result, the market cap of these seven stocks alone soared to a recent peak of $10 trillion. That staggering $9 trillion gain happens to account for nearly 30 percent of the entire gain of all the stocks in the Wilshire 5000 since mid-2012.

So yes, the stock market is an accident waiting to happen, and the seven FANGMAN stocks in particular have been where the Fed's massive liquidity emissions are most heavily concentrated. For reasons I will amplify in the following pages, the group as a whole does not even merit a 20 times PE multiple, owing to the fact that all seven are heading hard toward the iron law of single-digit GDP growth.

When the Fed is finally forced to stop its bond-buying spree and permit interest rates to rise to even a quasi-rational level—that is, once the "transitory" dodge about inflation finally comes a cropper, upward of $5 trillion of the hot air trapped in these FANGMAN stocks will come rushing out. As with Hemingway's famous description of bankruptcy—that it came two ways, gradually and then suddenly—the full bill for decades of hideous money pumping will arrive out of the blue, shocking the whole market and everyone invested in it.

Chapter 8

High Time to Flee the Casino

It should be obvious by now that the massive monetary inflation of the last several decades has manifested itself primarily in soaring asset prices. And that effect was cumulative, meaning that Wall Street is now a clear and present danger to the financial wealth and well-being of ordinary Americans. Stocks, bonds, options, meme stocks, cryptocurrencies—all have been contaminated and bloated beyond sanity by the Fed's incessant money pumping.

It is also important to understand that the eruption of financial asset prices since the mid-1990s represents a sharp departure from the initial period of fiat money after August 1971. During that earlier period, goods-and-services inflation predominated. The insidious and harmful nature of inflation was well and painfully understood by the American public by the time then Fed chairman Paul Volcker finally brought it to heel.

Now his successors have utterly obfuscated the handoff of this monetary poison to the financial asset arena. The inflection point was 1995, when the tide of imported deflation from cheap foreign goods began to lap hard upon the shores of the U.S. economy, thereby rechanneling the Fed's inflationary credit emissions from Main Street to Wall Street.

Here is the smoking gun: During the first quarter century of fiat money, from 1971 to the mid-1990s, nominal GDP grew by 8 percent per year. During the same period, the total market cap of the U.S. stock market as measured by the Wilshire 5000 reached $7.2 trillion, representing an 8.4 percent annualized gain from its 1971 level of $900 billion.

Consequently, the ratio of stock market assets to national income (nominal GDP) remained roughly constant, drifting upward only slightly from 80 percent of GDP in 1971 to 87 percent by 1996. That linkage was as it should be, of course, because over extended periods of time, the market value of assets is driven by the growth of the income they produce.

To be sure, there was a whole lot of goods-and-services inflation embedded in the nominal GDP growth during that quarter-century period until 1995. That's because there was no material, low-cost offshore source to absorb excess domestic demand for goods and services; the initial round of fiat money inflation ended up in both nominal GDP and the market value of stocks. Accordingly, even though the dollar was no longer anchored to gold, the ratio of stock market assets to income remained close to historic trends.

Alan Greenspan gave his now-infamous "irrational exuberance" warning in December 1996 and then promptly forgot about it. Following that, the total market cap of U.S. equities soared to $46 trillion as of early August 2021, leaving GDP far behind. The staggering $38.8 gain in stock values during the last 25 years is double the $14.5 trillion rise of nominal GDP, meaning that the stock market is now capitalized at an off-the-charts 200 percent of national income.

A good share of that rise happened during the past 16 months, when the U.S. economy allegedly was so battered by the pandemic lockdowns that upward of $6 trillion in bailouts and individual stimulus checks was thrown at it by Washington to ensure, they argued, that America wouldn't suffer a depressionary collapse.

What actually happened defies economic rationality. Despite the alleged near collapse of the U.S. economy, illustrated by a cumulative 60 million claims for unemployment benefits, the stock market has gained $13 trillion in market cap since the pre-Covid peak in December 2019. At the same time, and notwithstanding Washington's smorgasbord of free stuff, the GDP gain per annum during the same period was just $1 trillion.

That's right. Wall Street gained 13 times more than Main Street during the worst economic dislocation of modern times, dwarfing all previous historical markers. The $13 trillion gain is so bloated that it exceeds the entire value of the stock market as recently as November 1999. In comparison, the blow-off tops of the dot-com bubble in 2000 and the housing credit bubble in 2007 pale into relative insignificance.

The stock market has been roaring ever since Greenspan's infamous speech in December 1996. But after 25 years of accumulated speculative pressures, there is only one sensible thing to do.

Get out of the casino. Now!

Wilshire 5000 Market Cap and Percent of GDP

- December 1996: $7.2 trillion and 87 percent of GDP
- March 2000: $13.1 trillion and 130 percent of GDP
- October 2007: $15.6 trillion and 106 percent of GDP
- December 2019: $33.0 trillion and 152 percent of GDP
- August 2021: $46.0 trillion and 200 percent of GDP

The essence of the problem is that the value of the stock market rose by 6.3 times during the last quarter century of money-printing madness while national income increased by only 2.7 times. Because it is the dangerous and unsustainable product of rampant monetary inflation, this yawning gap will end in a devastating meltdown of stock prices. The alternative explanation—that Wall Street is capitalizing on improved fundamentals and better future performance prospects for the U.S. economy—doesn't remotely compute.

Self-evidently, the opposite is far more likely. The trend rate of real GDP growth has already deteriorated dramatically. It has plunged to just 1.5 percent per year since the fourth quarter of 2007. That's barely one-third of the rate that had prevailed in the decades before Greenspan cried "irrational exuberance" and nevertheless set stocks soaring. Moreover, during these last 25 years of sagging economic performance, the Fed's money-pumping policies have left permanent, deep scars on the Main Street economy. As we have seen, a huge chunk of America's industrial economy was offshored to China, accompanied by an eruption of debt and leverage of biblical proportions.

As Greenspan was jawboning the market in 1996 about how maybe, possibly, there was a little too much speculation in stocks, total public and private debt stood at $21 trillion and amounted to 250 percent of GDP. That was already way above the stable average of about 150 percent of GDP that had prevailed during the century before August 1971.

The "maestro," as the press called him, warned us but did nothing. After that, it was off to the races. Today, total U.S. debt—household, business, government, and financial—stands at a towering $85.9 trillion and a growth-crushing 370 percent of GDP. So the very idea that stock market capitalization in the last quarter century should have been breaking away from its moorings to national income is just plain nuts.

As we have seen, the only tattered rationalization for this explosion of market value is the current ultralow interest rates, but presumably, even central bankers understand that today's 1.5 percent nominal yield and negative 3 percent to 4 percent real yield are an artificial and temporary fluke, not a permanent or sustainable benchmark for valuing anything. On the contrary, the heart of the stock bubble eruption lies in three words—massive multiple inflation. Wall Street is literally floating on a combustible cushion of toxic financial ethers. One match and you have a street-leveling explosion from one end of Wall Street to the other.

What Happens Next

The fundamental consequence of 30 years of Fed-fueled financial asset inflation is that the prices of stocks and bonds have way overshot the mark. That's why what lies ahead is a long stretch of investor disappointment and losses as the fat years give way to the lean.

Well, that will be true for the preponderant share of the bullish investor herd that has been long the market or aggressive buyers of calls on the upside for decades and can't imagine any other state of play. They will be shocked to learn, but only after it is way too late, that the only money to be made during the decades ahead is on the short side of the market by buying puts on any of the big averages—the FANGMAN, S&P 500, Nasdaq-100, the Dow, and any number of broad-based exchange-traded funds (ETFs).

The reason is straightforward. The actual profits and incomes being generated by a sluggish, debt-ridden Main Street economy have been way overcapitalized, and it will take years for them to catch up to currently bloated asset values. Accordingly, even as operating profits struggle to grow, valuation multiples will contract for years to come owing to steadily rising and normalizing interest rates.

We can benchmark this impending grand reversal on Wall Street by reaching back to a cycle that began in mid-1987. That's when Greenspan took the helm at the Fed and promptly inaugurated the present era of financial repression and stock market coddling that he was pleased to call "wealth effects" policy. At the time, the trailing PE multiple on the S&P 500 was about 12 times earnings, a valuation level that reflected a Main Street economy and Wall Street financial markets that were each reasonably healthy and logically coupled.

To that end, the U.S. GDP in the second quarter of 1987 stood at $4.8 trillion and the total stock market was valued at $3 trillion, as measured by the Wilshire 5000, the most comprehensive index of all traded stocks. That is, Wall Street stocks were capitalized at 62 percent of Main Street GDP.

Today's screaming abnormalities and the disconnects that set in afterward resulted from the subsequent lock, stock, and barrel takeover of the central bank by Greenspanian monetary central planners. Over the next 34 years, during which that policy heist was being implemented with virtually zero accountability, a vast, unsustainable gulf has opened up between the Main Street economy and Wall Street's capitalization of publicly traded stocks.

During that three-decade period, the Wilshire 5000 market cap rose by 1,440 percent to $46.3 trillion. That's nearly four times the 375 percent gain in nominal GDP to $22.7 trillion. As mentioned earlier, the stock market, which was barely three-fifths of GDP on Greenspan's arrival, now stands at an off-the-charts 204 percent of GDP.

Just assume for a moment that the 1987 stock market capitalization rate against national income (GDP) was roughly correct. That would mean that the Wilshire 5000 should be worth $14 trillion today, not $46 trillion. That $32 trillion in excess stock market valuation now hangs over the financial system like the sword of Damocles.

In fact, I believe this is roughly the case and that the gulf between GDP and market cap has been growing wider and more dangerous since the Fed really jumped the money-printing shark after the Lehman meltdown. Since the precrisis peak in October 2007, the market cap of the Wilshire 5000 is up by nearly $32 trillion, while the national income to support it (GDP) is higher by only $8 trillion.

That's just plain ridiculous because, if anything, the stock market's capitalization of GDP should be falling, not soaring to historical heights. After all, since the financial crisis and Great Recession, the capacity of the U.S. economy to generate growth and rising profits has sharply diminished. As indicated, the real GDP growth rate since the precrisis peak in the fourth quarter of 2007 is just 1.5 percent per year, well less than half its historical trend rate of growth.

Back in October 2007, the stock market's capitalization was 106 percent of GDP. In just 14 years it has soared to the aforementioned 204 percent. Even as the growth rate of the U.S. economy has been cut in half, the cap rate of the stock market has doubled, and that makes no sense whatsoever.

So given that the stock market has gotten way, way ahead of the economy, the longer-range implication is no mystery. What lies ahead is a long spell during which financial asset prices will stagnate or even fall until they eventually recover the healthy relationship to national income that existed before the money-pumping escapades of Greenspan and his heirs and before assigns were deployed to fundamentally distort, bloat, and outright falsify financial asset prices.

For the purpose of illustration, the current $46 trillion market cap of the Wilshire 5000 would not return to 62 percent of GDP until U.S. GDP reaches nearly $75 trillion. At the average 3.3 percent annualized increase in nominal GDP since the fourth quarter of 2007, therefore, from this point, it would take 38 years to get there!

That's right. The massively overvalued stock market is currently capitalizing on an economy that might exist by the year 2060, if all goes well. In the interim, of course, no one would make a dime on stocks, let alone the 30 percent, 100 percent, and 1,000 percent annual gains that home gamers have come to expect.

Of course, even if the stock market is destined to revert to a more sustainable relationship to income, it's not likely to happen in a smoothly amortized 40 years of slow and steady financial water torture for gamblers and speculators. The path ahead is likely to be a lot more unpredictable and herky-jerky, even violent at times.

Still the destination—reversion to rationality—is reasonably clear. That's because the disconnect between Wall Street and Main Street has become so extreme as to be laughable.

For instance, by August 2021, the industrial production index stood exactly where it was in October 2007—a 14-year round trip to nowhere! At the same time, the Wilshire total market index (dividends plus price) posted at four times its October 2007 level. You can rationalize a thousand ways to Sunday, of course, by arguing the U.S. economy is becoming more service intensive and that for better or worse, much of America's manufacturing capacity has been offshored to China. And there is also the fact that the industrial production index represents real physical output, whereas presumably the Wilshire index also embodies the 26 percent rise in the price level (GDP deflator basis) since Q4 2007. But you can throw all those factors and several more at the chart below, and it still doesn't begin to explain how the broadest gauge of the stock market increased by 312 percent during that 14-year period while the sum of all manufacturing, energy, mining, and utility production in the U.S. economy increased by . . . zero.

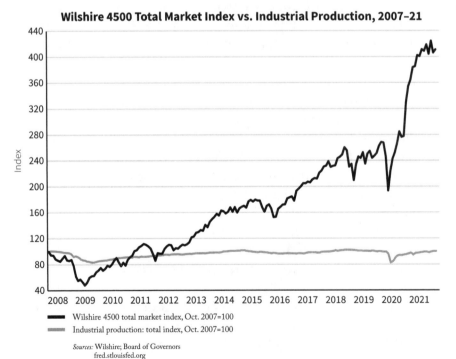

Wilshire 4500 Total Market Index vs. Industrial Production, 2007–21

Index

— Wilshire 4500 total market index, Oct. 2007=100
— Industrial production: total index, Oct. 2007=100

Sources: Wilshire; Board of Governors
fred.stlouisfed.org

Likewise, the massive leveraging up of U.S. nonfinancial business over the last several decades is utterly incompatible with the stock market cap rate's rise to 204 percent from 62 percent of GDP. In fact, here is what has actually happened to business balance sheets.

Back in 1972, total business debt outstanding of $634 billion amounted to just 46 percent of the gross value of U.S. industrial production, which was $1.38 trillion. By 2007, however, business debt had soared to $10.1 trillion and stood at 321 percent of gross industrial production of $3.15 trillion, and by 2020 the business debt figure had leapt even higher to $17.7 trillion, even as the value of industrial production had remained pinned to the flatline. That is to say, at the end of last year's Fed-fueled borrowing spree in the U.S. business economy, the business sector leverage ratio clocked in at an off-the-charts 592 percent of GDP.

In sum, the U.S. business economy is carrying 13 times more leverage than it did 50 years ago. Accordingly, growth and profits generation will become steadily weaker over time. The stock market capitalization rate of the national income, therefore, should—and will—be falling, not heading skyward as described above.

When Your Only Tool Is a Hammer . . .

It is appropriately said that to a repairman with only a hammer, every problem looks like a nail. By extension, to a Keynesian central banker with a printing press, there can never be enough liquidity.

Alas, the Fed's liquidity fire hose has no targeting mechanism, and eventually, that leads to big-time trouble. Indeed, the inflationary asset trouble that has been long brewing in plain sight is now arriving in a rush, and it afflicts the financial system on a worldwide basis. There are actually countless instances of simply hideous excesses because today's giant bubbles are global in scope and have been fueled by the syncopated action of all the major central banks.

For instance, China's giant housing developer, Evergrande, is a ticking time bomb of $300 billion in debts, customer deposit liabilities, and supplier payables. But it cannot be dismissed as an aberration in a distant land. The ultraeasy and cheap debt that fueled this monstrosity is available on Wall Street and everywhere else as well.

Evergrande simply carried its reckless, debt-fueled growth to such extreme lengths that it made a mockery of sustainable finance. For instance, it had $9 billion in trade and other payables a decade ago at the end of 2011, which represented an already hefty 513 days of payables in cost of goods sold (COGs). By the end of 2020, its trade-payables figure had soared to an out-of-this-world $149 billion or 976 days in COGs.

Once upon a time, anyone remotely familiar with the requisites of corporate finance would have recognized that as absurd. But after decades of central bank money pumping, the domestic and global economies alike are littered with Evergrande equivalents. As to Evergrande's other massive unconventional liabilities, we will leave it to Beijing to decide what to do with the roughly 80,000 employers, suppliers, and investors who foolishly bought the company's billions of high-yielding wealth management products and have now been stranded high and dry. They obviously didn't get the joke with respect to the company's massive trade liabilities or the fact that its net debt (debt less cash) soared to $85 billion from $5 billion in 2011, and that's after a $20 billion paydown funded by not paying its suppliers.

But as for the international (mostly U.S.) investors who bought upward of $20 billion in Evergrande's dollar bonds, let them learn from China's communists that risk does matter and that mindless yield chasing can have disastrous results. As it happened, U.S. punters didn't have the foggiest notion of the dubious economics of these thousands of vastly overpriced apartment high-rises built with Ponzi-scheme money. Our monetary central planners sent them chasing for yield because none was to be had on safe blue-chip bonds here at home. So they closed their eyes and bought Chinese junk and American bubbles with equal zeal.

Of course, Evergrande is by far the largest player in China's massive real estate development sector (29 percent of GDP), and the aforementioned figures on debts and payables were right there in the company's public disclosures, as was the fact that Evergrande was floating on a sea of tens of billions of customer deposits for 1.4 million unbuilt apartment units.

Then again, what kind of stable, sustainable "economic powerhouse" functions with nearly 1,000 days of payables and a backlog of liabilities (they already collected the cash) for unbuilt units nearly as large as the entire annual output of the U.S. housing sector?

Indeed, why has Wall Street been celebrating so-called Chinese capitalism for so long when it amounts essentially to an Evergrande of debt writ large? Back in 2000, China had a GDP of $1.2 trillion and total public and private debt of $1.7 trillion. Fast forward to the present, however, and those figures are $14.7 trillion and $49.3 trillion, respectively.

It doesn't get any plainer than that. China's debts have soared to 29 times over in the last two decades, far and above the 12 times gain in its nominal GDP.

Moreover, we don't know how much of that purported $13.5 trillion rise of nominal GDP is statistical wizardry or an embodiment of stupendous waste and malinvestment. But we are quite sure that when an economy grows its debt at nearly 20 percent per year for two decades running, raising its national leverage ratio to 355 percent from 140 percent of GDP, an eventual hard landing is virtually certain.

Likewise, we are also confident that Wall Street's failure to recognize that China is a world-historical Ponzi scheme like no other is not just a one-off case of Sinomyopia. The central banks have been inflating financial asset prices for so long, in fact, that freaks of economic nature such as the Chinese economy and Evergrande have been metastasizing in plain sight everywhere, even as Wall Street's drunken permabulls insist that all is well.

Lunatic Valuations

It's hard to overstate how much the stock market represents the greatest and most dangerous speculative bubble in history. In many ways, it is far more virulent than the blow-off tops of 2000, 1929, and even the legendary South Sea Company and Dutch tulip bulb manias of earlier times.

Moreover, the bubble has infected every corner of the market, from the high-flying tech stocks to the big cap S&P 500, to sector-focused ETFs, and to the speculative insanity on the market's periphery, reflected in meme stocks and the price eruptions fueled by online chatboard short squeezes and gamified trading among neophytes on smartphones.

In this context, the electric car maker Tesla is surely the poster boy for the kind of mindless, unadulterated speculation that has taken over Wall Street. On the single most important metric of valuation—free cash-flow multiple—Tesla's market cap has soared from 29 times as of June 2019 (latest 12 months) to an out-of-this-world 470 times for the period ending in September 2021.

You can't make this up. During the past two years, Tesla's market cap has exploded by 2,300 percent—to $1.2 trillion from $50 billion—even as its free cash flow barely doubled to $2.6 billion. I cite cash flow rather than a net income multiple because Tesla doesn't really have any of the latter. Every dime of the meager net income the company has reported during the past decade is attributable to regulatory credits, the greenmail GM, Ford, Chrysler, Toyota, and the rest are forced to pay to Tesla to obtain carbon credits needed to maintain the privilege of selling to the American public the internal combustion engine vehicles they actually want.

The irony is mind-boggling. Tesla's market cap as of October 2021 stood at 170 percent of the combined market cap of the entire global auto industry, from Toyota, Volkswagen, GM, and on down the list. Yet Tesla gives its high-cost cars away for zero profits, booking tiny amounts of income extracted by the government from the ample incomes its competitors earn by actually making profitable automobiles.

And no, Tesla is not some one-of-a-kind cult stock that has no implications for the rest of the market. In fact, today's massive multiple inflation has been universal, including among the big cap growth stocks that Wall Street pretends are solidly valued and have nowhere to go except up, owing to their immense profitability. The fact is, the Fed's rampant asset inflation has gone right to the heart of the stock market. It has drastically bloated the value of tech stocks, including that of the mighty Apple, which occupies the center of the red-hot FANGMAN complex: Facebook, Apple, Netflix, Google, Microsoft, Amazon, and NVIDIA.

Chapter 9

Apple and the Powell Put

The level of corporate profits and the valuation multiples applied to them today are totally different things. Back in June 2015, for example, Apple was valued at $715 billion on the strength of its unparalleled tech product franchise, reflected in $224 billion in annual sales and $50.7 billion in latest 12-month profits.

Still, there was a reason for the modest implied PE multiple of 14.1. Namely, the tech behemoth's growth rate was slowing—weighed down by the inherent limits embedded in its enormous scale and modest expectations for earnings expansion in the years ahead. Those modest expectations were accurate. Six years later, the figures for June 2021 came in at $347 billion in sales and $86.8 billion in net income.

Yes, that's a lot of profit, but only a modest measure of growth. In fact, Apple's six-year sales growth rate was only 4 percent per year, while its net income growth rate clocked in at just 6.8 percent. By any standard of historical corporate finance and equity valuation, Apple's June 2015 market cap at $715 billion and PE multiple of 14.1 were about right, given the modest progression of its sales and earnings since then.

However, in a casino-like stock market high on liquidity; dirt-cheap carry trades; the "Powell put," named after Fed chairman Jerome "Jay" Powell; and incessant buying from 18 million bored, wannabe traders on smartphones, historical standards have been shoved down the proverbial memory hole. Today, Apple's market cap recently weighed in at $3 trillion, meaning that its six-year valuation gain totaled a whopping

$2.32 trillion and that its PE multiple on latest 12-months GAAP earnings for September 2021 of $94.7 billion more than doubled to 31.7 times.

Stated differently, during the past six years, the company's market cap has grown at nearly 25 percent per year while earnings have risen by only 10 percent per year. The significance of a doubling of Apple's PE multiple cannot be denied. At the June 2015 PE multiple (14.1), Apple's market cap would currently stand at just $1.34 trillion. That means its actual current market cap reflects a $625 billion gain owing to earnings growth and a $1.70 trillion gain owing to multiple inflation since June 2015. In turn, this means that the preponderance (73 percent) of Apple's massive $2.32 trillion market cap gain during the past six years was created in the Federal Reserve building in Washington, D.C., not at Apple's Cupertino, California, headquarters.

Apple alone now accounts for nearly 8 percent of the total value of the S&P 500 of $37.1 trillion. This one firm is a $3 trillion market cap monster that drives the stock averages, ETFs, and indexed mutual funds ever higher. It has sucked in the fast-money hedge funds and the millennial naifs alike to join the single most crowded trade in modern history. Why in the world would you value a low-growth behemoth at 31.7 times earnings when those very earnings are owed to its legendary 38 percent to 40 percent gross margins that, in turn, are brewed in more than a dozen giant Foxconn factories located deep in the heart of China, a country whose economy itself is a massive real estate Ponzi scheme?

Obviously, if provoked sufficiently, Beijing could vaporize those fat gross margins coming out of the Foxconn factories and be not much worse for the wear. After all, the Foxconn wage bill for its Apple contracts amounts to less than 0.2 percent of China's GDP, while Apple-branded products have less than an 8 percent and steadily falling market share in China due to the intensifying commercial, political, and potential military cold war with Washington.

It is further crucial to note that a substantial part of Apple's huge PE multiple inflation was the product of Fed-fueled financial engineering on a vast scale. Indeed, Apple provides the very template for the manner in which corporate cash flows and balance sheet capacities have been artificially redirected into shrinking corporate equity and pumped-up stock prices.

Between September 2015 and June 2021, Apple's prodigious profits machine generated $507 billion in cash flow from operations before R&D and capital expenditures. Those two headings are the main investment channels that have fueled Apple's dominance, and they absorbed $84 billion and $76 billion, respectively, over the past six years. What that has meant, of course, is that after $160 billion in combined reinvestment in the business, Apple's operating free cash flow still amounted to $347 billion during the period.

Apple spent a staggering $339 billion, nearly the entire amount, on stock buybacks during the period, and another $77 billion on dividends. In all, it pumped $416 billion back into the stock market at a rate of 120 percent of its free cash flow. What's more, most of the $69 billion cash shortfall was borrowed. In fact, the company's total debt rose from $63 billion in 2015 to $124 billion at present. The most profitable company in human history cycled all of its free cash flow plus $61 billion in borrowed money into the Wall Street casino in order to fuel speculative mania in its stock. Need we say more?

By mid-2012, the U.S. economy had recovered all of the real GDP lost during the Great Recession and actually stood 3 percent above its precrisis level, while more than 57 percent of the 8.8 million private sector jobs lost during the downturn had also been recovered. At that point, American capitalism was on a sustainable natural expansion path and didn't need any training wheels or more "stimulus" from the Fed.

Nor for that matter did Wall Street. The total market cap of the Wilshire 5000 stood at $14.5 trillion, which represented 87 percent of GDP. That equals the aforementioned ratio recorded at the time of Greenspan's "irrational exuberance" moment in December 1996 and is only slightly above the 80 percent level of August 1971. Likewise, the S&P 500 stood at 1,360 against a latest 12-months net income level of $87 per share. Accordingly, the implied PE multiple for the big cap index of 15.5 was right down the fairway of stock market history.

Even the valuation of the market-leading FANGMAN stocks at the time made sense at $1.16 trillion. That accounted for just 8.3 percent of the total Wilshire market cap of all publicly traded U.S. equities, while the group's PE multiple weighed in at a sensible 15.5 times the group's combined net income of $75 billion.

In a word, it was time for the Fed to cool its jets at the printing presses and let financial markets and interest rates normalize. After all, during the previous four years, Bernanke had taken the Fed's balance sheet from $890 billion to $2.9 trillion and, in so doing, had pushed virtually the entire yield curve below prevailing inflation.

In fact, when it came to the benchmark security of the entire financial system—the 10-year U.S. Treasury bond—the yield in June 2012 stood at just 1.6 percent when year-over-year CPI had risen by 1.65 percent. Since market-driven price discovery is crucial to long-term growth, it was more than past time to enable investors to earn a meaningful inflation-adjusted return on long-term savings and to make Wall Street an honest casino again.

Needless to say, the Keynesian professors and government apparatchiks then running the Fed, which included Bernanke, Powell, Janet Yellen, and James Bullard, among others, were not about to leave well enough alone. Nor, dare say, even give a nod to earlier generations of central bankers, who would have been more than ready to pull back the punch bowl by mid-2012.

Instead, they doubled down. During the next nine years, they found one invalid excuse after another—up to and including the 2020 pandemic lockdowns, which were strictly a supply-side affair wholly outside the Fed's responsibility—to run the printing presses red hot. In all, they added $5.9 trillion to the Fed's balance sheet at a time when virtually no expansion was warranted considering Bernanke's so-called emergency infusions of Fed credit during the Great Recession.

That is to say, they should have averaged down and shrunk the balance sheet back to a normalized level, as Bernanke actually promised at the time and newly arrived Fed Governor Jerome Powell had publicly insisted on in early 2012. And by normal I mean about $1 trillion, which would have more than allowed for the standard 3 percent to 4 percent annual growth Friedman called for during normal times.

The indicated balance sheet shrinkage became instead a 13.2 percent compound growth rate—by far the highest level ever posted for a nine-year period, even during the inflationary 1970s. Even by the macroeconomic standards of these Keynesian witch doctors, the result was a bust. The nine-year real GDP growth rate came in at just 2 percent, the lowest growth over a decade stretch in modern history.

So even as the Fed heads prattled on about labor markets and improving growth rates, they studiously ignored the obvious question: Where was all that 13.2 percent per year of new fiat credit going if only a 2 percent Main Street expansion was coming out the other end? The Fed has no clue, of course, but a serviceable answer would be to say that most of it flowed into Wall Street and took the form of relentless inflation of asset prices.

Again, you need look no further than the market cap of the Wilshire 5000, which rose to $48 trillion at present (December 2021) from $14 trillion in June 2012. As it happened, that stupendous $34 trillion gain in the market cap of equities was coupled with a real GDP gain of just $3.2 trillion over roughly the same nine-year period, ending in September 2021.

You can't make this stuff up. The stock market rose by nearly 11 times more than real GDP. Stated differently, during that nine-year period of lunatic money pumping, the Wilshire

5000 market cap soared to 204 percent of GDP from 87 percent for no earthly reason related to income, profits, growth prospects, or other fundamentals. What drove the market to current nosebleed heights were a purely central bank–fueled speculative mania and PE multiple expansion without any plausible foundation.

That much is evident in the seven aforementioned FANG-MAN stocks that stand at the heart of the mania. Their combined market cap recently oscillated around $10 trillion, while the latest 12-month net income for the group weighed in at $289 billion as of June 2021. Thus their nine-year growth rate computes to 16.2 percent, even as the implied PE multiple for the seven companies has soared to 34.6. Moreover, when you remove Apple from the composite, the implied PE multiple for the other six companies as of June 2021 is 37 times earnings.

The net income of the six FANGMAN excluding Apple rose to $202 billion from $36.5 billion, or by 21 percent per year over the nine-year period. But there is not the slightest chance of that being duplicated again during the next nine years. That's because the overwhelming share of the profit gains represented one-time shifts of advertising from legacy media to Google and Facebook; the migration of retail sales from brick-and-mortar stores to Amazon; and the transplantation of computer power from stand-alone boxes to the cloud, dominated by Microsoft and Amazon.

For instance, between 2000 and 2020, the total global ad spend rose to $587 billion from $471 billion, representing a modest growth rate of 1.1 percent per year over the course of two full business cycles. More recently, the growth rate of total global ad spend between 2012 and 2020 was not much stronger at 2.4 percent, and here we are talking about nominal, not inflation-adjusted, dollars.

By contrast, the combined net income of Google and Facebook rose to $102 billion from $11 billion, or by 28 percent per year during the same nine-year period. The tenfold-higher growth rate reported by the online advertising giants versus total ad spending will be flat-out impossible to duplicate in the years ahead. The sheer math is prohibitive. During 2020, online advertising already accounted for 54.3 percent of the total global ad spend, or about $320 billion, the lion's share of which was accounted for by Google and Facebook. The balance consisted of $152 billion for TV, $32 billion for newspapers, $29 billion for billboards, $26 billion for radio, and $18 billion for magazines.

If overall ad spending rises by another 2.2 percent per year over the next eight years and digital ads manage to steal another 50 percent of the $263 billion that went to legacy media in 2020, total digital ad spending would amount to just $560 billion by 2028—assuming no recessions or other economic dislocations. Yet that would amount to just a 7 percent growth rate, barely a quarter of the growth Google and Facebook posted in net income over the last nine years.

And of course, that's to say nothing of potential financial setbacks owing to the regulatory pincer movement from both left-wing and right-wing political quarters currently aimed at the two ad-based social media giants. In short, the odds of 28 percent profits growth being perpetuated indefinitely are somewhere between slim and none.

As I will amplify next, the same kind of one-time growth considerations apply to the other members of FANGMAN as well. And none of these undeniable roadblocks to perpetual high growth are a state secret. They are simply being ignored by a casino crowd hopped up on Fed liquidity. The $9 trillion value gain by these seven stocks since mid-2012 accounted for nearly 30 percent of the entire gain of all the stocks in the Wilshire 5000 during that period.

So yes, the stock market is an accident waiting to happen and the seven FANGMAN in particular have been the sump into which the Fed's massive liquidity emissions are heavily concentrated. The group as a whole actually merits a PE multiple no higher than 16, a level that prevailed back in mid-2012 before the Fed jumped the shark with its unprecedented money-pumping spree. That's because all seven are heading hard upon the iron law of GDP-bound growth.

The degree to which the casino's speculative mania has been concentrated in the FANGMAN can also be seen by contrasting them with the other 493 stocks in the S&P 500. The market cap of the index as a whole rose to $36.3 trillion from $12.2 trillion in June 2012, meaning that the seven FANGMAN stocks account for 38 percent of the entire gain.

Stated differently, the market cap of the other 493 stocks rose to $26.4 trillion from $11.1 trillion, or by 2.4 times during that nine-year period, compared to the nine-times-over gain by the FANGMAN.

Moreover, if this concentrated $9 trillion gain in the seven go-go stocks of the present era sounds familiar, that's because we've seen this movie before. At the turn of the century, the so-called Four Horsemen of tech—Microsoft, Dell, Cisco, and Intel—saw their market cap soar to $1.65 trillion from $850 billion, a 94 percent increase during the manic months before the dot-com-era market peak.

At the March 2000 peak, Microsoft's PE multiple was 60, Intel's was 50, and Cisco hit 192. Those nosebleed valuations were really not much different than Facebook today at 30, Amazon at 68, Netflix at 54, and NVIDIA at 96.

The truth is, even great companies do not escape drastic overvaluation during the blow-off stage of bubble peaks. Accordingly, Cisco's peak market cap of $525 billion had plunged to just $75 billion two years later. By then, the Four Horsemen as a group had shed $1.25 trillion, 75 percent of their valuation.

This spectacular collapse was not due to a meltdown of their sales and profits. Like the FANGMAN today, the Four Horsemen were quasi-mature, big-cap companies that never really stopped growing, even as their rate of expansion downshifted sharply.

Amazon: Overvalued by Any Measure

At the end of the day, valuations do matter, and that's why the valuation of the very highest-flyer of the present bubble cycle, Amazon, is so hideously excessive. Indeed, as I explain further later, we seriously doubt that it will ever post earnings remotely consistent with its current $1.7 trillion market cap. That's because its gigantic e-commerce business is not a profit maker, and the overwhelming share of Amazon's modest earnings of $29 billion on $443 billion in sales is due to its Amazon Web Services (AWS) cloud business, a classic case of a one-time shift of technology that will soon reach its GDP-anchored limits.

It's worth remembering that when stocks appear to grow to the sky, skydiving is next on the agenda. For instance, during the years from 1998 to 2000, the Nasdaq-100 appeared to attain liftoff from a tenuous mooring to the net income of its constituent companies, rising by 300 percent to a peak of 4,700 in less than 24 months.

Then came the March 27, 2000 blow-off top. Twenty trading days later, the index was down by a gut-wrenching 30 percent, only to stutter long enough at 3,000 for buy-the-dippers to come in for one last killing, a slaughter that proved to be their own. By October 2002, the index had lost 83 percent of its peak value. At 800, it posted lower than way back in December 1996, when Greenspan first warned about irrational exuberance and no one paid attention, including the "maestro" himself.

That was a warm-up. Consider the same chart today, which is destined to become the Nasdaq-100 blow-off top of the near future. This time it took a tad longer to reach low-earth orbit at 16,000, but the index did touch 7,000 as recently as March 23, 2020, when the U.S. economy hit the skids under the lockdown shock, leading the Fed to run the printing presses round-the-clock.

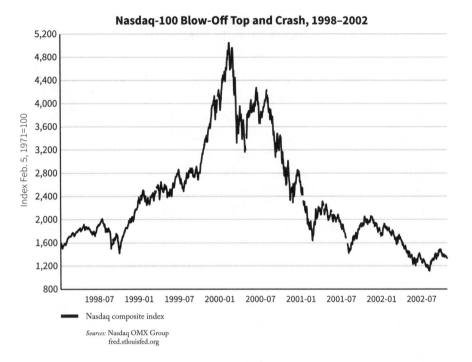

Nasdaq-100 Blow-Off Top and Crash, 1998–2002

Legend: ▬ Nasdaq composite index

Sources: Nasdaq OMX Group
fred.stlouisfed.org

Eighteen months later, Main Street is still short by more than 4 million jobs and GDP has barely reached its fourth-quarter-2019 level, yet stocks are up 100 percent, and retail investors are piling into this sucker's rally like never before. Of course, that's exactly what happened in early 2000, at which point the vertiginous declines soon followed.

Naturally, the pundits pound the table, insisting that this time is truly different and that powerhouse profit gushers such as Apple, Google, and Facebook are nothing like the dot-com stocks of 2000. Supposedly, the FANGMAN are some kind of financial Atlas that cannot fail, as they hold up the froth-ridden stock market on their own immensely profitable shoulders.

Nasdaq-100 Index, 2016–21

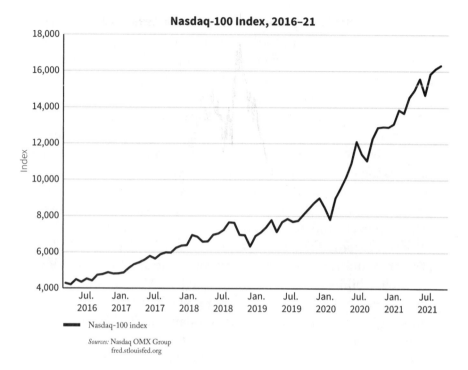

Nasdaq-100 index

Sources: Nasdaq OMX Group
fred.stlouisfed.org

That's cold comfort. When the market cap of the Wilshire 5000 rose to nearly $14 trillion from $7 trillion in the run-up to March 2000, it wasn't powered upward by the likes of famous flameouts such as Webvan, Kozmo, and Pets.com. That era's equivalents were in fact the aforementioned Four Horsemen of Intel, Microsoft, Dell, and Cisco, all large and highly profitable companies that have turned out to be among the most innovative enterprises created in modern times.

The problem was that they were massively overvalued, and it was those extreme valuations that accounted for the $6 trillion that came whooshing out of Wall Street when the last sucker finally hit the bid on March 27, 2000. Cisco was then valued at $500 billion on a latest 12-month net income of $2.6 billion. While that figure is by no means shabby relative to $15 billion in sales, the implied 192 PE multiple turned out to be utterly unsustainable.

Cisco's sales and profits actually never faltered and today stand at $55 billion and $10.2 billion, respectively. But that's just the problem. The company's compound growth rate of net income computes to an earth-bound 6.7 percent over the 21-year period. Such a pedestrian growth rate couldn't remotely have sustained its nosebleed PE multiple and, in fact, has resulted in its current market cap of just $235 billion. After two decades and counting, there is still no prospect of recovering Cisco's year 2000 value, in this lifetime or the next.

The reason, of course, is PE normalization. In this case, the company's hideously inflated 192 PE multiple imploded with the tech crash and now stands at 23.

The outcome for Microsoft was somewhat better, but the song remains the same. Its $23 billion in latest 12-month sales and $9.2 billion in net income posted in March 2000 were not a peak, as befits the technology powerhouse that the Redmond giant was then and remains today. But its March 2020 figures of $139 billion in sales and $46 billion in net income were nevertheless nothing extreme, reflecting compound annual growth rates of 9.4 percent and 8.4 percent per year, respectively, over the 20-year period.

Yet when you start with a 60 PE multiple in March 2000, it's hard for market cap to stay abreast of even moderate growth rates. Microsoft's market cap stood at $1.14 billion in March 2020, representing a mere 3.7 percent annual gain from the March 2000 value. The young online traders of today surely would pass on such a proposition, as they expect that kind of return daily, not over two decades. As it turns out, it was only the Fed's $4 trillion flood of free money after March 2020 that lifted Microsoft's PE back into the current zone at 36, adding a cool $1 trillion to its market cap.

Then there's Intel, undoubtedly one of the greatest high-tech enterprises ever created, yet an absolute cautionary tale in terms of investment valuation. At the year 2000 peak, Intel's market cap hit $300 billion against sales of $33 billion and net income of $10.5 billion. Despite years of continued technology innovation and dominance, the company could not live up to its 30 PE multiple.

During the last 21 years, its sales have more than doubled to $78 billion and net income stood at nearly $19 billion as of June 2021. Yet those outcomes compute to growth rates of just 4.1 percent and 2.8 percent, respectively. After a steady de-rating of its PE multiple to just 11.7, the small investors who piled into Intel in the spring of 2000 continue to wait, stranded with a market cap still 25 percent below its September 2000 level.

Stuck on Earth

Now consider again the supposedly gravity-defying rocket ship called Amazon. Like Microsoft in March 2000, Amazon is a world-beating innovator. It also happens that its current $1.71 trillion market cap represents exactly 65 times its $26.3 billion in latest 12-month net income (September 2021).

Unlike Amazon CEO Jeff Bezos's recent two-minute escape from the inexorable pull of gravity on board a private rocket ship, Amazon stock truly is earth-bound. Indeed, despite fattened sales due to the lockdown of $458 billion, the e-commerce giant has no possible way to earn its PE multiple thanks to the gravitational pull of actual GDP growth.

After all, Amazon as a firm is 28 years old, not a start-up. It hasn't invented anything explosively new in terms of end demand, such as the iPhone or the personal computer. Instead, 89 percent of its sales involve sourcing, moving, storing, and delivering goods—a sector of the economy that has grown by just 2.2 percent annually in nominal dollars for the last decade and for which there is no macroeconomic basis for an acceleration.

Yes, Amazon is taking share by leaps and bounds from the crumbling world of brick-and-mortar retail, but that's inherently a one-time gain that can't be capitalized in perpetuity at a 65-times PE multiple. And it's a source of "growth" that is generating its own pushback from the brick-and-mortar world, a headwind that has been only temporarily abated by the flight to online shopping among the pandemic home-bound.

Walmart's e-commerce sales, for example, have exploded since its purchase of online retailer Jet.com several years ago. In fiscal 2021, the Arkansas retail giant saw e-commerce sales hit $65 billion, six times the level of 2018. Likewise, Target's e-commerce sales now exceed $20 billion and are growing rapidly, as is the case for most other big-box retailers, including Home Depot, Lowe's, Kohl's, and a host of other survivors of the e-commerce onslaught.

All of these companies are learning how to leverage their massive existing asset base for duty on the e-commerce side. In the case of Walmart, for example, this includes using its 4,700 stores as customer pickup sites and even a free four-hour delivery option. The company is tapping its vast logistics system for e-commerce fulfillment duty, including its 147 distribution centers, a fleet of 6,200 trucks, and a global sourcing system that is second to none.

Certainly, the 2020 lockdown shock did accelerate Amazon's North American retail sales growth to 40 percent versus the prior year as consumers abandoned retail stores following government orders or fear of infection. But that's just the point. Amazon's robust sales growth represents a one-time capture of the shift to e-commerce. The 2020 shock only accelerated that process toward its completion.

During the prior two years, for example, North American retail sales grew by slightly less than 20 percent per year, a rate of gain that will now bend toward the single-digit line as the transition is completed and debt-ridden American households have just 2 percent to 3 percent more to spend on retail goods each year, if that.

Likewise, for those who believe that net income and pretax income are antiquated concepts, the story based on operating free cash flow is no less prohibitive. After nearly three decades of operation, Amazon (AMZN) still generates minuscule operating free cash flow. For the 12-month period ended in June 2021, it amounted to just $7 billion.

That's right. AMZN generated $59.3 trillion in cash flow from operations, but a staggering $52.3 billion was plowed back into the business as capital expenditures. Relative to its massive sales and nosebleed valuation, of course, this tiny cash flow number is almost farcical. It represents just 1.6 percent of sales and amounts to a free cash-flow multiple of 244!

That computes to a cash-on-cash yield of just 0.4 percent for anyone of a mind to buy Amazon at its current lunatic share price. And oh, that tiny yield is purely theoretical: Amazon has never paid a dime of dividends.

Needless to say, you can get a much better 1.5 percent yield today on a 10-year Treasury note, and Uncle Sam pays in cash. So why get in harm's way by taking on Jeff Bezos's relentless empire building and megalomania in order to stump up an even lower noncash yield?

And that gets to our larger point about Amazon's allergy to profitability. Between 2011 and the 12 months ending in June 2021 Amazon's net sales exploded to $443 billion from $48 billion, while its operating free cash flow only rose to $7 billion from $2 billion. On a humongous $395 billion sales gain, it generated just $5 billion (1.2 percent) of additional free cash flow. Indeed, apart from its cloud business, AWS, Amazon is essentially not a profit-making institution at all. Indeed, during the 12-month period ending September 2021, the company generated an operating cash flow of $54.7 billion but spent $56.9 billion on capital expenditures. That's a stunning $2.3 billion in negative free cash flow at the bottom line.

Chapter 10

Honest Markets

And that's where the Fed's destruction of honest price discovery and the resulting false signaling come in. In an honest free market, Jeff Bezos would be more than welcome to run a profitless growth machine, but it would also be valued accordingly. Even at the highest free cash flow Amazon has ever generated—$26 billion in its 2020 fiscal year—at a sensible 15 times capitalization rate, it would be worth about $500 billion, not $1.7 trillion. Bezos's personal stock would be worth $50 billion, not $200 billion!

We will readily grant that Bezos is a visionary and great capitalist innovator, builder, and disrupter, one who may be motivated by more than the last few billions of net worth. But we would also lay heavy odds on the probability that his business strategy might be dramatically different—and far more profit oriented—if his net worth were $150 billion lower.

Indeed, based on a rational valuation of Amazon's e-commerce business, Bezos's assault on the brick-and-mortar sector would be far less menacing and reckless. And that's giving full credit to the fact that online shopping and nearly instant delivery of goods are an enormous consumer boon that would be making great inroads in an honest free market, just not nearly as rapidly, wantonly, or disruptively because Amazon would be required to post a reasonable profit. To do that, its pricing would have to be far less predatory.

Until Amazon's gargantuan stock bubble collapses, however, I don't think the company's strategy of growth at any price is going to change. Nor do I see Amazon stock as a freakish outlier; it's actually the lens through which the entire stock market should be viewed because the whole enchilada is now in the grip of a pure speculative mania.

The vaunted securities analysis gurus Benjamin Graham and David Dodd, longtime spiritual mentors of billionaire investor Warren Buffett, wrote that the stock market should be seen as a discounting mechanism, one that in the short run is a voting machine but over the long run is a weighing machine. Today, however, the stock market is neither; it has become a virtual gambling hall.

The Bezos e-commerce business strategy is that of a madman—but one made mad by the fantastically false price signals emanating from a Wall Street casino that has become utterly unhinged by three decades of money-pumping policy. Since 2012, Amazon's stock price has bounded upward in nearly exact lockstep with the massive balance sheet expansion of the world's three major central banks—the Fed, the Bank of Japan, and the Bank of China.

Thus an egregiously overvalued Amazon is the prime bubble stock of the current cycle. What the Fed has actually unleashed is not the Schumpeterian process of creative destruction that Amazon investors imagine it to be. Instead, it embodies a rogue business model and a reckless sales growth machine that is nothing more than an example of destructive financial engineering at work and yet more proof that monetary central planning fuels economic decay, not prosperity.

Amazon stock is an utterly unsustainable bubble. When the selling starts, the vast horde of momentum traders who have inflated it relentlessly in recent months will make a beeline for the exits. The March 2000 dot-com crash will indeed seem like a walk in the park in comparison. Have no illusions. Long gone is the once-upon-a-time function of the stock market to assess, value, and capitalize the earnings and performance of listed companies while providing a venue for issuers and investors to transact the raising of capital.

Rather, today it's all about purely speculative trading and a mushrooming array of devices—among them index funds, ETFs, robotraders, and online trading mobs—all pointlessly churning existing equity securities and their derivatives. The driving force is not company earnings but the policy machinations and liquidity injections of the Federal Reserve and other central banks. What matters most is the anticipation of how other traders will position themselves in response to Fed actions and the implications of incoming economic data to Fed policy itself, not the economy writ large.

In recent times, the point of the monthly jobs reports, for example, was not the dubious economic significance of how many jobs were gained or lost but whether the headline figure was close enough to trigger an early start to the Fed's dreaded "tapering" process. In simple terms, the market was trying to assess the outlook for the continuation of $120 billion per month of fiat credit output at the central bank, not economic output and income on Main Street. So when it comes to valuing corporate earnings, *fuggedaboutit.* Out-of-this-world valuations reach all the way to the heart of the stock market with the FANGMAN, including the very monster of the midway, Amazon.

As Good as It Gets

The Covid-riddled year 2020 was like manna from heaven for a retailer that could dump boxes on America's doorsteps with no human contact with customers. Amazon's e-commerce business booked $340.7 billion in sales, more than the GDP of most member countries of the UN. Yet its operating income from all this sourcing, transporting, warehousing, picking, packing, shipping, and delivery activity amounted to a measly $9.4 billion, or 2.7 percent of sales.

At Amazon's ultralow tax rate of 12 percent, which amounts to just $8.2 billion in attributable net income in a year, that's as good as it gets. Indeed, the fact that Bezos's colossus is a profitless churner of economic activity and plenary disrupter of normal retail function is more than evident in the results for the last three years combined of its international segment. The overseas division of its e-commerce business generated cumulative sales of $245 billion and cumulative costs of, wait for it, $248 billion.

Even in North America, exploding sales have not led to any increase in profits at all. Amazon's e-commerce results in its home market were as follows:

- **2018:** $141.4 billion in sales and $7.3 billion in operating profits or a 5.2 percent margin
- **2019:** $170.8 billion in sales and $7 billion in operating profits or a 4.1 percent margin
- **2020:** $236.3 billion in sales and $8.6 billion in operating profits or a 3.7 percent margin

These giant sales numbers are driven by the migration of retail from brick-and-mortar operations to online transactions. The company's shrinking margins reflect a flawed business model that apparently attempts to make up in volume what it is giving away in costs to generate profitless sales.

In any event, the one-time migration to e-commerce is nearing the end game, so the appropriate capitalization rate for Amazon's pitiful high-water mark of $8.2 billion in net income from its global e-commerce business is surely an earthbound number. Give it a generous 17 multiple and you have a $140 billion market cap. So the question arises: How do you account for the other $1.56 trillion of Amazon's early August 2021 market cap?

Yes, the company's cloud business at Amazon Web Services (AWS) is a high-growth profit maker, with $12 billion in after-tax income (at a 12 percent tax rate) in 2020 on $45.4 billion in sales. But self-evidently, it does not merit the implied 130 PE multiple if you attribute the balance of Amazon's capitalization to the cloud business.

The fact is, the high growth rate of AWS also is down to a one-time migration from a local server and personal computing to the cloud, which will eventually bend to the GDP growth line as well. That's especially the case here because AWS is not really an inventor of technology. It's a brute force slinger of the massive asset base embodied in its giant server farms and in the tens of billions in high-tech equipment it purchases from technology industry vendors. So give AWS a frisky 30 PE multiple and you've got another $360 billion in market cap. Amazon might well be worth the aforementioned $500 billion, but it sure as hell is not remotely worth $1.7 trillion.

What we have here is an insane overvaluation, one driven by liquidity-saturated markets where the cult of growth at any price has become normalized and institutionalized. But still, if there is truly a pot of gold at the end of the endless growth rainbow, where is it in the case of Amazon?

A mere $8.2 billion in e-commerce net income (goosed by an ultralow tax rate that the Biden administration is determined to eliminate) during the e-commerce boom of a lifetime says in no uncertain terms that the stock market ain't on the level. After all, one of these days there should be economies of scale from conquering the better part of the entire retail world, but no such thing is in sight or even remotely plausible given Amazon's predatory business model. Indeed, to capitalize at $1.7 trillion the virtually profitless sales of an e-commerce monster that just keeps spending and expanding like some sci-fi blob is surely a measure of the mania loose in the stock market casino.

The fact is, every dime Amazon's e-commerce business takes in is being recycled into more distribution centers, package handlers, hired delivery trucks, and drone prototypes, which is the reason its capital spending exceeded its operating cash flow during the year ending in September 2021. And now another, apparently, is same-hour delivery service by out-of-work actors and students who happen to own a scooter and are willing to deliver meals packaged by Martha Stewart—who is also out of work at K-Mart—for a comparatively meager wage.

And that's not all. At the core of the company's e-commerce business is its $119 per year Prime membership system, which gives subscribers access to free shipping and numerous other benefits. The company's estimated number of Prime members in the U.S. has been growing by leaps and bounds—from 40 million seven years ago to 147 million at present and in excess of 200 million worldwide. Amazon is currently collecting about $25 billion per year in membership fees, yet if you pull these revenues out of its e-commerce financials, the true nature of the Amazon juggernaut becomes transparent. In 2020, e-commerce revenues less membership fees would have totaled about $315 billion compared to much higher operating costs of $332 billion. So Amazon essentially collects upward of $25 billion in membership fees in return for shipping a mountain of goods at a deep loss.

Based on that equation, Bezos will never make up with volume what he is losing in margin on each and every shipment. The Amazon business model is fatally flawed, and it's only a matter of the precise catalyst that will trigger the realization in the casino that this is another case of the proverbial naked emperor. Indeed, even as speculators celebrate Amazon's topline sales juggernaut, it is increasingly evident down below that the company is losing control and discipline. Since 2009, for instance, its payroll has grown from 25,000 to 1.3 million.

That 43 percent rate of employment growth was far higher than its 25 percent annual rate of sales gains, so revenue per employee has plummeted from more than $1 million a decade ago to just $300,000 during 2020. Once upon a time, the function of the stock market was to capitalize the current earnings and long-term prospects of listed companies traded on the exchanges. Amazon is living proof that this kind of price discovery is deader than a doornail.

Cathie Wood and the ARK of Crazy

The egregious inflation of stock prices at the very center of the market—encompassing the S&P 500 and Nasdaq-100 and epitomized by the FANGMAN stocks—is surely the mother of all financial contagions. So when it spreads into the periphery of zero-profit small-cap disruptors, a rotating cast of meme stocks, and speculative insanities such as trading on the Robinhood app or cryptocurrency website Coinbase, now you are in a realm of pure lunacy.

No rational adult should ever visit these so-called "markets" with his or her money. Yet the cult of the stock market has become so normalized that a washed-up fund manager with a long career of undistinguished results was able to reel in boatloads of capital during 2020, generating a stunning increase in assets under management (AUM) to $45 billion from $3.3 billion—in one year!

That's surely a flashing red warning sign and clanging horn combined. There is virtually no scenario in a world of sound money in which even the most adroit asset manager could attract a fourteen-fold gain in funds during the course of just 12 months. We are referring, of course, to Cathie Wood's lighter-than-air flying ARK, a series of eight ETFs that give the concept of daredevil recklessness an altogether new definition. These funds are chockablock with profitless, speculative plays that make a mockery of the old-fashioned notion that market capitalization represents the present value of current and prospective net income and cash flow.

Wood's flagship fund was up 149 percent during 2020 thanks to concentrated bets on Tesla, Zoom Video Communications, Teladoc Health, and Roku, hence the massive stampede of the retail investors into her funds. However, these four names also tell you all you need to know about the blithering madness on the loose.

These four stocks began the year with a combined market cap of $117 billion, a figure that rose to $846 billion by year-end 2020 and as of August 2021 stood at $900 billion. So yes, when you sink a skyhook into names that have gained nearly nine times in value over the last 20 months, your paper returns should look awesome. However, I'd say your capacity for leading the lemmings over the proverbial cliff is the more accurate description of the matter.

Here's the reason: At the beginning of 2020, these four companies had posted a latest 12-month net loss of $1.01 billion. So if you want to call it that, the "big four" ARK investments had a *negative* 117 PE multiple going into the year of the pandemic. The financial bleed-out was led by Tesla with $870 million in red ink, really a loss of $1.5 billion once you include the previously mentioned involuntary carbon credits purchased from it by the major carmakers. The only one of these four stocks to make money at all during 2019 was Zoom, which posted a slight $16 million in net income, giving its January 2020 market cap of $18 billion an implied PE multiple of 1,125.

So the starting point is simple. In a world of honest price discovery, no fund manager in their right mind would load up a huge share of their portfolio with three companies bleeding red ink and one trading in the stratosphere. More importantly, in an honest market, a weak recovery to $859 million in positive but low-quality net income by year-end 2020 would not have generated the aforementioned explosion of a combined market cap of $846 billion. After all, that computes to an average PE multiple of 1,000 for the group as a whole, a precariously unsustainable figure from which any seasoned money manager would flee without a second thought.

Still, the Fed kept pumping $120 billion per month of fiat liquidity into the market through late 2021, so the wannabe "diamond hands"—the self-named intrepid speculators who claim they will never sell—who own ARK funds hung tough, accumulating even more of these absurdly overvalued stocks. As of early August, the group's $900 billion market cap was owing to truly out-of-this-world valuations, including these PE multiples:

- **Tesla:** 330
- **Zoom:** 129
- **Roku:** 230
- **Teladoc:** essentially infinite against a $773 million 12-month net loss

Nor is this the half of it. Apparently, just to show that recklessness has no bounds, Wood has been recently loading up on the two sucker's wonders of 2021—Robinhood and Coinbase. Between them, these stocks had a combined market cap of nearly $110 billion after this year's IPOs, yet both of them derive the entirety of their revenues and scant net income from the fees paid by small retail investors on the Robinhood app and their kindred spirits in the crypto world.

During the first quarter of 2021, for example, Robinhood posted just $100 million in operating income in an environment that can only be described as a speculator's nirvana—namely, a 90-day interval in which Washington politicians blew out upward of $600 billion in stimulus checks at the same time the Fed was pumping $4 billion in free cash into the canyons of Wall Street each and every day.

A Frenzied Churning

What followed was a bacchanalia of at-home stock gambling: a rush of money that meant trading fees ended up in the coffers of these two fly-by-night wagering forums. In the case of Robinhood, that amounted to an annualized net income run rate of just $300 million, implying a PE multiple of 160. At the very least, 80 percent of Robinhood's revenues are from trading the stocks and options of real companies, even if they are wildly overvalued. By contrast, the entire $1.8 billion in revenue booked by Coinbase during the first quarter was from the frenzied churning of make-believe crypto money that has no practical purpose except as a virtual casino chip. Of course, such gambling surely will implode terminally when the last of the greater fools hits the bid on the 16,000th new crypto token invented by some 400-pound nerd trapped on a bed in his mom's basement.

Even then, it gets worse. We understand how twentysomethings might not realize that they are being scammed by silly ideas like the democratization of stock ownership. Or even theoretically appealing money tokens, which the powers that be are certain to crush when cryptos become even moderately inconvenient for their rule over the financial system.

But the real proof of the mania at large is that the mainstream financial press actually treats a charlatan such as Cathie Woods as a credible force to be reckoned with. A recent piece in the *Wall Street Journal* characterized her reckless gambling as the work of a veritable investment guru and spared no ink cataloging her fanatical following: "Fans of fund manager Cathie Wood have built websites that track her every investment move. They sell T-shirts with her picture in the style of the Barack Obama 'Hope' poster and with the ticker symbol of her flagship exchange-traded fund, ARK Innovation. On social media, they call her 'Mamma Cathie,' 'Aunt Cathie' and, in South Korea, 'Money Tree.'"

Her focus on meme-worthy investments and her ubiquitous presence on Twitter and financial news channels have thrust her alongside market influencers such as Tesla Chief Executive Elon Musk, venture capitalist Chamath Palihapitiya, and Barstool Sports founder David Portnoy, who use Twitter, YouTube, and podcasts to take their messages directly to a new generation.

You couldn't find a more unhinged trio of shooting stars than these three pretenders, but does Cathie Wood, proprietor of the hottest investment vehicles in today's manic markets, belong in even their dubious company?

Just consider why she continues to double down on Tesla. In a word, she insists to one and all that its share price will rise to no less than $3,000, a massive gain from today's already lunatic levels.

So let's see. Toyota is the one mass-volume auto company that has perfected the art of auto design, engineering, manufacturing, and distribution via some of the most sophisticated supply chain and factory automation and quality control mechanisms ever conceived, let alone made nearly perfectly operational on a global scale. This powerhouse Japanese automaker generated $288 billion in worldwide sales and $28 billion in net income during the June 2021 latest 12-month period, for which it was rewarded with a mere 9.1 PE multiple and a market cap of $253 billion.

And that grudging valuation was not due to the world's number one manufacturing company falling off the profits wagon. In fact, during the last decade, Toyota's net income has risen to $28 billion from $2.4 billion in 2011, representing 30 percent per year gain and leaving even the mighty Apple in the dust. Its 9.8 percent net income margin was double the 4.9 percent net margin among its next nine largest publicly traded automotive competitors. We review these crucial facts because they firmly underscore that Cathie Wood seems to be smoking something you can't get out of a vending machine (yet). To achieve a $3,000 share price, Tesla would have to generate, on a steady-state basis, $1.65 trillion in annual sales and $165 billion per year in net income—six times more net income than world-beating Toyota!

We arrive at these wondrous figures by assigning Tesla a full 10 percent, Toyota-sized net income margin and a 20 PE multiple, or twice what Toyota is now earning after posting something like $200 billion in cumulative profits over the last decade.

So with 990 million Tesla shares outstanding, that's the math. The skunk in the woodpile, however, is more than evident to anyone not caught up in the mania. It so happens that sales for the entire publicly traded global auto industry were just $1.38 trillion during the 12 months ending in June. This means the implied level of Tesla sales at $3,000 per share would be 120 percent of total industry revenues!

Inflationary Storms

And we are not omitting anyone. The $1.38 trillion auto industry total includes the combined sales of Toyota, Volkswagen/Audi, Daimler, General Motors, Ford, Nissan, Honda, Mazda, Subaru, and Renault. Moreover, the total worldwide profits of these 10 automakers amounted to $81 billion during the latest 12 months. Tesla would have to earn twice the profits of the entire industry to be valued at $3,000 per share as an electric vehicle maker.

Oh, and did we mention that Cathie Wood also contends that Bitcoin will hit $500,000? That would give a $10 trillion market cap to something that is an inefficient, clumsy medium of exchange and a positively dangerous, volatile store of value.

In short, the Wall Street casino is no place for hardworking Americans who desire to preserve wealth in the face of the inflationary storms that lie ahead. Three decades of Fed money pumping has resulted in massive and unsustainable PE expansion and grotesque overvaluation.

That's 21st-century style monetary inflation. And it's an economic nightmare that Washington's infernal inflation machine has visited upon America's once and former capitalist prosperity.

A Way Out—What Won't Work

The Fed has been coddling and backstopping the market for so long—and so egregiously since December 2008—that it has fostered a veritable cult of the stock market on Wall Street, Main Street, and most especially among the small-time online traders, many of them living with parents. For more than a decade, nearly all financial asset prices have risen so relent-lessly that today's punters actually believe markets will never correct because the central bank just won't allow it.

This has promoted a dynamic of one-way trades in which buy-the-dip investing has inundated every asset class and has been rewarded over and over and over again. Consequently, there are no bargains or safe havens left. When the Fed's in-flationary storm finally breaks, there will be exceedingly few places to seek refuge.

That will not stop the promoters from trying, of course. Asset classes such as real estate, cryptos, commodities, and alternative investments, including art, antiques, and a new wrinkle called a "nonfungible token" (NFT) will be proffered as a hedge against cratering stocks and bonds, but to no avail. That's because the Fed's inflationary credit emissions have seeped into the price of virtually everything that can be traded or wagered on, no matter how novel.

The Wall Street term for this convergence is "a correlation of one," a term that means that assets rise and fall together in nearly perfect sync and thus leave no refuge, no asset neg-atively correlated in which to hide. A rising torrent of fiat money has lifted all boats high above any safe place to anchor. The fact that it came to be over the course of decades of market corruption and asset price falsification by the Fed and other central banks is the single most important insight to carry into the troubled waters ahead.

The manner in which all asset prices have been ripped from any grounding in economic and financial fundamentals can be seen in the stupendous rise of the stock market since the December 2008 lows, when Bernanke permanently flipped on the printing press afterburners. Since then, the leading edge of the stock bubble, embodied once again by the Nasdaq-100, is up by a staggering 1,250 percent. That amounts to a 22.5 per-cent gain year in and year out for nearly 13 years running.

Is it any wonder that stock market cultists actually do think that trees grow to the sky? After all, during the same period, nominal GDP rose by just 3.5 percent per year. Indeed, if GDP roughly measures the humdrum business of work, sweat, production, and economic value creation, then why not hop aboard the Fed's financial fast train for an easy route to riches? This stock index, in fact, has risen 6.5 times faster than the plodding everyday economy—with the added convenience of having to lift a finger only occasionally to hit the "buy" key.

The important truth, however, is that the Nasdaq-100 is not an outlier, even if it is the home of the glitzy tech and growth stocks. To some substantial degree, all stock market sectors and most other asset classes have reflected the same dynamic—the severe decoupling of market value from their underlying substrate of economic output, income and profits. In a sense, the muscle memory of the markets has been infected by a toxic financial pathogen. That pathogen has literally extinguished financial rationality, prudence, and even common sense.

The consequence is that all financial assets are so radically mispriced that when the imminent inflationary blowoff and panicked Fed retreat send markets into a tailspin, the correlation of one will work in reverse as well. Virtually all financial asset prices have overperformed income growth by orders of magnitudes during the last several decades and therefore are now slated for an extended era of deep correction and persistent underperformance.

In that value reversal environment, the typical postcrash bargain basement will be unusually bereft of product. Preservation of capital—in the form of cash, Treasury bills, and gold—will be about all that matters because it will take years, and likely decades, for incomes and profits to catch up with even radically marked-down asset values.

The Nasdaq-100 compared to GDP is the smoking gun, a dramatic depiction of the disconnect between income (GDP) and asset prices. Yet most surely, neither the Fed heads nor their Wall Street acolytes have given two moments' thought to its implications, if they noticed it at all. The gravity of the matter can't be expressed more plainly: There is something massively rotten in Denmark when the income and profits base of the economy grows by just 55 percent over 12.75 years while the leading stock index rises by 1,250 percent. That juxtaposition defies every rule of rational finance.

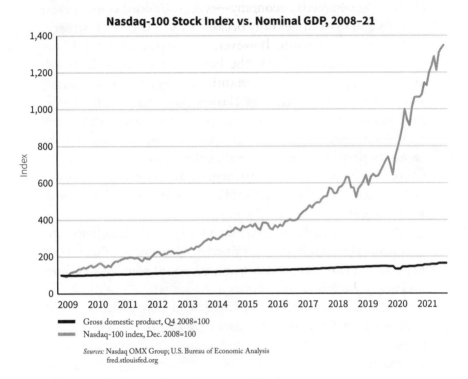

Nasdaq-100 Stock Index vs. Nominal GDP, 2008–21

■ Gross domestic product, Q4 2008=100
▬ Nasdaq-100 index, Dec. 2008=100

Sources: Nasdaq OMX Group; U.S. Bureau of Economic Analysis
fred.stlouisfed.org

The numbers imply not merely a garden-variety correction waiting to happen, but the immolation of 30 years' worth of excess asset value accumulation and all of the narratives, memes, canards, and casuistry that have been fostered by it.

The Trigger Will Be "Nontransitory" Inflation

As we have seen, for most of the past several decades, the Fed's reckless monetary inflation has manifested itself in soaring financial asset prices. What's relevant about that recent history, however, is that the Fed justified its money pumping by the absence of goods-and-services inflation above its misbegotten 2 percent target. Of course, the real reason for flooding Wall Street with fiat credits was the Keynesian conceit that this was actually helping the Main Street economy, coupled with an abiding fear that withdrawal of its massive stimulus and interest rate repression would trigger a raging hissy fit on Wall Street.

This is otherwise known as painting yourself into a corner. The geniuses at the Fed injected Wall Street with a fresh shot of monetary heroin every time a correction was even attempted, a maneuver that immensely rewarded the dip buyers but also inflated asset prices all the higher and left the central bankers buck naked with respect to their perennial cover story—a persistent inflation shortfall.

As I have previously shown, even an elementary analysis shows there isn't an actual inflation shortfall if a balance of price indices is consulted. The top line of all of them—standard CPI, the 16 percent trimmed mean CPI, the PCE deflator, the producer price index (PPI) for finished goods, and others—has been held down temporarily by cheap goods sourced in China and other low labor-cost venues.

What has changed dramatically in recent months is that this deflationary anchor has run its course. Accordingly, there is no prospect whatsoever that inflation will drop back below 2 percent, save for a deep recession. The "transitory inflation" idea upon which the Fed has hung its prestige is about to be utterly refuted.

Recent monthly CPI and PPI reports tell you all you need to know about this fallacious claim: The top line is way above its goals, and the internals tell you goods-and-services inflation is going to stay high indefinitely. It is only a matter of time before the Fed is forced into an ignominious retreat and has no choice except to shut down the printing presses in order to prevent high goods-and-services inflation from breaking out into a wage-price-cost feedback loop, decimating its credibility.

Needless to say, the impending Fed retreat from a decade of overheated money pumping is not remotely "priced in" by Wall Street. The Fed's unavoidable early and hard turn to monetary restraint, in fact, will come as a thundering shock, especially in the precincts of both Wall Street and under 35-year-old basement-dwelling online traders who have known nothing but a compliant, obsequious Fed. The clock is running out fast because goods-and-services inflation has finally worked up a real head of steam. When computed at an annualized rate over the past two years, there is no way to explain it away on account of "base effects" arising from the lockdown swoon in the spring of 2020. The two-year calculation averages out the dump last year and the rebound this year.

Consequently, the fact that the CPI for September 2021 was up by 3.4 percent and the PPI was higher by 8.9 percent per year on a two-year stacked basis means that the inflation sabbatical described earlier in this book is most definitely over. What's brewing under the inflation top-line, in fact, removes all doubt. Namely, the transitory factors that enabled the Fed to believe in the "lowflation" myth have evaporated completely.

Services inflation is running at 3 percent per year like it always has, and especially so since the 2 percent inflation target was adopted in January 2012 and subsequently became an obsessive fetish at the Fed. But the persistent deflation of durables and import prices, which consistently offset services inflation and kept the top-line inflation figure under the magical 2 percent, has decisively ended. In fact, the CPI for durable goods has been rising at a 10.2 percent annual rate since January 2020, while the dramatic turnaround in the data for prices of Chinese imports is about as crystal clear as it comes.

In virtually every month between January 2012 and January 2020, Chinese import prices fell, averaging a decline of just under 1 percent per year during the entire period when the Fed was whining about missing its inflation target from below. For crying out loud, that was a good kind of miss. It had nothing to do with any Fed policy impact on the domestic economy. Rather, it reflected Beijing's defensive response to the Fed's aggressive money pumping—a kind of foreign aid gift to the American consumer.

As we have seen, to prevent the yuan from shooting the moon and idling Beijing's spanking-new export factories, the People's Bank of China scooped up dollars in the trillions and swapped them for their own currency. That kept their export prices low and falling, even if it meant they were exchanging the sweat of their workers' brows for vastly overpriced U.S. bonds and other financial assets. But China has run out of cheap labor and has finally figured out that accumulating dollar assets is a mug's game. So domestic wages and costs are rising smartly. The yuan's exchange rate is up by 10 percent since September 2019.

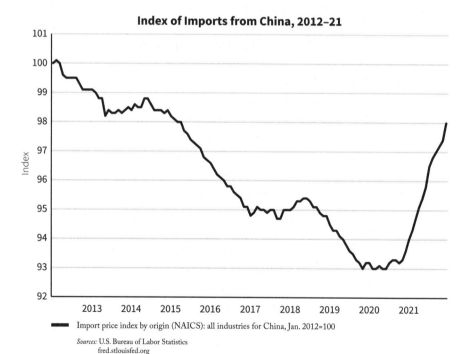

Index of Imports from China, 2012–21

Import price index by origin (NAICS): all industries for China, Jan. 2012=100

Sources: U.S. Bureau of Labor Statistics
fred.stlouisfed.org

Chinese import prices have nearly gone vertical and have already retraced 50 percent of their 2012 to 2019 decline. And that's to say nothing of soaring supply-chain and transportation costs that are also moving up the import price pipeline. In short, an inflation shock is coming, but not a 1970s-style double-digit gain on the CPI—at least not immediately. Instead, the shock we are talking about will occur inside the hallowed halls of the U.S. central bank and among their shills on Wall Street. It will be the realization that domestic inflation was never really as low as they thought, save for the one-time gale of imported deflation from abroad, and that now all cylinders—domestic services, nondurables, durables, and imports—are leaning hard into the inflation top line.

The Fed will soon lose its internal consensus. The open squabbling about whether the impending 3 percent to 5 percent per annum overall inflation is abating then will lead to a disorderly retreat. That means a premature end to bond purchases and a subsequent rise of interest rates across the maturity curve that will shatter the complacency of the stock market cultists.

So yes, we are heading into an inflationary blow-off top. But it's one manifested in wildly inflated financial asset prices, not chiefly the price of oil, commodities, and consumer goods and services as we saw in the late 1970s. Financial asset prices, in essence, are hanging from a hook erected by the Fed's massive suppression of interest rates since the spring of 2008. Once the Fed is forced to permit rates to rise, in the near future, the whole inflationary structure of financial asset prices will come tumbling down.

It is crucial to understand, therefore, that we are not heading for a replay of what we have called "your grandfather's inflation" of the 1970s. In that go-round, goods-and-services inflation led the cycle, while assets were correctly and sustainably priced at the beginning of the surge. Consequently, as the CPI and other goods and services measures took flight into the double-digit realm, there were plenty of places for investors to ride out the inflationary storm and even prosper as it unfolded.

Not Your Grandfather's Real Estate Hedge

Let's take the fourth quarter of 1970 through the same period in 1980 as the bookends of your grandfather's inflation; compounding can be an awful, insidious thing. The CPI rose by 8.1 percent per year during the period. By the end of 1980, the U.S. dollar was worth just 46 cents compared to 10 years earlier.

That's right. Your grandfather's inflation brutalized savers, but it didn't leave them bereft of ways to preserve and enhance their wealth. During that same 10-year period, the value of household real estate rose far more—by nearly 13 percent per year. Consequently, by the time of the inflationary blow-off top in late 1980, inflation-adjusted household real estate was 54 percent more valuable than it had been at the end of 1970. It was an inflation hedge par excellence.

The key reason for that, and one that is usually overlooked, however, is that real estate prices were reasonable and sustainable going into the 1970s because both the benchmark U.S. Treasury 10-year bond and mortgage rates were properly priced. For instance, between 1963 and 1972, the inflation-adjusted yield on the 10-year UST averaged 2.2 percent. Real estate prices had not been driven to uneconomic heights by cheap mortgage debt, like at present, and thus had room to run when the inflationary gale arrived.

By contrast, real estate today is massively overvalued, owing to ultracheap mortgage debt. Accordingly, when interest rates rise sharply during the inflationary blow-off top ahead, real estate prices will head southward. Owning real estate will offer no inflationary hedge this time.

The lynchpin of the massive inflation of real estate values in the past decade, of course, is the Fed's hideous repression of interest rates, centered on the inflation-adjusted yield of the benchmark 10-year Treasury. As shown in the chart below, the historically based real return depicted has been progressively expunged; during the 1990s, real returns averaged 3 percent or better and during the 2000 to 2012 period exceeded 2 percent most of the time, save for the bottom of the Great Recession.

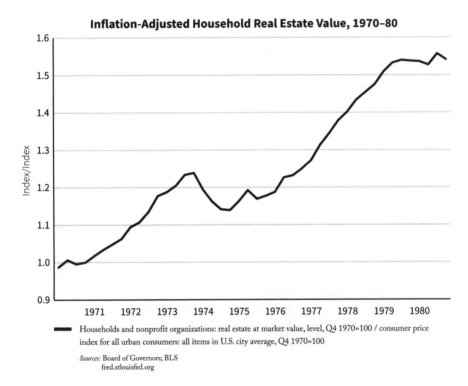

Inflation-Adjusted Household Real Estate Value, 1970–80

Households and nonprofit organizations: real estate at market value, level, Q4 1970=100 / consumer price index for all urban consumers: all items in U.S. city average, Q4 1970=100

Sources: Board of Governors; BLS
fred.stlouisfed.org

But after inflation targeting was officially adopted in January 2012—except for short intervals of barely positive real yields in 2014–15 and 2017–18—inflation-adjusted yields were pushed below zero and have remained deeply submerged ever since.

In July 2021, in fact, the real yield stood at a ridiculous negative 1.68 percent, and that's using the inherently smoothed year-over-year change in the 16 percent trimmed mean CPI for the calculation. Based on the Fed's preferred year-over-year change in the PCE deflator, the real yield is actually negative

2.60 percent. Either way, one thing is certain. Any financial instrument that prices off the Treasury benchmark, which is most everything directly or indirectly via the capitalization rate used by real estate investors, is drastically overvalued. That means when interest rates, cap rates, and PE multiples reset to some semblance of financial rationality and sustainability, there will be an extended period of draw-down in which the principal value of stocks, bonds, and real estate also will be sharply reduced.

As a result, the sparkling returns on real estate investment trusts (REITs) in recent years were a mathematical consequence of ultracheap interest rates, not the inherent characteristics of real estate or the REIT form of ownership.

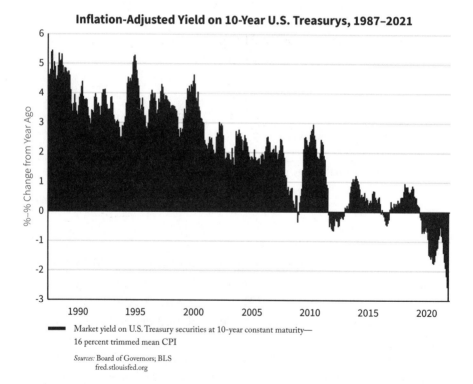

Inflation-Adjusted Yield on 10-Year U.S. Treasurys, 1987–2021

Market yield on U.S. Treasury securities at 10-year constant maturity—
16 percent trimmed mean CPI

Sources: Board of Governors; BLS
fred.stlouisfed.org

The 9 largest publicly traded REITs, which range in market cap from $30 billion to $130 billion, are listed below for the period January 2012 to the present. Their average total return—dividends plus price appreciation—was 332 percent over that period.

That computes to a sizzling annualized return of 16.7 percent. Within the group, the highest annual gain was 27.1 percent for Equinix, which is a data center REIT, and the lowest was 4.3 percent for Simon Property Group, which is the nation's largest mall owner.

Nine Largest REITs, Annual Total Return, 2012–21

- American Tower (communications): 20.0 percent
- Crown Castle (communications): 20.1 percent
- Prologis (industrial): 21.0 percent
- Simon Property Group (malls): 4.3 percent
- Equinix (data centers): 27.1 percent
- Public Storage (self-storage): 13.3 percent
- Welltower (health care): 10.0 percent
- Avalon Bay (residential): 10.1 percent
- Digital Realty Trust (data centers): 14.3 percent
- **Top nine REITs average:** 16.7 percent

For purposes of illustration, we can chart the course of American Tower Corporation (AMT), which is representative of how all of these REITs made such fulsome returns since 2012. AMT owns more than 180,000 cell towers throughout the United States, Asia, Latin America, Europe, and the Middle East.

Cell towers are a capital-intensive business that generates low returns. During 2020, for example, American Tower carried $47.2 billion of total assets, against which it generated just $1.82 billion in pretax income. (REITs are generally exempt from corporate income taxes.) That computes to a pretax return of just 3.9 percent, which is nothing to write home about and underscores the fact that the magic is in the cap rates and leverage, not the business of owning cell towers.

In this case, AMT is nearly a pure real estate play because it owns the land and the tower structure (i.e., the "building") but leases space on its towers to wireless service providers that install equipment to support their wireless networks and perform all aspects of the telecom operating business. The company has very little credit or customer risk because most of its revenue in each market is generated by just the top mobile carriers, which operate as quasi-utilities.

Not surprisingly, during an era of ultracheap debt and sky-high PE multiples, AMT has been a barn burner of an investment, especially since the Fed went full speed on the printing presses starting in the fall of 2008. Accordingly, during the 12.5 years between January 2009 and July 2021, AMT generated a total return (dividends plus price appreciation) of 20 percent per year.

We are talking about cell towers, which are built to customer order. The ordinary real estate risk of finding reliable tenants is virtually eliminated. Accordingly, on a risk-adjusted basis, this particular REIT's 20 percent annualized return since 2012 seems almost too good to be true.

In fact, it probably is. The lion's share of that sterling annual return is down to price appreciation, not AMT's modest 1.69 percent dividend yield. As it happens, the stock of AMT is currently valued at $130.7 billion, which represents a PE multiple of 57.9 times its $2.2 billion in latest 12-month net income. More importantly, for a real estate investment, its operating free cash flow was just $2.93 billion, representing a multiple of 44.7.

That's right. The company's dumb cell towers are valued at Silicon Valley tech start-up multiples despite a very modest free cash flow. And that's especially absurd considering that the growth rate of AMT's free cash flow has ground steadily lower over the past two decades. It recently barely avoided flatlining.

American Tower Free Cash-Flow Growth Rate per Year

- September 2004–June 2010: 25.9 percent per year
- June 2010–December 2018: 18.3 percent per year
- December 2018–June 2021: 1.3 percent per year

Implicitly, therefore, the company's free cash-flow multiple has been climbing skyward for two decades. During the period covered by the above growth rates, AMT's trailing free cash-flow multiple weighed in as follows:

- September 2004: 20.2
- June 2010: 28.3
- December 2018: 30.3
- June 2021: 44.7

Stated differently, at its current towering valuation, AMT is generating a meager earnings yield of just 0.44 percent per year, only a small fraction of the current inflation rate of between 3 percent and 5 percent, depending on which index you prefer. The sheer absurdity of that juxtaposition reflects the cult of the stock market at work. AMT has been crowned a growth wonder, leading speculators to either pay egregiously high multiples or accept razor-thin dividends and earnings yields. Nevertheless, they have been trained to believe that there is economic magic in cell towers and that per-share earnings and share prices will grow robustly into the future.

In fact, the company's historic net income and cash-flow growth have been driven by the brute force of asset accumulation. For instance, during 2020, it generated $3.88 billion in cash flow from operations, which was offset by $1.032 billion in capital expenditures and $3.8 billion in existing tower acquisitions. As a result, it was actually short $950 million in cash and paid $1.928 billion in dividends on top of that.

There is no surprise, of course, about how it came up with the nearly $2.9 billion needed to cover the shortfall from its investments and dividends. It borrowed the money, and cheaply too. In fact, AMT's year-end debt of $35.7 billion in December 2020 was $4.7 billion higher than the prior year. Moreover, 2020 was by no means an aberration. Rather, it is representative of the company's modus operandi. During its 2016 thru 2020 fiscal years, AMT's core financials computed as follows:

American Tower Cumulative Results, 2016–20

- cash flow from operations: $17.01 billion
- capital expenditures: $4.42 billion
- tower acquisitions: $12.058 billion
- dividends: $6.81 billion
- cash flow after investments and dividends: negative $6.29 billion
- debt as of December 2015: $17.1 billion
- debt as of December 2020: $36.7 billion

To be sure, borrowing heavily to fund "growth" and dividends did fuel its stock, which rose from $96 per share to $220 per share during the five-year period. But as they say in the nutrition business, that growth was essentially "empty carbs," calories without nutritional value. In reality, the company's trend return on capital employed was nothing to write home about and actually fell over the five-year period. Those sterling returns registered in the casino were purely a function of cheap borrowing to purchase additional earning assets (cell towers) and the willingness of the casino to pay higher and higher multiples for steadily declining rates of cash-flow growth.

Since December 2011, AMT debt has soared to $36.2 billion from $7.2 billion, even as its interest expense barely doubled. Accordingly, its annualized interest expense per dollar of debt has plunged:

- December 2011: 4.3 percent
- September 2015: 3.4 percent
- June 2021: 2.2 percent

In short, like so much else in the casino, the sterling 20 percent per annum returns mentioned at the outset were generated by the triple whammy of company financial engineers piling on debt and assets; the Fed's steady and relentless repression of interest rates, which lowered the carrying cost drastically; and stock market speculators betting that interest rates will never rise and that high growth through ever-increasing leverage can be capitalized in perpetuity.

When interest rates finally do rise and valuation multiples crater, one thing will be abundantly clear: No one makes 20 percent on leveraged real estate indefinitely. That's merely a delusion fostered by the cult of the stock market.

In effect, monetary inflation this time around has produced the inverse effect compared to your grandfather's inflation of the 1970s. The high return already has happened and is now embedded in asset prices, owing to superhigh PE multiples and cap rates. When the Fed finally turns to fighting goods-and-services inflation, real estate prices will get hammered. Rather than a hedge, they will be a graveyard of capital losses.

Bank Stocks Are No Place to Hide

The toxic effects of the Fed's relentless interest rate repression are not limited to the highflyers. Among the worst has been the absolute savaging of bank depositors and the resulting vast transfer of income from depositors to banks, which in turn has fueled an egregious, artificial ballooning of bank profits and stock prices.

For instance, the combined market cap of the top six U.S. banking institutions—J. P. Morgan, Bank of America, Citigroup, Wells Fargo, Morgan Stanley, and Goldman Sachs—has risen from $200 billion at the bottom of the financial crisis during the winter of 2008 and 2009, where it reflected their true value absent government bailouts, to $1.5 trillion currently. That 7.5 times gain, which was 100 percent orchestrated by the Fed, is an unspeakable gift to the wealthy who own most of the stocks and especially to top bank executives, who cashed in vastly appreciated options.

Needless to say, this massive bubble in bank and other financial stocks is unsustainable. When the Fed is finally forced to shut down its printing presses, bank stocks—normally considered a good bet in inflationary times—will be among the first to dive into the abyss.

While this might represent justice from a policy and equitable point of view, the extent of the harm to everyday Americans would be hard to overstate. That's because Wall Street is going for one more bite at the apple, claiming that the currently accelerating rate of inflation is good for bank stocks. Consensus stock price forecasts for J. P. Morgan (JPM) are up 20 percent by 2023 and for Goldman Sachs by 70 percent.

Yet this is just another 11th-hour lure from big money speculators looking to unload vastly overvalued stocks on unwary retail investors. Accelerating inflation supposedly portends higher growth and loan demand, but that's complete humbug because what's actually coming down the pike, as we have seen before, is stagflation. That fact will cap loan demand even as it squeezes net interest margins, causing bank earnings to plummet.

The impending demise of bank stocks is implicit in the manner in which the $1.5 trillion scam, currently reflected in the bloated market cap of the Big Six financial institutions, came about. The Fed dominates, especially the front end of the yield curve. It will brook no interference from market forces, as you can see in the yield on certificates of deposit (CDs).

Interest rates on 12-month CDs of under $100,000 dropped below the inflation rate in October 2009 and have been pinned there ever since. During the subsequent 137 months, the interest rate on CDs exceeded the year-over-year inflation rate during just seven months, and then by a pitiful average of just 25 basis points.

There is no other word for this than expropriation, the unconstitutional taking of property from tens of millions of households that needed to keep their funds liquid and didn't wish to roll the dice on junk bonds and stocks. On average, the after-inflation yield during the 11-year period was negative 1.40 percent.

Thus upward of one-fifth of the real wealth of depositors has been seized by Fed-enabled bankers during the last decade alone. Rather than admit to even a modicum of responsibility for this brutal economic injustice, the Fed heads actually have the gall to claim that they nursed America's bloated and parasitic banking system back to the pink of health.

The squeeze on banks has been far less intense, such that during the same 11-year period, net interest margins fell modestly from 370 basis points in October 2009 to 280 basis points by October 2020. Still, on an after-inflation basis, bank interest rate spreads—which are the heart of their profitability—remained positive throughout the period.

That's right. In the Fed-manipulated money and capital markets, it transpired that small retail depositors realized a minus 1.40 percent return after inflation, thereby helping banks to harvest positive spreads of 1.50 percent after inflation. We doubt a more perverse reverse-Robinhood redistribution could be imagined. Indeed, if any indictment of Fed policy is needed, it can be found in how that policy literally turned everyday depositors into the indentured financial serfs of the banking system.

Here is how a decade of extreme financial repression by the Fed played out in the banking system. From the fourth quarter of 2009 through the third quarter of 2020, CD yields fell by 75 percent, bank net interest margins dropped by 19 percent, and total bank assets soared by 79 percent.

Needless to say, the aforementioned combination did wonders for bank profitability. On the one hand, the Fed's money pumping fostered an eruption of debt and other securities issuance. The aggregate balance sheets of the nation's banks expanded to $21.1 trillion in total assets from $11.8 trillion during this 11-year period. Even with lower interest rates and yields on these assets, total bank interest income rose to $576 billion during the latest 12-month period ending in March 2021 from $545 billion in 2009.

Meanwhile, the rates banks paid depositors plunged by 50 percent to 75 percent depending on deposit type and size. Accordingly, total bank interest expense plunged to just $56 billion during the March 2021 latest 12-month period from $146 billion in 2009.

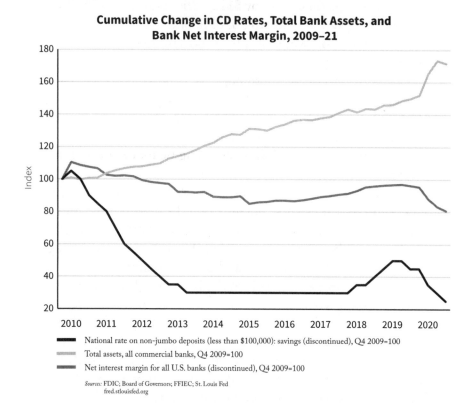

Cumulative Change in CD Rates, Total Bank Assets, and Bank Net Interest Margin, 2009–21

— National rate on non-jumbo deposits (less than $100,000): savings (discontinued), Q4 2009=100

— Total assets, all commercial banks, Q4 2009=100

— Net interest margin for all U.S. banks (discontinued), Q4 2009=100

Sources: FDIC; Board of Governors; FFIEC; St. Louis Fed
fred.stlouisfed.org

In a word, the nation's bankers not only emerged unscathed from the financial crisis, owing to Washington and Federal Reserve bailouts, but during the subsequent decade surely believed they had died and gone to bankers' heaven. Thanks to a 6 percent gain in interest income over the above depicted 11-year period and a 62 percent drop in interest expense, the dollar level of bank net interest margin soared.

In return for essentially doing nothing other than scooping up their share of the tsunami of corporate and government debt and collecting nearly cost-free deposits, the net margin of the banking system rose to $521 billion for the March 2021 latest 12-month period from $399 billion in 2009. That's right. By crowding around the Fed's easy-money trough, the net margin of the banking system rose by $122 billion, or 30 percent. Not in a million years would this have happened under a regime of sound money and honest free-market pricing in the money and capital markets.

Fed apologists claim these huge profit gains were designed to spur bank lending and thereby encourage businesses—especially small businesses without access to the bond markets—to fund increased growth and new jobs. But that excuse for money printing has been a big lie for decades. It has now turned into a farce.

As recently as the 1990s, loans and leases accounted for 60 percent or more of total bank assets. But that ratio steadily declined during the last two decades and plunged after the post–March 2020 explosion of Fed money printing, falling to just 47 percent during the most recent quarter. Instead of making loans to businesses, banks have loaded up with government and corporate debt, the price of which is effectively underwritten by the Fed, as well as excess reserve deposits at the Federal Reserve itself.

As to the former, the banks have surely been the handmaids of Washington's borrowing spree. There was $1.4 trillion in U.S. Treasury and federal agency debt on bank balance sheets in the fourth quarter of 2009; the current level stands at $4.2 trillion. In effect, the Fed midwifed a $2.8 trillion or 195 percent gain in bank holdings of government paper, thereby enabling Washington to dispense more public stimulus and subsidies even as the banking system collected the coupons and arbitraged them against virtually zero cost deposits.

The negative impact of the Fed's massive bond buying is especially evident, however, in the excess reserve accounts of the banks. These are held as deposits at the Fed, which currently pays the banks a mere 0.15 percent rate of interest on excess reserves (IOER).

These excess reserve "assets" are the result of deposits by primary dealer banks at the Fed, which are payments to them for its $120 billion per month of bond purchases. Since these "assets" don't count in the calculation of bank capital ratios, the banks are apparently happy to collect $6 billion in IOER payments for doing absolutely nothing rather than invest them in loans, leases, or securities, which do require the setting aside of bank capital and do involve some degree of risk.

As a measure of the extent to which the money markets and banking system have been distorted by the Fed's money-printing madness, these IOER deposits are something out of a wholly different financial universe. Since December 2007, excess reserve deposits at the Fed have risen by a staggering 4,460 percent!

You truly can't make this up. Between its "prudential" regulation of bank capital ratios and its lunatic rate of bond buying under quantitative easing, the Fed has pumped $4.2 trillion of hot air into the egregiously bloated $21.1 trillion balance sheets of the U.S. banking system.

Commercial Bank Reserves
Deposited at the Fed, 2002–21

- December 2002: $7.2 billion
- December 2007: $9.4 billion
- December 2012: $1.5 trillion
- December 2014: $2.4 trillion
- August 2021: $4.2 trillion
- **Percent increase since December 2002:**
  4,460 percent

The net result, of course, is that bank executives and shareholders have been laughing all the way to, well, the bank. Since the first quarter of 2010, once bank earnings stabilized after the massive write-offs following the financial crisis, quarterly pretax earnings have quadrupled from $25 billion to $97.5 billion, roughly $400 billion annualized.

In the case of the Big Six institutions, the rebound has been similar. The combined net income of J. P. Morgan, Bank of America, Citigroup, Wells Fargo, Morgan Stanley, and Goldman Sachs has performed as follows:

- 2009: $43.3 billion
- 2013: $75.8 billion
- latest 12 months, March 2021: $146.4 billion

Yet the overwhelming share of that gain is the fruit of Fed-fostered arbitrage of interest rate markets. In truth, the U.S. banking system is massively overcapacitated. In a free market operating with sound money, bank profits would be dramatically lower than today until excess capacity was liquidated.

As it is, the banking system runs massive payrolls, occupancy expenses, technology bills, vendor support expenses, and other overheads, economic resources that would otherwise be more productively employed elsewhere in the economy. Economists call this deadweight economic loss, but the practical effect of it is the perpetuation of banking zombies.

Unfortunately, the perpetuation of excess banking capacity isn't the half of it. What also has occurred is that a preponderant share of these bloated, Fed-enabled banking profits has been recycled straight back to Wall Street in the form of massive stock buybacks and dividend payments.

During the eight years encompassing 2013 through 2020, the Big Six collectively generated $726 billion in net income, of which 84 percent was recycled back to Wall Street. This figure includes $375 billion in share buybacks and $231 billion in dividend distributions.

Stated differently, the Big Six alone pushed $606 billion in cash back into Wall Street, mainly based on interest rate arbitrage facilitated by the Fed. The sheer magnitude of that figure speaks for itself: How in the world is it conceivable that the Big Six generated enough real value to justify that three-fifths of $1 trillion dollars be returned to shareholders?

Indeed, the figures for J. P. Morgan alone tell you all you need to know. From 2013 to 2020, while the economy was creeping forward at about 2 percent per year, JPM generated $211 billion in net income and pumped $90 billion of this into share buybacks and another $74 billion into dividends.

Not bad for a financial institution that got $25 billion from the Troubled Asset Relief Program (TARP) and hundreds of billions of Fed bailout lines during 2008 to 2009 and that continuously benefits from an implicit too-big-to-fail subsidy that, according to an International Monetary Fund (IMF) study, amounts to about 80 basis points on its interest-bearing liabilities.

Then again, J. P. Morgan currently has $2.784 trillion in deposits and interest-bearing debt outstanding, meaning the subsidy currently amounts to about $22 billion per year. Likewise, Bank of America (BAC) generated $142 billion in net income from 2013 to 2020 and returned $111 billion (78 percent) to shareholders in the form of buybacks and dividends. At the same time, its balance sheet currently carries $2.21 trillion in deposits and interest-bearing liabilities, meaning that by the IMF formula, its too-big-to-fail subsidy amounts to $17.6 billion per year.

As it happens, that estimated subsidy figure amounts to virtually the entirety of BAC's $17.9 billion in net income in 2020, from which it paid $14.7 billion back to shareholders in buybacks and dividends. Cynics might wish to call this a Ponzi scheme of the first order, but the real danger is actually more fraught. During the last decade, JPM's price-to-book value has more than doubled and Bank of America's has increased fourfold.

In the case of Morgan Stanley and Goldman, the story is much the same. The former generated $55 billion in net income during the 2013 to 2020 period, of which $41 billion or 74 percent was pumped back into Wall Street as buybacks and dividends. For Goldman, the figures were $62.7 billion in cumulative net income, of which 84 percent or $52.9 billion was returned as buybacks and dividends.

Wall Street speculators, of course, piled on for the ride, causing Goldman's price-to-book ratio to double from its late 2011 level and Morgan Stanley's to nearly quadruple.

Perhaps Wall Street's vicious response to the Fed whenever it has even thought out loud about cooling off its printing presses is not so extreme after all: the two leading Wall Street investment banks are among the most egregious beneficiaries of those very printing presses running overtime.

That is to say, back in late 2011 when Bernanke was still assuring the world that quantitative easing (QE) was a temporary emergency measure and that the Fed's then bloated balance sheet at $2.8 trillion would be soon rolled back to pre-crisis levels, the market assumed that neither of these financial behemoths was worth their bloated book value. At least back then, stock market operators knew that without QE there would be no tsunami of bank earnings.

Since then, of course, the Fed's balance sheet has tripled to $8.8 trillion and Wall Street dramatically reset its expectations. They now assume that for all practical purposes the Fed's massive bond buying and interest rate repression will never end.

Yet it will end, because the Fed has hung itself out to dry. The inflation genie is out of the bottle. The Fed soon will have to shut down its printing presses and permit interest rates to rise, and sharply. That will send bloated bank profits and corresponding market caps careening in a distinctively southward direction.

Chapter 11

"TINA"—Safe Havens No More

The health care and food sectors, often considered "safe" stocks when growth stocks decline, provide another damning case in point. The UnitedHealth Group (UNH), for instance, is the monster of the midway in health care, with $270 billion in annual revenues (2020) and $14.5 billion in net income. The thing is, the company's market cap currently stands at $401 billion, yielding an implied PE multiple of nearly 28.

A decade ago, UNH sales, net income, and market cap stood at $99.3 billion, $4.9 billion, and $49.1 billion, respectively. The implied PE multiple back then—when the economy had fully recovered from the Great Recession and the Fed was on the verge of adopting the madness of 2 percent inflation targeting—was just 10.

Nor was that valuation inappropriate. During the decade since 2011, the company's revenues and net income have grown at 10 percent and 11 percent per annum, respectively, growth rates that do not warrant a 28 times PE multiple in any way, shape, or form.

Indeed, when you look at the true litmus test of economic earnings—operating free cash flow—the drastic overvaluation of the nation's largest health care conglomerate is clear. A decade ago (September 2011, latest 12 months figures) the company's free cash flow stood at $7.7 billion, implying a valuation multiple of 6.4 times. Today's latest 12-month free cash flow of $18.5 billion is valued at a multiple of 21.7.

That is to say, based on a free cash-flow growth rate of just 9.2 percent per year, the company's valuation multiple has more than tripled. This outcome is not remotely justified by the company's actual production of cash earnings.

As it happens, even that characterization is on the charitable side. During the past eight years, UnitedHealth has reinvested $58.3 billion of its operating cash flow in the business. However, fully $44 billion, 75 percent of that total, went to acquisitions rather than direct capital expenditure, a fact that underlines the true growth specialty of UnitedHealth.

During the past decade, the company's goodwill has soared to $86.6 billion from $26.6 billion, increasing 12.5 percent per year. Not surprisingly, debt rose to $48.2 billion from $14.6 billion, or by approximately 13 percent per year during the same period. In short, much of UnitedHealth's apparent modest growth in terms of sales, net income, and free cash flow is owed to debt-financed acquisitions for which it paid far more than actual net asset value, illustrated by soaring goodwill accounts.

Notwithstanding all of the self-serving ballyhoo about its vaunted "synergistic acquisitions," the company's current net income return on assets of 7.28 percent is no higher than it was a decade and $48 billion worth of purportedly synergistic acquisitions ago. The more than tripling of UnitedHealth's free cash-flow multiple over the last decade is no outlier. Rather, it's par for the course among most of the large cap companies outside of the tech space.

It's really just more compelling evidence that soaring market caps are fostered by the Fed's largesse, not the traditional market push and pull of the Main Street economy, which clearly is struggling in comparison.

At the heart of the stupendous financial bubble fostered by the Fed and its caravan of central bank money printers from around the planet is a simple proposition—namely, that interest rates on the benchmark U.S. Treasury and related blue-chip bonds are ultralow, so PE multiples are justifiably wafting high into the historical nosebleed section, divorced from common-sense rules of financial valuation because of what stock promoters today call TINA.

That is to say, "there is no alternative" (TINA) to stocks, so close your eyes and buy the present value of a risk-adjusted earnings stream that cannot possibly justify its purchase price. No matter, prices will keep going up because, like magical beanstalks, that's what stocks do.

Investing has finally been reduced to trusting in the Fed, the monetary Father Almighty, creator of rising asset prices on Wall Street and everlasting prosperity on Main Street. If stock prices should falter lower, by no later than the third day they shall arise again, ascending skyward to reward the quick (bullish speculators) and dispatch the dead (bearish nonbelievers), world without end, amen.

Actually, there is something to TINA, but it's the very opposite of buying hideously overpriced stocks. In truth, there is no alternative over the long run to a real return on society's pooled savings. Without that, capitalism will wither on the vine, and prosperity as we have known it will, at length, perish from the earth.

A Reckoning Deferred

So here is the reality behind TINA as a stock-buying mantra. For the better part of three decades, real yields have been falling but now have reached preposterously unsustainable levels. In fact, inflation-adjusted yields on the benchmark security of the entire financial universe went negative in May 2019 and currently stand negative 175 basis points below the zero bound. Obviously, a world of permanently negative 175 basis-point yields is an impossibility. At length, it would generate essentially zero new savings, causing the whole capitalist economy to go tilt.

Accordingly, it is only a matter of time—and not much time—until the late economist Herb Stein's law proves itself yet again: that which is unsustainable tends to stop, and the longer the reckoning is deferred, the harder the landing when the end finally comes. It goes without saying that when the most important price in the financial universe is drastically misaligned owing to central bank repression, the resulting mispricing ricochets through the entire warp and woof of the financial system.

As we saw earlier, we are speaking not merely about the tech sector, where growth has been absurdly overvalued on the ultralow cap rate theory, but about large-cap stocks, especially where multiple escalation has been rampant.

Take the case of the giant global food company, Nestlé. As of August 2021, it was valued at $350 billion against net income and free cash flow of $13.6 billion and $10.4 billion, respectively. That is, it was valued at nearly 26 times net income and 33.5 times operating free cash flow.

With multiples like that, you might be forgiven for expecting they represent a reward for superior growth over a sustained period of time. But you would be dead wrong. During the last 10 years, Nestlé's net income and free cash flow have grown at just 2.4 percent and 6.2 percent per year, respectively.

Of course, what has grown smartly is the rate at which it pumped cash back into Wall Street and the amount of debt it took on to do so. Thus during the eight years from 2013 thru 2020, Nestlé generated $86 billion in operating free cash flow after capital expenditures, but spent fully 92 percent of that, or $79 billion, on stock buybacks and dividends.

The fact that the company was not motivated to reinvest its cash flow and balance sheet capacity in productive assets is evident in the book value of its property, plant, and equipment (PP&E), which stood at $30.3 billion in December 2013 and came in lower—at $29.6 billion—in December 2020. What did grow by leaps and bounds during that same period, of course, was debt, which increased to $45.8 billion from $24.5 billion during the same period.

In short, large-cap companies outside of the tech sector have not had to invest aggressively during the last decade in order to catalyze soaring share prices and market caps. Recycling virtually all of their free cash flow into Wall Street and rampant multiple expansion was more than enough to do the trick.

This outcome occurred in the investment-grade world at a company run by the relatively prudent Swiss. But take the case of the Kraft Heinz Company. These once-storied food companies were combined by gun-slinging financial engineers on the backs of cheap junk debt financing. In so doing, they managed to thoroughly wreck both operations in frantic pursuit of cost cuts and "synergies" needed to service their mountainous debts.

And I do mean ultracheap junk debt was the culprit here. Owing to the combination of tiny yields after inflation and a historic realized loss rate of about 3 percent—after recovering from a 4.2 percent initial default rate—junk bond yields have essentially hit zero. So the Fed is deep in the zombie breeding business.

After all, when you give junk-rated companies long-term capital at rates that leave investors with virtually nothing after inflation and losses or essentially zero return to investors, you are going to get a lot of demand from a mushrooming herd of zombie issuers—that is, companies that would otherwise be liquidated and their resources redeployed more productively elsewhere in an honest free market.

Owing to its $4.5 trillion money-printing spree since September 2019, the Fed has essentially vaporized after-inflation returns in the sovereign debt and investment grade sectors. In the resulting desperate hunt for yield, speculators have plowed into the junk bond market, driving yields to a paltry 3.95 percent as of mid-August 2021.

We don't know how you could falsify bond prices any more blatantly than that. Notwithstanding the Fed's dubious insistence that elevated inflation readings are "transitory," the fact is that the CPI posted a 5.4 percent year-over-year gain in September, a figure that will be even higher in the months ahead. So they've done it. These fools have driven the junk-bond yield to negative 145 basis points after inflation, and it will be going deeper into the red from there.

Too Much Cash

Among all the financial market distortions and misallocations that result from the Fed's money-pumping policies, we are hard-pressed to think of something more stupid and more counterproductive than negative real yields on junk bonds.

The fact is, in a world of sound money and honest price discovery in the bond pits there wouldn't be an appreciable junk bond market at all. Companies with truly risky but worthy investment projects would sell equity, and investors looking for reliable yields would have plenty of government and investment-grade corporate bonds with adequate risk-adjusted returns from which to choose.

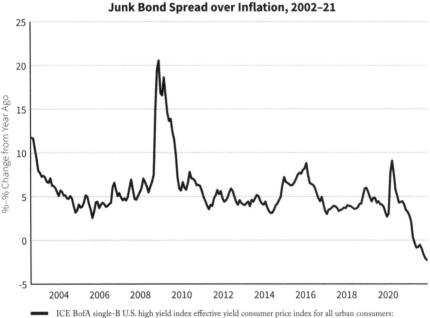

Junk Bond Spread over Inflation, 2002–21

ICE BofA single-B U.S. high yield index effective yield consumer price index for all urban consumers: all items in U.S. city average

Sources: ICE Data Indices, LLC; U.S. Bureau of Labor Statistics
fred.stlouisfed.org

Accordingly, not in a month of Sundays would the 2021 June year-to-date result have happened—namely, the issuance of nearly $300 billion worth of high-yield debt, according to Dealogic. That's more than 40 percent ahead of last year's pace. The reason so much junk has been scarfed up at what amounts to guaranteed losses after inflation and defaults is no mystery. As at least one analyst still possessed of a modicum of common sense told the *Wall Street Journal* the following: "Gennadiy Goldberg, U.S. rates strategist at TD Securities, said the inversion indicates investors are chasing returns far and wide in a low-rate environment, even in riskier places. 'This is a function of too much cash in the system and too few attractive assets for investors to put their cash into,' he said."

You don't say! Yet the fact that investors are flocking to put themselves into harm's way is only half the story. If it were just about the risk of loss due to runaway investor stupidity, we'd say let them enjoy their just deserts. But the other side of the coin is that these hundreds of billions of junk bonds and junk-bank loans—there are now about $3 trillion combined outstanding—essentially fund leveraged buyouts, leveraged recaps, and other financial engineering schemes. The overwhelming bulk of these deals have no economic utility or added value. Instead, they merely function to strip-mine corporate cash flows and debt capacities in order to recycle the cash to public shareholders and private equity insiders.

In this regard, the *Wall Street Journal* story noted that some asset managers are buying these yieldless junk bonds just the same in the expectation of capital gains. That's right. Debt securities, which are supposed to generate a modest yield and no change in principal value (price), are being purchased for appreciation! It's a straight-up bet that endless easy money from the Fed will eliminate any possibility of future recessions and permit existing heavy junk-debt burdens to be refinanced at ever lower rates, thereby triggering upgrades by the rating agencies.

Train Wreck

That's the theoretical underpinning of the Kraft Heinz train wreck, anyway. Back in 2015, the two predecessor companies were slammed together by Wall Street financial engineers, private equity firm 3G Capital Partners and the sainted Warren Buffett. This followed the 2013 leveraged buyout of Heinz for $23 billion by the same crew.

The deal itself did nothing for the business challenges of the predecessor companies. Pro forma sales of $28 billion never remotely materialized and have flatlined at about $26 billion since the merger. What the merger did do, of course, was enrich insiders and shareholders. During the period from 2016 through the first quarter of 2021, the company generated $15.8 billion in EBITDA and $4.86 billion in capital expenditures, yielding free cash flow of $10.95 billion.

Meanwhile, dividends paid to shareholders during that same period totaled $14.06 billion, or 128 percent of the company's free cash flow. That's what I would call plain strip-mining by financial engineers, all made possible by massive interest rate repression.

The company's financial ratios now stand at the edge of an abyss. For the latest 12-month period ending in June 2021 total debt stood at $28.3 billion, yielding a leverage ratio of 9.7 times free cash flow. The company has also sold off upward of $4 billion in business units to remain solvent, including its namesake cheese business. What happened was that the financial engineers who controlled the merged, debt-ridden companies attempted to slash costs per their spreadsheet "synergy" analysis. But in cutting north of 7,000 jobs, or half of the Heinz workforce, they ended up ruining their brand value instead.

At length, the whole scam became fully public, and the company was forced to take a $15 billion write-down on its storied brands. Critics have long contended that 3G Capital's cost cutting went too far and came at the expense of growth.

They were right. Starting in the first quarter of 2017, the company's U.S. organic sales declined from a year earlier for six quarters in a row. ("Organic" sales strip out portfolio changes and currency impacts.)

Yes, this is financial engineering and junk bonds at work. Since the merger, $24 billion in cash dividends have been paid to shareholders and hundreds of millions of fees have been showered upon Wall Street and insiders. The result is a deal that would never have happened on the free market under a regime of sound money and that shipwrecked a company that functions as a dividend mule, at least as long as it can avoid Chapter 11 bankruptcy.

Self-evidently, Kraft Heinz is not an aberration. Deeply subeconomic interest rates have enabled firms to continue to pile on more and more debt while managing to barely stay afloat. Such zombie firms retard economic growth by locking up labor and capital resources in low-productivity firms that do not even earn their cost of capital. Nevertheless, as the Fed and other central banks have pushed rates to rock bottom, zombies have been able to survive far longer than in the past with less pressure to reduce debt and curtail economic activity.

Chapter 12

A Bubble-Ridden Stock Market

So the question remains: Are the central bankers who have fostered these hideous financial bubbles really this obstinately dense? After all, Wall Street is actually so saturated with anomalies, irrationalities, and sheer absurdities that you would have to be literally deaf, dumb, and blind not to notice.

One of the obvious cases of speculation run amok is what we would call cult stocks. The absurd valuations of these stocks demonstrate in spades why the short side of the market will be the only safe place to make money in the years ahead.

We are speaking here of everyday companies with market caps and PE multiples that make a mockery of the very notion of honest price discovery or even intelligent thought. Our poster boy in this regard is Chipotle (CMG). It is the nation's largest burrito joint, with 2,850 restaurants that have largely saturated its niche. But owing to the massive growth of its store count since it was spun out of McDonald's in 2006, it has been vastly overvalued all along, while during the last several years its valuation has gone from the absurd to the insane.

To wit, between 2011 and the present, its market cap has soared from $16 billion to $54 billion, or by 405 percent. You'd think this $43 billion valuation gain means it has been slinging an avalanche of burrito bowls from coast to coast. But not really. The growth of its market cap over that decade outpaced its net income growth by 2.4 times and its free cash-flow growth by 4.4 times.

Yet that's not the half of it. Actually, Chipotle was already vastly overvalued way back in 2011. Its $10.6 billion market cap represented a superfrisky 49 times its December 2011 latest 12-month net income of $215 million and an even more ridiculous 41 times its free cash flow of $260 million.

Alas, since then its valuation multiples have gone absolutely bonkers, even as its profits and cash flow were humdrum at best. During the last decade, CMG's net income and free cash flow have grown at only 11.1 percent and 7.2 percent per year, respectively. What that means is that its valuation multiples have literally jumped the shark. Its June 2021 latest 12-month net income of $586 million computed to an implied PE multiple of 92 times and its $502 million in operating free cash flow yielded a valuation multiple of 106 times.

That's right. Wholly prosaic single-digit free cash-flow growth of 7.2 percent per year over the last decade has been rewarded with a nosebleed triple-digit multiple that is 15 times its growth rate! That's so absurdly high that even the hottest Silicon Valley start-ups could never earn it out.

The insensibility of CMG's valuation can also be seen by allocating its market cap and store-level gross profits among its 2,850 units. Those figures compute to slightly under $19 million of market cap per store against gross profits of just $520,000 per store. For crying out loud. These are "fast casual" eateries with no tablecloths and what barely passes for silverware, which average just 2,600 square feet in size and generate an average ticket of only $17 per customer from their core demographic of 25- to 34-year-old millennials.

A real restaurateur who had to make payroll and earn a return on his assets and time wouldn't pay even $3 million for one of these stores. Self-evidently, $520,000 of gross profit—even before marketing and overhead—isn't remotely worth $19 million in the real world, only in the fantasy world of the Wall Street casino.

Cult Stocks

This gets us to the cult thing. After decades of Fed liquidity-pumping and market-propping action, the normal mechanisms that keep financial markets reasonably disciplined, honest, and stable have essentially been euthanized. Carrying costs have historically been a powerful check on excessive speculation because leveraged speculation doesn't pay when funding costs are too high and when the risk of a sudden rate spike can quickly bring about ruin. But today, in the name of "transparency," the Fed foolishly tells the Wall Street gamblers in advance as to when and by how much it intends to alter the cost of overnight funding from the zero bound, where it has been pinned for 13 years. It has thereby essentially set the cost of gambling chips at nothing.

Even more importantly, the Fed has bailed out the stock market so many times in the face of even mild corrections that short sellers have essentially been defenestrated while the amount of capital available to fund short sellers has literally withered on the vine.

In the case of Chipotle, for example, after its last food safety scares in 2015 and 2016, its PE multiple had dropped to 42 times and upward of 12 percent of its shares were sold short. Yet after the Fed's latest money-pumping spree, apparently all has been forgiven. Chipotle's PE multiple has doubled to the aforementioned absurd 92 times, while the shorts have been taken out behind the barn and shot. Short interest today stands at an all-time low since the company came public in 2006 at just 2.8 percent of outstanding shares.

And that really tells you all you need to know. One of the most egregiously overvalued companies on the U.S. stock market cannot even generate a modest level of short interest because the Fed's constant interventions have turned markets into one-way gambling venues. Investors are literally being herded into risk by these misbegotten Fed policies. For instance, the year-to-date total return on investment-grade corporate bonds has been a minuscule 0.05 percent and minus 1.4 percent for U.S. Treasuries. By contrast, junk bonds had returned nearly 5 percent to investors this year through August, and triple-C-rated bonds have gained almost 10 percent. Not surprisingly, the stampede into junk bonds and loans is on course to set another record in 2021, even though the returns after inflation are now actually negative.

That's right. Nearly 90 percent of the junk market is trading at yields below the year-over-year 5.4 percent CPI inflation rate. Over the last 50 years, the highest this number ever reached was 7 percent.

Larry McDonald, who saw it firsthand last time around as a trader at Lehman Brothers in the run-up to its demise, summed up the current madness as well as can be done in his book *A Colossal Failure of Common Sense*:

> Each year that goes by while central banks force investors to reach for yield—any paltry plus return on capital will do these days—complacency builds over time to an extreme—dangerous level. Mark my words—there were dozens of Bernie Madoffs, Al Dunlaps, and Jeff Skillings sipping mint juleps in the Hamptons and the beaches of the south of France this summer.
>
> Central bankers are these guys' best friends, that is the reality no one wants to admit. As long as central banks do NOT allow the cleansing process of the business cycle to function over longer and longer periods of time—credit risk will continue to build under the surface. Each month, week, and year we allow this charade to move forth—the corners capital flows into are deeper and deeper soaked with moral hazard toxicity. Today's players on the field make "Dick Fuld"—former Lehman CEO—look like a choir boy walking out of Sunday mass.

Indeed, if they don't hear the bell ringing on Wall Street now, we are surely dealing with a mass loss of auditory function. There are actually many highflyers that even make Chipotle's valuation look like a model of sobriety.

We are referring to the fact that Tesla's Elon Musk recently became the richest person on the planet with a net worth of more than $250 billion. But remember, his principal asset—the car-maker Tesla—has never made a dime producing and selling electric cars.

Government Teat

That's right. Tesla is basically a financial milkmaid squeezing the green teats of 11 mostly blue states that require automakers to sell a certain percentage of zero-emissions vehicles by 2025. If they can't meet the standard, the automakers have to buy regulatory credits from another automaker that meets those requirements such as Tesla, which exclusively sells electric cars.

It has been a lucrative business for Elon Musk and has brought in $3.3 billion over the course of the last five years, nearly half of that in 2020 alone. Accordingly, the $1.6 billion in regulatory credits Tesla received last year far outweighed its net income of $721 million, meaning that Tesla actually lost $879 million making and selling cars or about negative $1,800 per vehicle delivered.

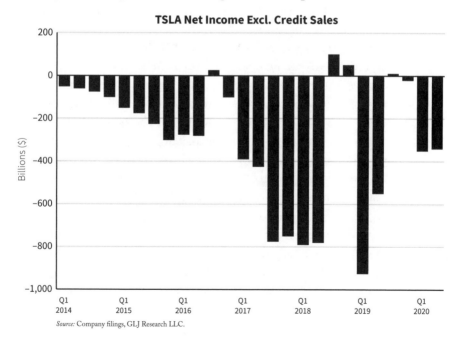

TSLA Net Income Excl. Credit Sales

Source: Company filings, GLJ Research LLC.

It doesn't take a genius, of course, to see that all of these regulatory credits are as evanescent as the morning dew and that every single car maker—for better or worse—is bending over to the climate change hysteria and plunging into the electric vehicle business. Recently, Ford announced a massive $11.5 billion investment in an electric vehicle and battery production complex, the largest new auto investment in North America in recent history.

The Truth about Tesla

Therefore, the proper capitalization rate for the regulatory credit portion of Tesla's net income and free cash flow is basically nothing. Rather than a recurring income stream that can be capitalized into permanent asset value, it's a disappearing gift of the state that will soon be over and done. As it is, Tesla has zero net income after excluding regulatory credits, but even when it comes to free cash flow, the absurdity of its current $1.2 trillion market cap is plain as day. For the June latest 12-month period Tesla reported $2.61 billion in operating free cash flow, but if you remove the regulatory credits paid to it by GM, Ford, and others, the figure amounts to just $1 billion. Tesla is being capitalized at 1,200 times its free cash flow from the car business!

Moreover, during the past five years, its reported cumulative free cash flow of negative $2.2 billion actually amounts to negative $5.8 billion when you adjust for the $3.6 billion in nonrecurring regulatory credits booked by the company. So we have a stock valued at more than 175 percent of the entire global auto industry combined that has actually incinerated nearly $6 billion in cash during the past half-decade while pretending it is in the auto business!

Tesla is not merely a colossal scam and Elon Musk is not just the greatest snake oil salesman since P. T. Barnum. No, Tesla is still another, even more spectacular poster boy for a stock market that has lost its marbles completely owing to the unrelenting flood of fiat liquidity still being pumped by clueless central banks.

The problem is that these kinds of insane valuations, which can be found across the length and breadth of the stock market, are not merely bubble excretions that will be wiped out during the next crash. They are actually evidence that the price discovery function has been totally euthanized by the Fed's massive and relentless falsification of financial asset prices.

As a result, nothing in the real world is being discounted. Not the tidal wave of goods-and-services inflation steaming down the pike or the unprecedented supply chain disruptions roiling the entire global supply system. And certainly not the utter breakdown of governance in Washington where fiscal rationality has long since vanished.

Instead, the stock market has become the domain of chart monkeys and algos where the only thing that matters is 5-, 20-, 50-, 100-, and 200-day daily moving averages (DMAs). It is the product of an utterly aberrant 12-year era in which central banks have instilled the traders and machines with overweening confidence that buying the dip is always and everywhere profitable.

Indeed, the green arrows pointing to the market's bounce off the 50 DMAs during the past 18 months tell you all you need to know. That is, an economy whipsawed by lockdowns, Covid-hysteria, and a fiscal bacchanalia like never before imagined by even rabid Keynesians is not one that should have hosted a 35 percent rise in the stock market, especially since the starting point was already ridiculously high.

Thus at the pre-Covid peak on February 19, 2020, the S&P 500 stood at 3,375 or 24.3 times its latest 12-month earnings. That was already far above the 15 times historical norm in an economy freighted with debt and state-imposed barriers to investment and growth.

Yet on the strength of relentless dip buying, the index reached a peak of 4,700 on November 5, 2021, representing an absurd 29.6 times earnings.

The only thing that now stands between the S&P 500's index level and a thundering crash is the market's BTFD ("buy the f****** dip") muscle memory. The latter has been built up over 12 years of false tutorials by a central bank that has now backed itself into an impossible inflationary corner.

But muscle memory can atrophy when it is subject to relentless battering, as has repeatedly occurred in recent months, and it becomes obvious that there is no fiscal or monetary posse riding to the rescue. That's where we are now. Waiting for BTFD to die.

Options Explosion

In the wider scheme of things, here is what has happened since the March 2009 bottom. The U.S. economy has grown by a miserable 2 percent per year—the lowest recovery cycle rebound rate in history—and is now just 27 percent larger than it was then. Yet the algos, chart monkeys, and BTFDers have driven the S&P 500 index up by 550 percent. When the 200 DMA breaks, it will be all over except the shouting, and that moment is now not so very far away.

One of the reasons that the stock market has become this red-hot gambling casino is the explosion of options trading in both broad indices and single stocks. Since the turn of the century, the increase in average daily volume has been staggering and relentless, rising by 13.3 times. Options volume now far exceeds actual cash transactions in the underlying securities. Nine of 10 of the most active call-options trading days in history have taken place in 2021.

As shown below, almost 39 million option contracts changed hands on an average day (as of September 2021), up 31 percent from 2020 and the highest level since the market's inception in 1973, according to figures from the Options Clearing Corp.

Average Daily Contract Volume of Stock Options

- 2000: 2.9 million
- 2004: 4.7 million
- 2007: 11.4 million
- 2012: 15.9 million
- 2017: 16.7 million
- 2018: 20.5 million
- 2019: 19.4 million
- 2020: 29.5 million
- 2021 YTD: 38.6 million

As to the actual market in the underlying stocks, a recent *Wall Street Journal* article summarized the current condition:

> So far this month, single-stock options with a notional value of roughly $6.9 trillion have changed hands, well above the $5.8 trillion in stocks that traded, according to Cboe data through Sept. 22.
>
> By one measure, options activity is on track to surpass activity in the stock market for the first time ever. In 2021, the daily average notional value of traded single-stock options has exceeded $432 billion, compared with $404 billion of stocks, according to calculations by Cboe's Henry Schwartz. This would be the first year on record that the value of options changing hands surpassed that of stocks, according to Cboe data going back to 2008.

This is with reference to the entire market, but the story is even more lopsided when it comes to the institutional gamblers and investors playing at home. For instance, Apple options with a notional value of more than $20 billion have changed hands daily this year compared with roughly $12 billion of the iPhone maker's stock. About $80 billion of Tesla options have changed hands daily this year, roughly quadrupling the figure for the stock, according to the *Wall Street Journal* analysis.

That's right. Speculators are using the implied massive leverage in stock options to make bets on already absurdly valued cult stocks like Tesla. Of course, in turn, the Wall Street dealers writing these call options need to delta hedge their short position on these calls by purchasing the underlying Tesla or other stock, thereby driving prices even higher and causing ETFs that own the stock to buy more too. It's the closest thing around to a self-licking ice cream cone!

As the *Wall Street Journal* article further elaborated, the fact that homegamers increasingly embrace risky options trading is unmistakable. By one measure, options trading by individual retail investors has risen roughly fourfold over the past five years: "I'm hooked on the options," said Britt Keeler, a 40-year-old individual investor based in Winter Park, Florida. "You could lose it all really quick but you could hustle and kinda hit the jackpot. . . . Everyone is using leverage. And they're using it because you can make a ton more money," Keeler said.

Or as Mr. Patel, a 27-year-old nurse in Columbus, Ohio, explained, "I had no idea what options were last year . . . You can make quick 100 percent, 200 percent, 300 percent [gains] within minutes if things go your way."

Relentless Money Pumping

Needless to say, just as bullish call options have helped fuel rallies in stocks such as GameStop, AMC Theaters, and Tesla itself, traders banding together to buy bearish put options could similarly help drive big declines in individual companies. And then, of course, Wall Street put options writers would delta hedge by selling the underlying stocks, which would then trigger liquidations among the $6 trillion or so in ETFs holding these stocks, creating even greater selling pressure.

Thus the Fed's relentless money pumping has turned the stock market into a coiled spring of irrational exuberance and momentum chasing. The desperate need for a serious correction to an accelerating 12-year spiral has been thwarted over and over by the BTFD muscle memory in the market that has lost all contact with economic and valuation fundamentals. Indeed, since March 2009, equity investors have come to realize that any correction would finally lead to a bounce and a new upward run. In the beginning, it took a long time before positive trading emotions and Pavlovian rewards emerged, but as the bull run accelerated the rewards came faster and faster.

Until very recently, all the dips—even microdips—were almost instantaneously bought by the herd of traders and small retail investors driven by Pavlovian reflexes, thereby reinforcing the power of positive feedback loops. The problem, of course, is the risk that a solid exogenous shock will break the chain of dip buying and options-based speculation and eventually trigger a put-buying stampede, especially among the younger traders who have never experienced a down market.

Their online gurus will tell them they can ride out the storm and can safely hang on to their FANGMAN, Tesla shares, and meme stocks by buying "protection" via puts on their portfolios. That, of course, will trigger more delta hedging among options dealers, more ETF liquidations, and more temptations for the fast money to engage in open shorting of a market suspended on a skyhook.

We have no idea whether the asymptotic high has yet been reached or what the "exogenous shock" might be that causes the present coiled spring to lunge into reverse. But with each passing episode of sharp sell-offs and only partial buy-the-dip rebounds, the odds of a meltdown reversal continue to rise.

The Cryptoverse: Bastard Son of Fiat Money

As we have seen, the Fed's relentless money-printers have unleashed a financial contagion of biblical proportion. There simply are no asset classes that have escaped the resulting inflationary whirlwind and most especially not the very newest asset class—cryptocurrencies.

Ironically, crypto is held up as a monetary antidote for fiat money gone wild. From a philosophical vantage point, I would embrace honest, private money over state-issued money every day of the week and twice on Sunday. But whatever their theoretical merit and pretensions as private money, cryptos too have been swallowed whole and thoroughly corrupted by the storm of speculative madness unleashed by the central banks.

As they now function, cryptocurrencies are not money in any way, shape, or form. To the contrary, they are merely the latest boiling-hot speculative asset class and yet another bastard spawn of the central bank money printers. They are not an alternative to bad central bank money; they spring from the loins of those very same banks.

That's why the utter denial of speculative excesses by the Fed is so completely ludicrous. For crying out loud, if they can't bring themselves to acknowledge that the FANGMAN stocks are wildly overvalued, you would think that at least the absolute speculative madness in the cryptoverse would get their attention. In theory, crypto is their sworn enemy, after all.

So consider this: On May 12, 2013, the total market cap of the few cryptos that existed at the time, including the pioneer, Bitcoin (BTC), was $1.6 billion. Exactly eight years later, on May 12, 2021, that figure stood at $2.51 trillion—a staggering gain of 1,570 times over.

Cryptocurrencies at this juncture have no monetary use. Only fools believe they are a store of value, and as a medium of exchange, they are clunky and inefficient. For any purchase less than, say, a $135,000 Tesla electric car, a good old wire transfer, check, or chunk of actual cash has a far lower transaction cost as a percent of the purchase price.

Then there's the volatility. Since September 2016, Bitcoin has risen by 40 percent or more over eight months and fallen by 20 percent or more during the course of five months, with lesser but still large alternating gains and losses during most of the rest of the period.

That's no store of value unless you are a confirmed buy-the-dipper, and in that case, you are talking not about a store of value but about pure speculation. Real money is not at all like stocks. It doesn't go up forever; it actually goes nowhere forever. By contrast, the pitching and heaving cryptoverse is simply a legal online casino. It has attracted trillions of dollars' worth of wagers only because the financial markets are so saturated with excess liquidity that today's wildly intoxicated gamblers have an unquenchable thirst for new ways in which to roll the dice.

Chapter 13

Joke Coins

The second quarter 2021 financial filing of Robinhood, the smartphone stock-trading app, tells you all you need to know about crypto trading. More than 14 million Robinhood users, or roughly 63 percent of the company's customer base, traded cryptos in the second quarter. Robinhood earned $233 million in fees from routing these cryptocurrency trades to high-speed trading firms. Dogecoin—a crypto that literally started as a joke and features the winsome face of a smiling, internet-famous pooch—accounted for nearly two-thirds of the volume.

That $233 million in crypto trading revenues fleeced from the desperate small investors was up 46 times over from just $5 million in revenues from crypto asset trades during the second quarter of 2020. And no, these foolish folks are not doing God's work of price discovery in the quest to give birth to a new money better than central bank fiat. It's just that many of the meme stocks they once traded were played out. So the cryptoverse became the go-to wagering arena of choice during the period.

Indeed, a brief overview of cryptocurrency evolution should tell policymakers all they need to know about the widespread speculation raging right under their noses. According to CoinMarketCap, there are now 16,633 different crypto coins trading on 456 exchanges, all of which have sprung up out of nowhere during the past five years or so.

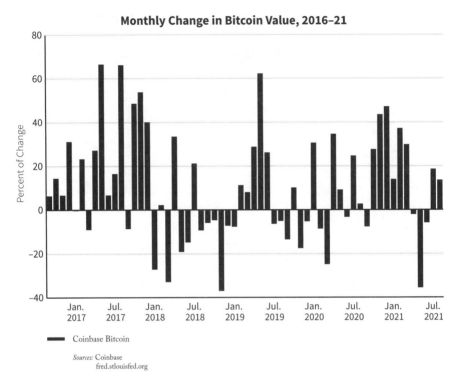

Monthly Change in Bitcoin Value, 2016–21

Coinbase Bitcoin

Sources: Coinbase
fred.stlouisfed.org

The crypto-evangelists would have you believe that the radical volatility pictured above is just the hard work and labor pangs of new money being born. Supposedly, it will eventually settle out, and capital and use will flow to a few winning coins, perhaps even one winner, at length. But that's wishful thinking, financial romanticism on steroids and not solid analysis. If crypto tokens had the essential characteristics that make money what it is—natural scarcity and difficulty of adding to supply—there absolutely would not have been 16,633 of them minted virtually overnight. Actually, there would be not 1,000 of them, or even 500, or even 80 such money tokens.

In practice, new cryptos are the very opposite of scarce and hard to mint. They are simply the digital excrescence of the proverbial fast-buck artists who have piled onto the latest gambling craze. Crypto coins are being literally invented by the score by energetic prospectors, some with no more tools than a keyboard and an internet connection and no more schooled in the business of money than the proverbial 400-pound nerd lounging on a bed in his mom's basement somewhere.

Just to get a sense of the absurdity of it all, the following cryptos are presented based on their rank by market cap as of mid-August 2021:

- "PancakeSwap," ranked #31, which trades at $21.19 per coin with a market cap of $4.5 billion
- "Helium," ranked #62, which trades at $18.51 per coin with a market cap of $1.8 billion
- "Wootrade," ranked #145, which trades at $0.688 per coin with a market cap of $335 million
- "HEX" coin, ranked #201, which trades at $0.1825 per coin with a market cap of $332 million
- "Alchemy Pay," ranked #246, which trades at $0.0788 per coin with a market cap of $242 million
- "Troy" coin, ranked #401, which trades at $0.008807 per coin with a market cap of $78.6 million
- "MimbleWimbleCoin," ranked #470, which trades at $5.36 per coin with a market cap of $58.3 million
- "CUMROCKET," ranked #489, which trades at $0.04046 per coin with a market cap of $53.9 million
- "AhaToken," ranked #614, which trades at $0.01016 per coin with a market cap of $30.2 million
- "Infinitecoin," ranked #718, which trades at $0.000229 per coin with a market cap of $20.1 million
- "Glitch," ranked #726, which trades at $0.2527 per coin with a market cap of $20 million

- "Pickle Finance," ranked #773, which trades at $10.61 per coin with a market cap of $17.1 million
- "ZeroSwap," ranked #794, which trades at $0.3137 per coin with a market cap of $16.2 million
- "STEM CELL COIN," ranked #811, which trades at $0.0471 per coin with a market cap of $15.1 million
- "Wall Street Games," ranked #867, which trades at $0.00000009457 per coin with a market cap of $12.5 million
- "AntiMatter" coin, ranked #966, which trades at $0.3224 per coin with a market cap of $9.2 million
- "MoonSwap," ranked #993, which trades at $0.3145 per coin with a market cap of $8.3 million
- "CoinPoker," ranked #996, which trades at $0.03003 per coin with a market cap of $8.2 million
- "Abyss," ranked #1,000, which trades at $0.03586 per coin with a market cap of $8.1 million

The above is just a random smattering of the more notable tokens. There are still more than 16,000 crypto coins to go!

Needless to say, nobody but nobody would be interested in this insanity, save for the fact that these gambling chips have been going up in price, sometimes massively and with breathtaking speed.

For instance, Infinitecoin had a market cap of $742,000 on January 3, 2021. By May 9, it had hit $61.1 million. So somebody had fun pocketing an 8,200 percent gain in four months. That is, if they didn't suffer the 67 percent loss to $20.1 million that happened by August 14.

Likewise, CUMROCKET traded at a market cap of $126,000 on May 4, 2021. That value rocketed by 3,000 times over to $385 million the next day, only to plunge to $40 million by May 30, before resurrecting to $400 million on June 5, which then bled out to $53 million by August 18.

Nevertheless, a click of the mouse at the CoinMarketCap website will tell you all about trading CUMMIES, as they are called:

> The live CUMROCKET price today is $0.039278 USD with a 24-hour trading volume of $1,165,697 USD. CUMROCKET is down 10.25% in the last 24 hours. The current CoinMarketCap ranking is #495, with a live market cap of $52,417,542 USD. It has a circulating supply of 1,334,519,634 CUMMIES coins and a max. supply of 10,000,000,000 CUMMIES coins.
>
> If you would like to know where to buy CUMROCKET, the top exchanges for trading in CUMROCKET are currently CoinTiger, PancakeSwap (V2), Bilaxy, and PancakeSwap. You can find others listed on our crypto exchanges page.

Needless to say, this wild oscillation goes on hour after hour on a 24/7 basis for thousands of coins in the cryptoverse. It could be considered another form of Covid-era indoor recreation, save for the fact that trillions of dollars are at risk and massive amounts of financial and human capital are being diverted into one of the purest and most accessible forms of gambling ever invented.

So yes, there is a reason folks are buying "Pickle Finance," "MoonSwap," and "Abyss," and it has nothing to do with the search for an alternative to the bad money of central banks. To the contrary, the cryptoverse is the radioactive end game of bad money. It's a financial burial ground where hordes of gamblers supported by easy central bank money ultimately are going to die. Far from being a store of value, the cryptoverse has become a blooming, buzzing mass of speculative energy. Below is the evolution of the aggregate market cap of all cryptos tracked by CoinMarketCap, valuations that are updated virtually by the nanosecond.

For each date shown, which represents an interim high or low, I provide the aggregate market cap for the entire cryptoverse and the percentage change from the prior inflection point.

Combined Value of All Crypto Coins

- May 1, 2013: $1.6 billion, 0.0 percent
- December 1, 2013: $14 billion, +769 percent
- June 19, 2016: $14 billion, 0.0 percent
- January 8, 2018: $759 billion, +5,360 percent
- December 12, 2018: $113 billion, –85.1 percent
- June 29, 2019: $342 billion, +202 percent
- March 19, 2020: $157 billion, –54.1 percent
- May 12, 2021: $2.506 trillion, +1,497 percent
- July 20, 2021: $1.198 trillion, –52.2 percent
- August 17, 2021: $2.031 trillion, +69.5 percent
- November 7, 2021: $2.760 trillion, +39.5 percent

So what will become of the $2.8 trillion in crystallized wagers that existed in early November 2021? Simple. The cryptoverse is not a financial maternity ward where new kinds of money are trying to be born. It's the epicenter of a historic mania that makes all prior manias, going all the way back to the Dutch tulip bulb mania of the 1630s, look like exceedingly tiny potatoes.

Someday, to be sure, the technology behind crypto, known as the blockchain, may prove to be a better venue for financial transactions than the existing banking machinery. If so, so be it. Blockchain technology may prove itself to be a digitized venue of commerce that is more convenient and adaptable than today's methods of selling art, recording deeds, trading baseball cards, or minting collectible nonfungible tokens (NFTs).

But neither of these possibilities has much to do with the crazed speculation in today's cryptoverse. To remind, there are now more than 16,600 wannabe monies that are nothing but wagering tokens, valued as follows:

- two cryptos with market caps above $500 billion,
- twenty-two cryptos with market caps over $10 billion,
- one hundred-eight cryptos with market caps above $1 billion,
- four hundred fifty cryptos with market caps above $100 million, and finally,
- 16,233 additional cryptos that trade at some value somewhere on the rapidly mushrooming 456 distinct crypto exchanges currently in existence.

Legalized Gambling

The truth is, what we have is internet-based legalized gambling on a global scale, which for the moment is free from the boot heels of state gaming commissions, SEC nannies, and the cops alike. That is to say, it is the most free-wheeling, rambunctious home imaginable for the massive flood of central bank liquidity poured into the financial system with reckless abandon, especially in recent months.

To put a number on it, here are the market caps of the top 30 cryptocurrencies tracked and reported in real time. None of these "currencies" makes anything, stores anything, or (in 99 percent of the cases) transacts anything. They are just plain old gambling chips with market caps that depend on greater fools and precious little more.

In a recent fourth-month period, market caps have gone up or down as follows:

Selected Crypto Market Caps as of April 25, 2021, versus August 18, 2021

- Bitcoin: $998 billion versus $840 billion
- Ethereum: $289 billion versus $354 billion
- Binance Coin: $81 billion versus $66 billion
- XRP: $59 billion versus $52 billion
- Tether: $50 billion versus $64 billion
- Cardano: $39 billion versus $68 billion
- Dogecoin: $34 billion versus $40 billion
- Polkadot: $31 billion versus $23 billion
- Uniswap: $19 billion versus $15 billion
- Litecoin: $16 billion versus $11 billion
- Bitcoin Cash: $16 billion versus $12 billion
- Chainlink: $14 billion versus $11 billion
- Solana: $12 billion versus $21 billion
- VeChain: $12 billion versus $8 billion
- USD Coin: $11 billion versus $27 billion
- Stellar: $11 billion versus $8 billion
- THETA: $11 billion versus $7 billion
- Filecoin: $10 billion versus $7 billion
- Wrapped Bitcoin: $8 billion versus $9 billion
- TRON: $8 billion versus $6 billion
- Monero: $7 billion versus $5 billion
- Binance USD: $7 billion versus $12 billion
- Terra: $7 billion versus $12 billion
- Neo: $6 billion versus $3.5 billion
- Klaytn: $6 billion versus $4.3 billion
- IOTA: $5 billion versus $2.7 billion
- EOS: $5 billion versus $4.7 billion
- PancakeSwap: $5 billion versus $4.5 billion
- Aave: $5 billion versus $4.9 billion
- Bitcoin SV: $5 billion versus $2.9 billion

These 30 cryptos alone had a trading value of $1.80 trillion on April 25 but weighed in just a few months later at just

$1.67 trillion. What's a mere $130 billion loss of wagering value in the world's largest 24/7 casino?

In fact, many of these cryptos trade a substantial share of their market cap every 24 hours. For instance, during a recent 24-hour span, Tether traded $81 billion in volume against a market cap of just $64 billion; Avalanche traded $1 billion, or 21 percent of its $4.7 billion market cap; and my favorite, Sush-iSwap, traded $580 million against a market cap of $1.6 billion.

If you are a "long-term" crypto investor looking all the way out to, say, a seven-day horizon, you could try shorting Uniswap, which was already down 15 percent in that span. Or go long Solana, which was up by 75 percent in just a few days. Of course, there's always Dogecoin awaiting another promotional tweet from none other than Elon Musk.

I have no objection at all to free citizens betting on black at the roulette wheel, playing craps in the back alley, or swinging for the fences in the crypto space. But remember what this is and what it isn't. Foremost, this is not gentlemanly stock-market gambling where 75 years of nanny-state policing by the SEC and prosecutors at the Department of Justice have taken all the sharp elbows out of the game. Crypto exchanges are real wild west free markets, a place where every manner of manipulation ever known to speculative man has been revived and with malice aforethought.

So yes, the lambs will soon find themselves in the slaughterhouse, and they won't know what hit them. But so what? At least we might get a live fire demonstration of what booming and busting "markets" should look like when there's no government oversight around to gentrify the gambling.

And more importantly, we will find out that in a raging world of fiat, fiat is all there is. That is to say, today's crypto madness, like the rest of the virulent financial asset inflation, is the consequence of the explosion of central bank balance sheets. During the last quarter century, global central bank balance sheets have risen from about $2 trillion in 1997, to $7 trillion by the eve of the financial crisis in 2007, and then to upward of $35 trillion at present. Relative to GDP, this hypersurge of money printing has turned the statistics upside down.

In 1997, the world's central bank balance sheets stood at about 6 percent of the worldwide GDP of $32 trillion, a figure only slightly higher than the 3 percent to 6 percent range that had prevailed prior to the Greenspan era.

A decade later, however, that ratio had grown to an unprecedented 12 percent of global GDP, and then it was off to the races. Central bank balance sheets now represent more than 40 percent of world GDP, and until recently, they have been expanding by roughly $400 billion each and every month, with $250 billion of that coming from the United States and Europe alone.

That's right, at the recent $4.8 trillion annualized rate of global securities purchases (quantitative easing, or QE), the combined balance sheets of the world's central banks are growing faster than the world's nominal GDP. And that's just plain madness.

Torrent of Liquidity

Our own Federal Reserve leads the global convoy of money printers. During the two-year period ending in June 2021, nominal GDP rose by $1.4 trillion, while the Fed's balance sheet expanded by $4.5 trillion during the same span. So yes, there is a reason the crypto asset class is flying skyward, just like more conventional assets. Namely, the real economy can't possibly absorb the central banks' torrent of liquidity. So it never leaves the canyons of Wall Street and the other global financial markets. Instead, it is channeled into the greatest speculative mania that the world has ever seen.

Just consider the massive liquidity pumping of the world's four largest central banks—the U.S. Federal Reserve, the European Central Bank, the People's Bank of China, and the Bank of Japan—during the last 14 years.

Taken together, their balance sheets have grown to $29.3 trillion as of April 2021 from $4.9 trillion in 2007. That $24.4 trillion, a fivefold increase, actually exceeds their $19 trillion collective gain in dollar GDP, which rose to $54 trillion from $35 trillion over the same period.

Central Bank Balance Sheets

	2007	April 2021	Percentage Gain
U.S. Federal Reserve	$0.8 trillion	$7.7 trillion	+863 percent
European Central Bank	$1 trillion	$9.1 trillion	+810 percent
Bank of Japan	$1.5 trillion	$6.6 trillion	+340 percent
People's Bank of China	$1.6 trillion	$5.9 trillion	+269 percent
Big four central banks combined	$4.9 trillion	$29.3 trillion	+500 percent

That this massive outpouring of central bank liquidity has inflated financial markets on nearly a lockstep basis is beyond dispute. As shown in the chart below, the correlation between the pace of Big Four central bank balance sheet expansion and the rise of the global stock market index (MSCI AC World Index) is 0.94 since 2009—nearly perfect.

In this context, the cryptos are just instances of the leading edge of the global financial asset bubble—places where the most reckless can congregate to swing for the fences. As is the case with the owner of one of its biggest promoters, cryptos and Tesla stocks alike are not earning assets; they are just vehicles for unadulterated speculation that rise solely because central bankers enable speculators to push the hunt for the last greater fool to the edge of sanity.

A Thief in the Night

More likely than not, the exogenous shock will be administered by the Fed itself. It is now way, way behind the goods-and-services inflation curve after it added insult to injury by continuing to pump $120 billion per month of monetary kerosene into Wall Street through the end of 2021, all the while claiming that inflation is transitory when it most surely is not.

The PCE deflator for the third quarter of 2021 by all rights and reason should have been a wake-up call. It came in red-hot at 4.3 percent on a year-over-year basis—the highest level in 30 years. It is only a matter of time, therefore, before the Fed is forced into a belated, unexpected, and jarring tightening mode that will fall hard and unexpectedly upon the speculators and day-traders like a thief in the night.

Year-over-Year Change in PCE Deflator, 1991–2021

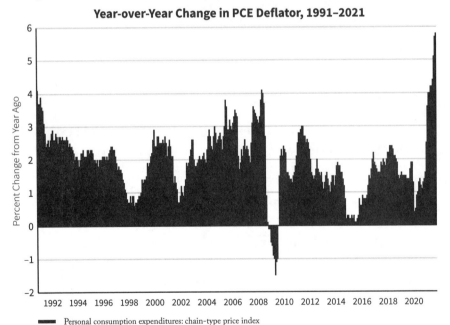

Personal consumption expenditures: chain-type price index

Sources: U.S. Bureau of Economic Analysis
fred.stlouisfed.org

In this context, remember that during the past three decades, the part of the PCE deflator that the Fed can most directly influence—the domestic services component—has almost never run below its magic 2 percent target.

In fact, since the official adoption of inflation targeting in January 2012, the PCE deflator for services has risen at a 2.4 percent annualized rate and in the most recent 12-month period was up by 3.3 percent. The Fed's only hope that the overall PCE deflator will fall back in line to 2 percent is that by some miracle, the surging level of goods inflation will suddenly collapse.

Yet you don't have to be squinting at the commodities and industrial inflation dashboards to recognize that's a pipe dream. Goldman Sachs, for instance, recently projected $90 per barrel of oil.

At the end of the day, the Fed is engaging in rank monetary insanity. The supply side of the economy is riddled with shortages, supply chain disruptions, inventory depletions, and raging price increases, yet these fools kept pumping in $120 billion per month of monetary kerosene until the 11th hour.

It amounts to a colossal accident waiting to happen, and then the corrupted investment world of Wall Street will be turned upside down. Interest rates have hit a four-decade supercycle low and will be rising intermittently but relentlessly as the Fed and other central banks struggle to contain the inflationary monster they have spawned.

In that environment, four things will be true and profoundly different from the past several decades. They compose the essence of a sensible financial strategy for the "payback time" world lurking just around the bend:

- Interest rates are going up on a secular basis for years to come, so paying down debt rather than borrowing will be the winning financial strategy for most households.
- Savers will finally be able to earn a modest return on bank certificates of deposit (CDs) and

short-term Treasury bills without taking principal risk on longer-term bonds, junk debt, crappy paper from China, or absurdly overvalued stocks.
- Buying puts on the broad market, such as the S&P 500 or Nasdaq-100, will consistently generate favorable returns because the market has nowhere to go except sideways or down.
- For those with a strong stomach and risk capital to deploy, shorting cult stocks could be immensely rewarding.

What Will Work—Practical Steps to Preserve Wealth

If you remember the 2007 housing crash and ensuing stock market debacle, you may remember hearing the phrase "all correlations go to one." It's a complicated idea, but the gist is that at extreme turning points in the financial markets, many types of investments, such as stocks, bonds, and real estate, are correlated. That is, they tend to move in the same direction, full speed ahead.

If they do, that's a correlation of +1. Of course, that's the opposite of what the investment textbooks recommend. They urge the opposite—that is, a portfolio in which the major asset components move in an inverse direction, amounting to a correlation of –1. In normal times under a regime of relatively honest money, this standard investment advice makes a great deal of sense. The idea is that if there is a sudden turn in a major part of the portfolio—say, stocks fall sharply in value—a weighting of the uncorrelated investments such as bonds will rise enough to compensate for those short-term losses.

Most retirement investors, for instance, own bonds in their portfolios in the hopes that a sharp decline in stock valuations can be offset by the movement of other people's money to the relative safety of bond holdings. Sudden demand for safety can cause bond prices to go up, just as with stocks.

Likewise, the antidote to the downside risk posed by high-flyers in a stock portfolio, such as tech stocks and today's super-hot FANGMAN stocks, is held to be blue-chip staples such as Procter and Gamble or Nestlé, which tend to hold their earnings and value during an economic and market downturn.

Similarly, some investors choose a more aggressive route—such as shifting a portion of their wealth to gold. This is essentially a portfolio insurance notion, meaning that in a real panic, people are likely to abandon not only stocks but the dollar itself. In that scenario, gold as a safe haven would see its value rise dramatically, protecting the overall portfolio.

Finally, the most aggressive approach to achieving a cor-relation of –1 is taking short positions in popular, widely held stocks via short mutual funds—that is, making bets that cer-tain stocks must fall in value in the relative short term.

The problem today, unfortunately, is that construction of a classic negatively correlated portfolio is well-nigh impossible owing to the massive distortion of financial asset prices fos-tered by the Fed and the other central banks. Massive bond buying in the form of trillions in quantitative easing, as we have seen, has driven bond prices to ludicrous, overvalued heights. They now represent a clear and present danger to any portfolio, not a traditional form of balance and safety.

Likewise, while it is inherently risky to short stocks be-cause they must be "covered" if those stocks go up instead, it has now become impossibly risky because central banks have actually destroyed the short side of the market. In fact, such insanely overvalued stocks as Tesla and the meme stocks GameStop and AMC have been driven to ludicrous heights by Fed-enabled speculators who have made a gang sport of attacking short-sellers who have properly bet that vastly overvalued stocks will fall in price.

Accordingly, shorting of even the most hideously overval-ued stocks has become prohibitively dangerous. In the near term, prudent investors cannot even hedge their portfolios with a classic portion of loser stocks for fear that a short raid by an online mob of neophyte chatboard speculators will do them incalculable harm.

In short, the classic goal of all these counterintuitive investing strategies, making money in a general stock market decline by pursuing a correlation of –1, is now largely beyond reach. Where we are, therefore, is in the midst of a repeated case of 2007 and 2008, which demonstrated that at moments of such blind panic, all assets can and will fall in value at once.

Back then, speculative stocks fell in value, but so did supposedly "safer" large-cap stocks, bonds, and even gold. Instead of the protection one expected from negative correlation, it turned out there was no place to make money or to even protect money. At the time, many pundits lamented that there was "nowhere to hide," which is another way of saying all correlations were headed toward +1.

Needless to say, when all investments move in the same direction at nearly the same speed, investors face a conundrum. The only safe place from an asset preservation viewpoint turns out to be cash, an asset that inherently loses value to inflation and, under today's central bank–pegged ultralow interest rates, provides hardly a smidgen of even nominal return on investment.

It should not be forgotten that during the worst moments of the 2008 credit crisis, cash itself was called into question.

As crazy as it might sound now, after the Lehman meltdown in September of that year people didn't even trust money market accounts, as famously exemplified by the panicky flight from the $62.6 billion Reserve Primary Fund, the original money market fund that launched the industry in 1970.

It turned out that Lehman owned a lot of securitized mortgage bonds backed by janky home mortgages (i.e., subprime) that were suddenly underwater when defaults began to surge. In turn, Reserve Primary owned Lehman commercial paper, which was effectively backed by the cratering securitized mortgages. So a contagion seemed inevitable, triggering a massive run on money markets, normally among the safest short-term investments available. Investors were taking cash out of this massive money market fund, Reserve Primary, and others like it and using the cash to buy U.S. Treasury paper. It didn't matter that money markets before were considered "near cash" and ultrasafe. People wanted out, and fast. Reserve Primary eventually settled with investors and ultimately dissolved.

That was the starting gun for a true financial crisis. Before long, not even banks trusted other banks. The whole system of daily money flow in the trillions seized up, causing a severe old-time "panic" in which labor and inventories and big-ticket consumer purchases plummeted in October 2008 and the winter months that followed.

It's foolish, of course, to use the past as any kind of indicator of the future. Chances are low that we will have another stiff, historic credit contraction that plays out in exactly the same way. But there is an overwhelming chance that once a panic begins, once again no asset will be deemed safe. All correlations again will go to +1, and swiftly so.

What complicates matters this time is that the bond market, historically a fortress for scared money, is surely overdue for a deep price correction. Remember, when yields fall, bond prices rise. Once you have extended periods of extremely low interest rates, the implication is that bond prices are drastically inflated and cannot rise further. The only direction left for bond prices is down. Way down.

Historically, the Federal Reserve has at least nominal power over the benchmark interest rate. In the next crisis that will be seriously in doubt. That's because asset values have been so drastically inflated that once the selling starts, the Fed will be powerless to stop the stampede. The resulting severe price correction in the bond market will affect millions of investors and trillions of dollars.

Chapter 14

Short-Term Chaos

Suddenly higher interest rates will spark a selloff in stocks, causing capital to rush out of both the stock and bond markets at once. The only constant in any of these scenarios is likely to be chaos, at least in the short term. On top of all that, a huge number of so-called passive investors—holders of index funds and index-driven ETFs—could create a serious accelerator effect on capital flight.

At the time of the financial crisis in 2008, there was hardly $1 trillion in ETFs, a figure that now stands at more than $7 trillion. That's one thing that's truly "different" about this market compared to even the recent past. Millions of investors today are completely hands-off by choice, allowing computers to dictate stock-to-bond ratios via automatic index funds.

If those ratios get tested, it's possible that many of those once-passive investors will wake up and decide to "do something" about their losses. Millions of people at or near retirement age could find that assumptions that worked for decades are suddenly a danger to them personally. The chaos would increase exponentially. Imagine a herd of angry bulls loose in a city full of china shops. That herd might charge in any direction, destroying all in its path.

So what can you—a lone investor in this chaotic rush of good intentions and inevitably bad outcomes—do to protect yourself?

The starting point of wisdom is to recognize that this time is truly different, and not in a good way. Financial asset markets have been so thoroughly inflated and distorted by the central banks that there is no viable asset-side strategy available.

Accordingly, the route to safety and financial salvation lies on the debt and income sides of the ledger, not some traditional notion of repositioning and hedging one's asset portfolio. Stated differently, central bank inflation of assets has been so destructive that what remains for average investors is the hard slog of earning more, spending less, and paying down debt wherever possible.

Here is a four-step approach to help you prepare and hopefully not join the panic once it begins. Only on the other side of chaos is there a real chance to make your wealth once again grow, but first you have to live to tell the tale.

Step One: Cut Debt Now

You've likely been meaning to get out of personal debt for years, and that's a laudable goal. That goal is quickly turning into a must for most Americans. The Federal Reserve Bank of New York recently put total household debt in the United States at $15.24 trillion. Housing debt, meaning mortgages and home equity debt, is nearly $11 trillion of that, and the rest is consumer debt such as credit card balances, auto debt, student loans, and personal loans.

Those debts are bearable now only because of artificially low interest rates. Once interest rates start to rise, many overstretched consumers will be instantly swamped by rising variable-rate adjustments. Defaults will spike. It will be nearly impossible to secure a new loan should you need it to refinance your existing obligations.

Credit Cards

Your marching orders here are to get out of any and all credit card debt, pronto. If it's a relatively small amount and you have some savings, pay it off. If you have more than one credit card open, consider closing all but one.

You should close the newest cards, not your oldest line of credit. Part of your credit score is based on longevity of credit and part is how much you have borrowed as a ratio of credit available, among other factors. If you feel you need a specific amount of short-term credit, try to get your oldest card limit increased while paying off and closing your newer cards.

Get to zero, however, on all of them as soon as possible. This is priority one. Credit card interest rates will go much higher once general lending rates are forced higher, setting off a resounding cycle of consumer defaults. In turn, rising defaults will cause your friendly credit card lenders to drastically tighten their lending standards.

Housing Debt

Next, tackle any home equity lines (HELOCs) you may have open. Unlike a mortgage, most HELOC products are variable and will rise in cost with a rising benchmark interest rate. Yes, there can be a tax advantage to keeping home equity debt, but you may find that the break you get isn't worth the risk of being unable to pay it off when you like.

Likewise, if you have an outstanding mortgage and it is a variable rate product, convert it to fixed as soon as you can. Some borrowers like the flexibility of a variable rate and the freedom it allows to invest in a larger, more attractive property. However, a sharp increase in the interest rate will cause all mortgage rates to spike higher. Your variable rate could turn from lifeline to noose overnight. If you wait too long to choose a fixed rate, you may find the banks are suddenly setting lending requirements much higher. Mortgage defaults and foreclosures will be commonplace, an echo of the experience from 2007 to 2009.

Student Loans

This is a tough one. Generally, student loans are fixed, lower-rate products. If you have federal loans (not private loans), it's possible to renegotiate them to match your earning ability. To the degree this is true about your student loans, better to focus on credit cards and HELOCs first. But make sure your loans are in fact fixed and federally backed, not private. If you have private student loans, treat them like your HELOC—an unnecessary risk.

Medical Debt

These outstanding bills, if you have them, come last. Most people seem unaware that hospital charges are 100 percent negotiable. First, demand an itemized list of charges to make sure you are not being charged for services you don't recall or that seem bogus. Look up doctors who are billing you via the hospital and verify their efforts on your behalf. Sometimes you can be billed just because your surgeon sought advice but the doctor in question didn't even see you. Often, specialists are not covered by insurance and charge much higher fees. Negotiate all of this directly with each doctor's office.

If everything checks out and you still can't pay it, ask for a discount. A goodwill reduction in the overall bill is well within the power of the hospital finance manager if he or she thinks you will pay the difference in a reasonable amount of time. The alternative they face is sending your bill to an external collector. The hospital will get even less going that route, pennies on the dollar, so give it a shot. You have more leverage than you think.

Finally, most big hospital chains will happily allow you a full year to pay down a bill at zero interest, so long as you call and request a payment plan. (Do this after getting the bill lowered!) As always, hospitals and most doctors would vastly prefer to get at least something from you than almost nothing from a bill collector, never mind the ill-will that bill collectors generate with an otherwise good patient.

Step Two: Build Cash

Most Americans get fast cash the most expensive way possible—by using debt. The coming financial crisis means that people really have to change that mind-set. Debt will get very expensive and hard to procure when a true panic ensues. Naturally, you will need an emergency fund.

Researchers recently studied the issue of emergency funds and came to a curious conclusion: Some households would be fine with savings as low as $2,467. That's the number needed by people who live close to the U.S. poverty line to avoid falling into true hardship in an emergency.

For the rest of us, of course, the figure is larger. How much larger? Consider what you truly must spend in a single month: Mortgage, car payments, utilities, food, and so on. It's probably a number that corresponds pretty closely to your current income after taxes. Once you have your debt situation squared away, assume that you will need three to six months of that "monthly money" in a safe place (more on that below) just to feel comfortable in a financially chaotic year or, possibly, several years. The Great Recession lasted a year and a half!

If you're still working and don't expect to be laid off, a short-term emergency fund might be enough. Many financial advisors tell nonworking retirees that a year's worth of cash on hand is a more reasonable goal.

The point is that nobody wants to be forced to sell stock at the bottom of a downturn just to pay living expenses. First of all, you are likely to have to pay capital gains taxes on any sales, and second, there's a good chance you may have to sell stock that has lost an immense part of its current value or even your original acquisition cost. While there will be a carry-forward tax break on any outright losses, it's painful to sell under duress and take a loss just to keep the lights on.

Reduce Spending

What if things go south more quickly than expected? In that case, simply saving more from your paycheck or investment income might not be enough. Here are some steps to help you get on track with your cash goals sooner. One way to make money appear is to spend less in a radical way, at least over the short term. Go over your budgets and look for items that are nice to have but are generally avoidable spending.

That might be eating out or ordering meals in, a convenience that grew on a lot of us during the worst of the pandemic but is not strictly necessary. If you took out three or four streaming subscriptions, cancel them. You can always re-subscribe later on. If you opted for the highest speed internet, consider a lower speed, end the TV package no one watches, and try getting by on your cellular internet connection for a spell.

Inventory your closets and garage and figure out what items you have that you haven't used in a good while or equipment and tools you never use. Are they still serviceable? Knowing what's wearable or in good repair can reduce your urge to buy new items for a time. Sell things you don't need online.

Sell Household Items

That's right. As you inventory your closets, pantry, and garage, go ahead and start piling up items you haven't worn or things you bought but don't use. It's kind of astounding the sheer amount of stuff most Americans have in their homes, so much stuff that many of us opt to pay to store it all elsewhere.

The knee-jerk reaction to clutter is to donate. That's admirable, but the tax advantage of doing so has evaporated under recent changes in tax law. If you want to scratch up an extra $1,000 in a weekend, consider a yard sale. If you have larger stuff, take it down to a flea market and rent a small booth.

Price it right and negotiate your way to an empty yard in a day or less. A lot of estate sales, for instance, tell lookers on the first day that everything will be 25 percent off the next—if it's still there. That tactic tends to quickly separate the casual browser from the buyers.

Get a Second Job

If you have time but not money, monetize your time. The easiest way to make some quick cash is to get to more work.

That doesn't necessarily mean waiting tables, though if you have experience in restaurant work, most eateries are certainly hurting at the moment.

You don't need to build a whole side hustle or second career here. Remember, your goal is to create an emergency cash position, get comfortable, and then quit. If that means taking on overtime or picking up some shifts elsewhere for a few months, worse things could happen to you.

Rent Out Space

For some people, a second job or side hustle might be too high a hurdle time wise. For many retirees too, going back to work is just not an option. If that's you, consider renting out a room in your home.

If you live in a college town, there are likely hundreds of short-term renters seeking a place for eight months of the year. Contact graduate schools and ask if they have a bulletin board or newsletter for incoming students. Charge the square-foot going rate for an apartment or dorm and you could raise $1,000 a month for as long as classes are in session.

Step Three: Review Your Investments

If you have your debt managed and a fair amount of cash on hand, it might be time to review your current investments in preparation for what will surely be an extended and rocky stretch in the markets.

Many retirement-oriented investors have been long on stocks for decades. That has been a winning strategy for millions of Americans, so much so that a new phrase to describe them—"401(k) millionaires"—has entered the lexicon.

The problem with this approach is that your millionaire status, if by chance you have achieved it, is by no means guaranteed. If stocks drop sharply across the board, so will investments in retirement products such as 401(k) plans and IRAs.

There's nothing guaranteed or safe about money invested in these plans. They are not pensions, after all, but the same investments that are held in taxable accounts. The only difference is that they have not been taxed during all these years of inflated bull markets.

Building Cash in 401(k)s

The lack of tax drag on these investments has been a boon for millions of Americans, but the downside is absolutely real and as forbidding as it is for anyone investing outside them.

The good news is that you can much more easily rearrange your risk profile in a tax-deferred plan. In a taxable brokerage account, any sales will be subject to capital gains taxes. Retirement accounts, however, are shielded from investment taxes. If you sell now, you will only pay taxes later as you withdraw funds to pay your bills.

If you look at your overall wealth as two big buckets—taxable and tax-deferred—put them into a single spreadsheet instead. Looking at all of your money in one view, it may suddenly seem reasonable to increase your cash holdings by selling off stocks and mutual funds inside your tax-deferred accounts rather than your taxable accounts. You won't pay taxes on those sales, and you may be able to do enough rebalancing to cash in retirement accounts to feel comfortable without touching taxable accounts at all.

A Taxable War Chest

So what about your money in the non-tax-deferred bucket? You may want to keep some of your money invested and avoid capital gains taxes, but it's important to remember that once panic sets in, these investments will lose value.

Maybe you have an emotional attachment to a stock you've owned since college, or a fund you inherited from dear old Mom and Dad. If that's the case, make peace with the fact that the rest of the world won't care and the value of that investment will surely fall with the market.

A good strategy to help you through the pain will be to build up an investment war chest in your taxable accounts. Once you have debts under control and an emergency fund, go ahead and put cash into your taxable accounts and earmark them for buying shares—after prices have gone down. That could help offset any potential losses from a market decline and may help your mental state when markets finally scrape the bottom. Bear in mind, the collapse could be in slow motion, a series of dips and recoveries and then a total collapse. A 50 percent haircut would be not merely unsurprising; it's almost guaranteed.

Where should you hold your cash? Broadly speaking, short-term Treasury debt in the form of T-bills will be safe. You can own them directly through TreasuryDirect.gov rather than via a costly third party, such as a mutual fund. If you prefer a fund, seek out a low-cost index product that invests solely in short-term government debt from Vanguard or Fidelity Investments.

Savings accounts have gotten a bad rap over the past several years thanks to very low interest rates, but you are not likely to find any place safer to put money in the medium term. That's because all bank accounts are guaranteed by the Federal Deposit Insurance Corporation (FDIC) up to $250,000 per account. Credit unions are insured in the same way by the National Credit Union Administration (NCUA).

This only gets to be a hassle if you have more than $250,000 in cash in the bank, which is few people. However, it is possible to have more than that in cash in a brokerage account, especially if you choose to rebalance to cash in preparation for a market decline. Many brokerages now offer "sweep" accounts that wrap bank account access seamlessly into the brokerage login. Your money is actually held at one of several partner banks and never in amounts exceeding federal insurance maximums.

If you have cash in the bank and want a slightly better than piddling return, consider buying a certificate of deposit (CD).

Some banks offer what's called a "bump up" CD that could benefit you if rates move higher. Note, however, that terms on these products are complex and absolutely will not favor you over the bank itself. Another route is a CD ladder—that is, owning several short-term CDs in a maturity sequence and rolling them over into new CDs as they mature. Doing so allows you to capture rising interest rates over time.

Step Four: Consider Hedging

Finally, there are a number of ways to hedge your investments in order to soften the blow of a falling stock market. As discussed above, just owning cash can be a powerful tool once stocks finally bottom. More than a few billionaires made their bones in deep-value scenarios where absolutely everyone else has given up on stocks but they had the cash on hand to buy shares at bargain-basement prices.

If you doubt this can happen, consider this stunning fact: Ford Motor at about $20 per share today traded for less than $2 a share in February 2009. The last time Ford was worth that little was the early 1980s. A stock market rout in that sense can be like a time machine for a prepared buyer, and a prepared buyer is one with cash on hand to buy at market bottoms.

A Role for Gold

You are likely to hear a lot about cryptocurrency as the ultimate hedge against all kinds of financial ills. Please ignore all that. There's really nothing to hold up the crypto market in a serious downturn and there's no guarantee that you'll get your money out safely on the other side. For one, a rush to own government bonds in a market panic would likely drive the dollar higher in value, not lower, and the whole crypto scheme is predicated on the idea of the dollar being second (or third) banana in a brave, new, postfiat world.

If you still want to have some kind of non-dollar-denominated hedge, it's simpler to own gold, which is a well-understood and heavily traded commodity widely recognized as the "antidollar" in most circumstances. Plus, it's just plain easier to buy and sell gold in the current regulatory environment.

You can choose physical gold if you like and if you have access to a reputable dealer. Make sure you can secure your physical gold in a safe or bank vault and don't overdo it. If a truly stunning reversal for the U.S. dollar is in the cards, a small gold holding as a percentage of your assets should be enough to offset it.

If buying coins or small bars of gold is not your style, consider owning gold through an exchange-traded fund. There are several large, well-known gold funds on the market, some of which hold actual physical gold to back their paper. The downside is that you cannot touch the gold, but the upside is that you have essentially daily liquidity if you choose to change your gold position.

Buy Portfolio Insurance

One way to insure a portfolio is to buy long-term puts on highly appreciated speculative stocks. A put option is a contract to sell an asset at a certain price by a specified date. In this case, the buyer of the put believes that the price of the stock will fall.

If you aren't sure which stock to buy a put on, or the technical aspects of trading options seem forbidding, another way to bet against stocks is to own an inverse ETF. Inverse ETFs are essentially mutual funds that own short positions. You don't have to actually sell anything short personally, but if an overall index—say, the S&P 500—declines in value, the value of the inverse ETF goes up.

Of course, if the index rises, the inverse fund will fall. That's why it's important to keep your holdings in inverse products at levels that provide insurance against the balance of your portfolio and nothing more and to only build a significant put position once it is clear that the markets have truly topped out and that central banks have no dry powder left to rescue them.

Use TIPS

Finally, if you expect to keep bonds in your portfolio, consider owning a weighting of Treasury Inflation-Protected Securities (TIPS). These are U.S. government bonds that are guaranteed to maintain value in an inflationary environment. The federal government is not going away. At some point, the dust will clear, and bonds will again pay a worthwhile return above inflation.

Until then, keep safe cash close and liquid, and be ready to reinvest. Asset prices at some point will be reasonably cheap for the risk taken, but that will only matter if you have taken the aforementioned steps to hunker down and safely ride out the coming financial storm.

Index

Page numbers followed by *f* and *t* refer
to figures and tables, respectively.

Simple **Heart Test**

Powered by Newsmaxhealth.com

FACT:

▸ Nearly half of those who die from heart attacks each year never showed prior symptoms of heart disease.

▸ If you suffer cardiac arrest outside of a hospital, you have just a 7% chance of survival.

Don't be caught off guard. Know your risk now.

TAKE THE TEST NOW ...

Renowned cardiologist **Dr. Chauncey Crandall** has partnered with **Newsmaxhealth.com** to create a simple, easy-to-complete, online test that will help you understand your heart attack risk factors. Dr. Crandall is the author of the #1 best-seller *The Simple Heart Cure: The 90-Day Program to Stop and Reverse Heart Disease.*

Take Dr. Crandall's Simple Heart Test — it takes just 2 minutes or less to complete — it could save your life!

Discover your risk now.

- **Where you score on our unique heart disease risk scale**
- Which of your lifestyle habits really protect your heart
- **The true role your height and weight play in heart attack risk**
- Little-known conditions that impact heart health
- **Plus much more!**

SimpleHeartTest.com/Heart

My RETIREMENT *Date*

How would you like to know the exact date you can expect to retire? Well, this **FREE** assessment will help you learn exactly that. And more importantly, we give you some fun tools that you can use so you'll retire quicker, safer, and wealthier than you ever imagined . . . along with simple investment strategies to help ensure you NEVER run out of money during your retirement. Enjoy!

Find out *your* retirement date!

Go To:

MyRetirementDate.com/Money

Powered by NewsmaxFinance.com

9.50

Essay Index

THE WINDOWS OF WESTMINSTER

RT. HON. STANLEY BALDWIN

THE WINDOWS OF WESTMINSTER

BY

HAROLD BEGBIE
A Gentleman with a Duster

*In an age of political infidelity, of mean passions, and petty thoughts,
I would have impressed upon the rising race not to despair, but to seek
in a right understanding of the history of their country and in
the energies of heroic youth, the elements of national welfare.*
—DISRAELI

ILLUSTRATED

Essay Index

BOOKS FOR LIBRARIES PRESS
FREEPORT, NEW YORK

First Published 1924
Reprinted 1970

STANDARD BOOK NUMBER:

8369-1447-3

LIBRARY OF CONGRESS CATALOG CARD NUMBER:

77-104993

PRINTED IN THE UNITED STATES OF AMERICA

INTRODUCTION TO THE AMERICAN EDITION

THE domestic politics of England must always be of some interest to intelligent people in other countries; but at the moment the political struggle taking place so quietly in her midst has a particular interest, I think, for all democratic nations, more especially for the United States of America.

It is a struggle such as divided the nations in the Great War. On one side are the Socialists, who have learned their economics in the German school, and, who like the Germans, believe in making the individual subservient to a State despotism; and on the other side are the Conservatives, who believe in evolution, and who cherish the ancient traditions of personal liberty, individual enterprise, and free discussion.

Much may be said for the thesis of either side. Germany had made herself one of the greatest nations in the world. Given a strong and inflexible Government following despotically a single idea, and any fairly intelligent people that does not mind the loss of personal freedom and is indisposed to quarrel with perpetual supervision by government officials, may reach a high degree of culture, both physical and mental, and may exercise a preponderating influence in the affairs of the world. Socialism has certainly something to say for itself.

But Conservatism has something to say for itself. It is an attitude of the human mind towards life which is essentially spiritual. It acknowledges that the German Empire had reached a formidable height of greatness, and that in many ways it was vastly superior to the stumbling and untidy democracies of Europe; but it examines that disciplined German greatness and that manufactured German superiority, and asks the question of Jesus: *What shall it profit a man if he gains the whole world and lose his soul alive?* In other words, State despotism, in the opinion of Conservatism, is destructive of moral character.

Socialism in England is of a mild aspect and does not yet lend itself to dramatic treatment; but it represents all the same that way of looking at political problems which inspires the Bolsheviks of Russia. It is a creed which is rather fashionable among earnest young men at the universities, and among its devotees are some of our most decadent painters of bad pictures and many of our most decadent writers of absurd poetry. It has a note of newness which is attractive to weak minds, and a strain of wildness and revolt which is meat and drink to foolish stomachs. Curiously enough it is as popular in the dullest red-brick chapels of Dissent, where it was born, as in the most flagrantly unmoral studios of Chelsea, where it is hailed as the apostle of free love and the iconoclast of all bourgeois respectability. One seems to feel that it is a notion which can capture the heart of the self-righteous as easily as it can turn the head of the most abandoned. Under the Red Flag, Calvin and Horace Walpole are met together, Wesley and Oscar Wilde have kissed each other. And at the back of these discordant disciples of an economic heresy are gathering an ever increasing multitude of the workers—men and women who are out of love with the present system, who find life hard and difficult, and who are as ready to be deceived by the bunkum artists of political agitation as any dolt at a country fair by the patter of a Jewish cheapjack.

In every country of the world the political forces are more and more grouping themselves in this manner. Two utterly antithetical principles are every day emerging with greater distinctness from the clash of humanity's economic struggle with the forces of nature. Men and women are beginning to see life only from these two standpoints. Revolution is opposing itself to Evolution. The State is setting itself against the Individual. Mechanism is preparing to crush Personality. This struggle, this clash of two antagonistic principles, is manifesting itself in England in a manner peculiarly English. It is not such a struggle as gave to Thomas Carlyle so many picturesque opportunities to convert the unpleasant vehemence of the French Revolution into memorable literature. There is nothing Latin in its atmosphere, and nothing Slav in its gestures. It will never satisfy the so-called Mr. Trotzky nor fill the beautiful heart of Mr. Litvinoff (if that is still his latest *alias*) with pious ecstasy. It is, one must confess, a rather dull struggle. It differs from other tremendous battles of the political mind as a game of chess differs from a prize-fight. Nevertheless there is in the calm atmosphere and quiet stillness of this English battle an intellectual value enabling the democracies of other countries to see more clearly and distinctly the features of the contest in which the whole world is now more or less involved. However *bourgeois* Mr. Ramsay MacDonald may have appeared to the impatient eyes of Lenin, he is the undoubted herald of a Communist army, which intends to destroy the present basis of society, and much more thoroughly than Lenin succeeded in doing, to do away with capital and private enterprise, and to make of the British Empire a number of self-determined Soviet Republics.

If the American reader will glance through these windows of Westminster, from which I have attempted to remove some of the dust accumulated by past controversies, he will see that the protagonists of English Conservatism stand for many of those things which are dear to the Constitutionalists in his own country, and that the features of English Socialism, under their mask of moderation, are identical with the features of Revolution in every country under the sun. He will see that the English Socialist is attempting to do gradually and peacefully what the Revolutionist in other nations is attempting, or has attempted, to do at one disastrous blow. And he will see that the English Conservative is opposing himself to the moderate and plausible Labour Government because he knows that the ultimate object of this Government is to put genius into chains, to enthrone mediocrity, and to substitute for personal liberty, free discussion, and Parliamentary institutions the despotic dictatorship of a few determined pedants.

It will be clear to American readers that a triumph for English Socialism would mean the disruption of the British Empire, and that the falling apart of such an immense political structure would have grave and powerful reactions in every quarter of the globe. The American Continent could not view without disquiet, for example, a military Asiatic power seizing the empire of India, and perhaps thrusting out its well-disciplined legions as far as Australasia. It could not feel itself so free to work out its great destiny in peace if England counted for nothing in Europe, and her example of revolution was being followed in many other nations. No Monroe Doctrine can isolate America from the real politics of the human race. No Fordney Tariff can protect the American citizen from his natural relationship with the rest of mankind. By the Will of God, the United States are, in particular, shareholders in the world mission which England has obeyed for so many centuries, and of which the American Constitution is itself a consequence. Easier would it be for England to survive some great political catastrophe in the United States than for America, with all her wealth, power, and population, to survive the downfall of the British Empire.

Therefore it is not a presumption, I hope, to think that people in America may be glad to read this book and to make themselves acquainted with the present crisis in English politics. Most of the men whose opinions I have endeavoured to express in these pages are the chief captains of our Constitutional legions. They will either destroy the work of our Socialists or themselves vanish from the stage of human history. They are not so much the leaders of a political party as the apostles of the democratic principle. If they are destroyed, their places will be taken by a tyranny—either a Communist tyranny, or a Fascist tyranny. Let the American reader who believes in democracy assure himself of this truth—let him, also, put out of his mind all prejudices against old-fashioned Toryism, which is as dead as George the Third—and he will come to feel that these Conservatives in England are fighting his battle as well as their own, and that they will be as heartened by his interest in their difficult struggle as the British troops in France were heartened by the appearance of the American Armies in 1917.

America and England are the strongest pillars of peace and sanity left standing by the World War. Between them they uphold the great cause of human civilisation. Let them know each other well, and understand each other's part in world politics, and democracy may hope to survive, with sufficient strength to fulfil its difficult destiny, all the recurrent onslaughts of despotism, whether they come openly and frankly from a foreign militarism or secretly masked and cloaked, like an assassin, from the secret hiding-places of an international conspiracy.

D.

LONDON, July, 1924.

INTRODUCTION

Perhaps as long as there has been a political history in this country there have been certain men of a cool, moderate, resolute firmness, not gifted with high imagination, little prone to enthusiastic sentiment, heedless of large theories and speculations, careless of dreamy scepticism; with a clear view of the next step, and a wise intention to take it; a strong conviction that the elements of knowledge are true, and a steady belief that the present world can, and should be, quietly improved.

—WALTER BAGEHOT.

*States, as great engines, move slowly—*BACON.

*My own origins were living within me; by their light I could see clearly that this England was pre-eminently the home of a decent happiness and a quiet pleasure in being oneself. I found here the same sort of manliness which I had learned to love in America, yet softer, and not at all obstreperous; a manliness which when refined a little creates the gentleman, since its instinct is to hide its strength for an adequate occasion, and for the service of others.—*GEORGE SANTAYANA.

"I AM a Conservative," said Disraeli, "to preserve all that is good in our Constitution, a Radical to remove all that is bad"—a phrase which perhaps represents the politics of most reasonable people. But difficulty arises even for reasonable people when we attempt to decide what things in our Constitution are good, and what things are bad.

This is clearly a matter not to be decided from the slight altitude of a soap-box; nor, with so many half-breeds in the political flock, is it easy for an unqualified layman to separate even the sheep from the goats. Let any great question arise in this debatable region, and, if wigs are not immediately on the green, at least there is considerable and widespread evidence of fog in the public mind.

Only one way exists out of the political confusion which arises in this matter, and which is so dangerous to the welfare of the State. It is a return to first principles. What are the principles which govern Conservative policy? and what are the principles which govern Socialist policy?

For the moment I leave Liberalism out of court. The people of Great Britain have decided, so far as one can see into their minds, to choose between Conservatism and Socialism. I can perceive, at any rate, no manifest sign that democracy is up in arms for the present champions of Liberalism, or that it is caring a button about those unfortunate temperamental differences which appear to afflict the political relations of Mr. Lloyd George and Sir John Simon with a noticeable peevishness. It seems to me quite certain that democracy has decided to take its Liberalism henceforth with a grain of salt, and that while Mr. Lloyd George, the political father of Sir William Sutherland, may always be sure of triumphal processions and requests for his autograph, he is extremely unlikely to become possessed, in the next few critical years at any rate, of the latchkey of Number Ten.

With Liberalism thus out of the way, except as a nuisance to the Conservative and a convenience to the Socialist, it is a comparatively easy matter to state the differences which separate the two chief parties in the State. The principles of Conservatism differ sharply, distinctly, and entirely from the principles of Socialism. Democracy, however confused its thinking, and however apathetic its vision, should be able not merely to perceive that great difference, but also to feel it in its bones. Conservatism is the very breath of English history. Modern Socialism is a mushroom forced by Russian atheism on the dunghill of German economics. The one is at least an element in every Englishman's patriotism; the other, the poisonous vodka with which international enthusiasts stimulate their blissful vision of a world proletariat in chains to a world bureaucracy.

But not every Conservative uses his brain, and not every Socialist shows his hand.

The danger of the present time lies in a Conservatism false to its traditions and a Socialism masking its aims. Democracy may here very easily be confused. It may decide, in its good-natured and easy-going way, that Labour should be given another chance; and it may easily come to think, in the absence of a vigorous propaganda, that Conservatism is little more than a picturesque survival from the Middle Ages.

Conservatism, then, has two duties: honourably and courageously to live up to its traditions; fearlessly and earnestly to tear the mask of moderation from the Bolshevik features of Labour. Unless it sets itself to discharge both of these duties, it seems to me that Labour will return to power with so great a majority that even Mr. J. H. Thomas will be forced to take the white-slip from his waistcoat and to roll up his shirt-sleeves in the interest of Moscow and the Red Flag. There is only one generation, Americans say, between shirt-sleeves and shirt-sleeves.

At this point we return to the matter of principles. What are the authentic principles of Conservatism? and what are the authentic principles of Socialism?

The pages which follow attempt to answer these questions. The reader will find various views of Conservatism expressed by the various members of the Conservative party with whom I have discussed the matter; but he will see that underlying all these superficial differences of outlook and opinion there is a sure and solid foundation of political principle, a strong unity of purpose which Disraeli summed up as a threefold object—the maintenance of our institutions, the preservation of our Empire, and the improvement of the conditions of the people.

It reveals to us the prescience of this great statesman of Conservatism that he so constantly and emphatically insisted upon the need of maintaining our institutions. In those days even the wildest of reformers never seriously assailed the institution of Parliament or questioned the value of free discussion. But a day has now come when our Parliamentary institutions are regarded as the invention of a hypocritical *bourgeoisie*, and free speech is openly denounced as the cant of a tyrannical commercialism. It may not win loud cheers to remind democracy that Parliament is the only bulwark it possesses against the suffocating despotism of a Mussolini or the destructive brutality of an active Revolutionary minority; but it is nevertheless an urgent duty of the Conservative to profess his faith in the efficacy of our historic institutions, and to tell the people why Conservatism regards those institutions as essential to the liberty, the happiness, and the growth of the British nation.

At the end of the book the reader will find a statement of those authentic principles which unquestionably inspire Socialism, but which are not often honourably and courageously proclaimed by the tacticians of the present Labour Government. My object, let me explain in thus setting forth the principles of Socialism in a book mainly concerned with an exploration of the mind of modern Conservatism, is not so much to ridicule or to denounce Socialism, but much more to awaken the intelligence and the moral energy of those who profess and call themselves Conservatives to realise the nature of the conflict awaiting them.

I would ask the reader to think of me as one who honours the principles of Conservatism, but who regards the Conservative Party with the detachment of a man whose chief intellectual interests lie outside politics. I am interested in politics only so far as they touch English character. I pay attention to politicians only when they seem to me earnestly engaged in some matter which vitally affects the historic character of the English people. At the moment I am on the side of Conservatism, because the menace of the Socialist seems to me both real and near; but I must confess that I am anxiously on the side of Conservatism, lest it should fail to safeguard those things for which I care with all my heart. I could support a new-born Liberalism or a converted Labour Party which promised, not merely to fight the Socialists effectively but promised also to maintain our ancient institutions, to preserve and develop our incomparable Empire, and to improve the physical and intellectual conditions of our heroic people.

The fate of the country is largely in the hands of men and women who have lost the shrewd and natural instincts of ignorance without gaining the difficult and compensating wisdom of culture. We are an urbanised nation of half-educated people, and it is a mark of the half-educated to be sceptical, apathetic, unimaginative, and capricious. The awakening of such a nation as this to the true nature of the many great moral and economic changes confronting civilisation is one of the most urgent duties of our time, as it is also one of the most difficult.

I have written this book in the hope that it may help people to understand and appreciate the fundamental principles of historic Conservatism, and also in the hope of stimulating those whose duty it is to keep democracy informed of the ever changing political situation to show much more energy, and perhaps, if I may say so without offence, somewhat greater intelligence, in their work of educating the mob of all classes.

CONTENTS

ILLUSTRATIONS

The Windows of Westminster

MR. STANLEY BALDWIN

THE RIGHT HON. STANLEY BALDWIN

Born in 1867. Son of Alfred Baldwin. Educ.: Harrow and Trinity College, Cambridge. M.P. (Unionist) since 1908 for the Bewdley Division of Worcestershire. Financial Secretary to the Treasury, 1917–21. President of the Board of Trade, 1921–22. Prime Minister and Exchequer, 1922; Prime Minister and first Lord of the Treasury, 1923–24. Resigned after the election of 1924, retaining the Leadership in the House of the Conservative Party. Mr. Baldwin had the responsibility, as special commissioner of the Treasury, in securing an adjustment in Washington in 1923, of the war indebtedness of Great Britain to the United States.

© Farrington

RT. HON. STANLEY BALDWIN

I

MR. STANLEY BALDWIN

He carries his English weather in his heart wherever he goes, and it becomes a cool spot in the desert, and a steady and sane oracle amongst all the deliriums of mankind. . . . It will be a black day for the human race when scientific blackguards, conspirators, churls, and fanatics manage to supplant him.—GEORGE SANTAYANA, *Soliloquies in England.*

Words, money, all things else, are comparatively easy to give away; but when a man makes a gift of his daily life and practice, it is plain that the truth, whatever it may be, has taken possession of him.—LOWELL.

. . . I prefer the liberty we now enjoy to the Liberalism they promise, and find something better than the rights of men in the rights of Englishmen.—DISRAELI.

MR. BALDWIN, who is before everything a countryman, conserves at the depths of his personality something that is now regarded by numerous people as a superstition. He believes that men may be used by the invisible forces of the universe as instruments for the good and elevation of mankind.

A man, in his opinion, however commonplace, however lacking in any of the qualities of genius, may nevertheless co-operate with the divine energy in the supreme work of evolution—the production of a higher human creature; that is, provided he sincerely desires selflessly to serve his fellow-men, and earnestly seeks his strength from the sole source of spiritual power.

He does not regard religion, even in its cruder forms, as dope for the people. He gratefully accepts it as the sustaining breath and the inspiring beauty of the moral life. His conservatism, which is more impassioned than many people suppose, is an aspect of this profound faith in a rational universe. He is a man, to use the phrase of George Sand, tormented by divine things. This is the compulsion which keeps him in the rather sordid and depressing atmosphere of modern politics.

Here is a plain, blunt, simple-hearted countryman living laborious and exhausting days in that forbidding atmosphere, which can have but one attraction for a selfless man, while his whole heart hungers and thirsts after the countryside from which only a mystical compulsion has expatriated him. He told me once how many years it is since he saw the blossoms in Worcestershire—six or seven lost springtimes, if I remember rightly. I said to him that his feeling for the country interested me because it was not governed by the sporting calendar. He replied, "The country that I love will still be there when sport is dead."

Speak to him of almost any part of England, and he will tell you that he once walked from such a village and over such a range of hills to some historic market-town in that neighbourhood; and perhaps he will tell you of a talk he had with a field labourer or an old village woman in the course of his walk. Like Edward FitzGerald, he loves these chance encounters on the roads of England, and seldom fails to discover in such occasions new reasons for rejoicing in his English blood. The idea that Charles Dickens exaggerated brings a smile to his eyes. Grub Street and Chelsea may think so, but not the man who goes into the highways and byways of English life.

There is about him nothing that suggests either the provinces or London. For good or for evil, his personality entirely lacks the flick of a cocktail. He is genuine cider. The small pinched-up eyes, with their uplifted brows, have the shrewdness of the shepherd rather than the sharpness of the merchant; the deep, grave, kindly voice has no note of drawing-room or art coterie, but the tone of a slow, pondering, decisive country mind. He is a man of action, but his activity suggests the fields and not the city. He is quick with humour and not a sluggard in the matter of wit; but both his humour and his wit never suggest the smoking-room and the dinner-party, but rather the open sky and a prospect of shining hills.

I think he has something of the peasant's obstinacy,

and is not altogether free from a certain obtuseness. He would light his pipe a dozen times and never perceive that his guest is not smoking. He can offend the feelings of his colleagues and never be aware of it. To take the closest of his friends fully into his confidence is as difficult a matter for him as to utter his opinions in public. He is hand and glove with no man, and listens rather than speaks, watches rather than leads. It is said of him that he is better at perplexing his own party than at harrying the enemy. Also it is said of him that while his heart entitles him to the respect and even the affection of mankind, the quality of his intellect is such as constantly to flabbergast his best friends.

In the spring that has just departed, I sat one afternoon on the terrace of the House of Commons talking with a youthful Conservative who is as full of fire as a loaded cannon. While he was pouring into my ears an argument for greater energy in the Conservative ranks, there emerged from the little doorway just behind our bench two elderly members of the Labour Party. These dusty-looking old men, without speech between them, advanced slowly to the next bench on our left, laboriously took possession of it, and as laboriously produced their pipes, filled them with tobacco and lighted up. Then they stretched out their legs, crossed their hands over their stomachs, and rested their weary eyes on the buildings of St. Thomas's Hospital across the water. At regular intervals one of them slowly lifted a tired hand, removed his pipe from his lips, and leaning heavily forward spat upon the pavement.

Presently there shot out of the same little door from which they had emerged, a man who swung instantly away to the left, and with his thumbs in the armholes of his waistcoat, his shoulders humped, and his head bent, proceeded to walk at a great pace up and down the east end of the terrace, which is reserved for members of Parliament.

What little sunlight there was fell upon his sand-coloured hair and gave it a reddish look, which accentuated the yellowish pallor of his face and the colourless character of his lips and eyebrows. A certain spruceness about him refused to harmonise with the leaden-hued stone of the Palace of Westminster. Nor was his stride in harmony with the melancholy austerity of the place; it was the quick and impatient stride of a man bent on business. Occasionally he raised his eyes and looked upward at the packed clouds, and the gulls falling through the misty air towards the river; but for the most part he walked with his eyes on the ground.

One of the pipe-smoking Labour members drew his companion's attention, by a prod of the elbow, to this pedestrian, who was the Conservative leader, and they both stared after him, and continued to stare after him for a long time, but blankly and without any vital interest.

This incident struck me as characteristic of the present position of politics. The more solid and old-fashioned representatives of Labour are in a disillusioned state of mind: they are both bored and disheartened: they cannot fit themselves into the club life of Westminster: the whisky-drinking in the tea-room is no distraction for them from the overpowering dulness of the Chamber; many of them would fain be home with wife and weans.

Mr. Baldwin also finds it difficult to fit himself into the work of the present Parliament. He, too, must sometimes escape from the boredom of speeches which change nothing, and from the incessant whispers and talk which besiege a party leader. He must get into the fresh air, exercise his muscles, and restore the natural and precious solitude of a man's soul. But whereas the two Labour men appeared to be worn out with fatigue and disappointment, Mr. Baldwin was evidently longing for real action and a decisive issue, impatient of wasted time, exasperated by the delays of a too-prolonged entr'acte in the great drama of human progress, longing to play his part in the future of mankind.

Not many people outside the small circle of his immediate followers are aware of the dream which he cherishes in the solitude of his soul, or of the nature of that compulsion which keeps him so doggedly and composedly at a post not always comfortable and sometimes even profoundly distasteful to a man of delicate feelings. He is so cheerful and bluff in social intercourse, and in public life apparently so easy-going and so slow to move, that many politicians take him to be a good-natured man of average ability who has never seen a vision, never nursed an ideal, and never hitched his waggon to a star. They are quite unaware of his true nature.

A clue to that nature may be found in two services which he rendered to the country during the term of his office. He, more than anybody else, broke up the Coalition. Why did he do so? He had seen that the government of the country was losing the moral character which had distinguished it during the Victorian period. He believed that if this moral decay continued it would be fatal to the greatness and glory of England. To strike at it, and root it out for ever, meant striking at some of the most brilliant intellects in the Coalition, and destroying some of the most promising of political careers in both parties. But he believed that it would be better for the country to have a less brilliant government, and for his party to go into the wilderness, even for a long period, than to continue a system which was poisoning the whole atmosphere of public life.

The effect of his decision led immediately to two reforms of the very highest significance. He swept away the dominance of the Press, and he cleansed the

Honours of their shame. From the moment of his accession to power the doors of Downing Street were shut fast against certain newspaper proprietors, who had come to regard ministers as servants of their will, servants, too, not above accepting gratuities in one form or another—Press magnates who had been able not only to compel the gift of titles for some of the basest men in politics, but even most dangerously and fatally to deflect the foreign policy of this great country from its traditional course.

For these two services, of which the public is not yet sufficiently aware, the nation owes Mr. Baldwin a great debt. The corruption of our public life had reached a festering height which threatened the health of the whole nation. There was an air of Tammany in Westminster, a touch of Bottomley in the party organisations. All that was morally bad in politics had gathered a courage and intensified an insolence which were carrying every successive barrier of decency and virtue before them. Men who could never have personally addressed the second secretaries of Salisbury and Gladstone were the close intimates, the gossips, and the go-betweens of the greatest ministers of state. There was no limit to the demands of these insurgents. They were not content with securing honours for themselves and their parasites, not even content with dominating the organisation of their parties and degrading the once noble profession of journalism; they were determined, these gross and ignorant men, to govern the British Empire.

From this disgraceful state of things Mr. Baldwin delivered the reconstructed Conservative Party. He has restored the old standards. He has repaired the ancient barriers. Never again, so long as he is loyally supported by the best elements of his party, will the flood of Fleet Street return to Whitehall. Public life is again clean, if it is not yet altogether fearless; and I know that Mr. Baldwin could have to-morrow the powerful friendship of a certain Press magnate, at present engaged in striking every day at his reputation, by merely asking him to luncheon. That invitation will never be given.

These things, as I have said, are a clue to Mr. Baldwin's nature. He is a man who believes that the evolution of the human race is an evolution towards knowledge and power, and that absolutely essential to that evolution is a growth in the moral nature of man. England's part in this evolution, as he reads history, is the contribution of a very sturdy and yet tender moral character. He once told me that he loves to find evidence of this moral character in the works of the great English humorists—whose humour is always struggling to rise above grossness and salaciousness into the pure air of sweetness, tenderness, and kindness.

"What nation, save ours, could produce a Lamb and a Dickens?"

One of the questions that most disturbs him is how to keep the urban Englishman true to the rural type. He would like to see our dark and denaturalising cities dismembered, and their factories planted out in the country, with model villages surrounding them. He believes that every Englishman is better for a bit of garden, and that flowers play a deeper part in the affairs of men than either the historian or psychologist suppose. His love of the English is heightened by the knowledge that even in spite of the miseries and depressions of crowded cities, you may still find in their slums people who are true to the type which existed in a pastoral age. "No man, who knows our people," he said to me one day, "can be a pessimist; nor should he be an alarmist. But there is work to do. It is work for those brave people. Their true nature must be given a chance. The big cities are apt not only to shut out the wide horizon of the Empire, but to sap the force and gaiety of English character. We do not want masses. We want Englishmen."

In all his thinking there is this thought of English character, and its value for mankind. He is never tired of hearing a story that exemplifies the kindness or the courage of English character. And sometimes he will attempt in a few brief phrases to hit off the salient characteristics of the Englishman.

Our emphasis in this matter, he contends, is on sincerity. No one is so contemptible in English eyes as a hypocrite. We can do with a rogue who is a jolly rogue, and who makes himself ridiculous in his roguery; but we cannot abide a humbug, particularly an oily or a pompous humbug. We play our games fairly. We love the man we can trust. We are sceptical about emotion, contemptuous of sentimentalism, and strong haters of cant. A man must ring true before we admit him to the outer suburbs of our intimacy; before we take him to our hearts, or follow him as a leader, he must be bone good. "Bone good" is a phrase that he utters with a rejoicing ring.

Such an Englishman as he has sketched does not talk often of the sorrows and sufferings of the poor; certainly never with a glib loquacity. It would turn his blood to vinegar even to think of using those sorrows and sufferings to advance his own political fortunes. Moreover, it is of the very essence of such a man to be practical. He will not let his feelings run away with him. He will not contemplate measures which might possibly make matters worse. He asks himself what can be done to relieve their sorrows and sufferings, what can be done to raise the whole standard of British democracy, and he does not move until he is sure that his remedy is in harmony with the processes of evolution.

Years ago, when he was a young man in his father's works, Mr. Baldwin conceived the ambition to be Prime Minister of England. It was part of his romantic

youthfulness and soon disappeared in the increasing
pleasure of his daily duties. He got to know the
workers intimately, and found in their hearts the same
atmosphere and the same music which he had always
found in the Worcestershire countryside. They became
for him the living England of his deepest affection.
To know them enriched his own life, widened his sympathies, strengthened his faith, and purified his patriotism. He began to think of politics once again, and this
time seriously, but with no personal ambition; his sole
idea was the thought of being useful to these very
lovable people. His father retired from Parliament
after sixteen years' service, and Stanley Baldwin succeeded him in the seat. He, too, has now served for
sixteen years. Throughout this time he has been
faithful to the first idea which took him into politics,
but of late years with a new passion, and with a much
stronger compulsion. Of this compulsion I have
already spoken, but it is now necessary to speak of it
with greater clearness.

It manifested its force, with a new and deep intensity,
when, quite unexpectedly, and to his immense surprise,
he found himself called upon to play a decisive part in
Conservative politics. He asked himself how it should
be that a man so habituated to the humility of back
benches could thus suddenly find himself called upon to
occupy the chief place in the counsels of his party, and
the government of his country.

The answer he made to this question cannot be given in words. Men of his make do not easily talk of such matters, nor have we yet, perhaps, invented the modern equivalent for mystical phraseology. It is enough to know that he took office with a deep sense of responsibility to the creative Power, and with the hope that in spite of his shortcomings he might in some humble fashion be used to further the greatest causes of humanity.

He struck his first blow quickly and decisively. Public life was cleared of evils which threatened it with the worst calamities. That done, he found the compulsion in his soul driving him forward to a labour which kindled all the enthusiasm of his thoroughly English nature. He saw that to do its work in the world Conservatism must draw its strength from the confidence and affection of the working-classes; and he believed that with more energy and enthusiasm in the ranks of the Conservative Party, that confidence might be won gloriously in spite of all the gibes of academic Liberalism and all the alien ferocity of Communism. Was it not a suggestion of value that he, a man who had long lived with and loved the working people of England, who knew that the common people of England, the shepherds of Cumberland, the steel workers of Sheffield, and the ploughmen of Norfolk, that these nameless ones and not Mr. Lloyd George nor Lord Haig had won the greatest war for human freedom ever fought

in the history of mankind—was it not a suggestion
of value that because of this great love for, and confidence in and knowledge of the English people he had
been called, so unexpectedly, to the head of the oldest
party in the State?

To understand his attitude towards the working-
classes is to understand all that is best in the mind of
modern Conservatism. With his strong love for the
simple man goes a great antipathy for the *intelligentsia*
of Labour. He feels that these bookish champions of
democracy have no real affection for the workman, that
their hearts, such as they are, are given to economic
theories, and that they are ready to sacrifice the personal freedom of the individual citizen and the domestic
happiness of the multitude in the interest of ideas which
have never yet worked in any nation under the sun. He
regards them as usurpers in the affections of the working-classes.

His anger is stirred by their hypocrisy in affecting
a sympathy with the sorrows of the working-classes
which in truth they have never genuinely felt. His
resentment is quickened by that method in their propaganda which would make the working-classes see in
the Conservative a selfish and arrogant champion of
vested interests as far removed from any sympathy
with the poor as Dives from Lazarus. His contempt
is moved by their association, secret or openly avowed,
with those foreign mercenaries of revolution who sow

among our working-classes the poisonous tares of class hatred and irreligion, with no other purpose than the ruin of English character and the destruction of the British Empire.

But for the best men in Labour he has respect, and sympathy, and even affection. Indeed, it is one of the most interesting features of the present political situation that between Conservatism and Labour there exists a sympathy which is entirely lacking between Liberalism and Labour. Mr. Baldwin regards this genuine sympathy as a continuance of the feeling which existed in old times between the squire and the villager, between the old-fashioned employer and his man, and he believes that the best men in the Labour Party, with the best men in the working-classes, do still trust the Conservative as a man who keeps his word, is kind of heart, and is sincerely anxious to do his duty.

But while he feels this sympathy for the old-fashioned trades unionist, and is conscious, with so many other Conservatives, of a real affection for certain men in the Labour Party, he sees clearly that not very far ahead of the road on which they are both now travelling there is a signpost pointing in two contrary directions, the one towards a slavish Communism, the other towards an intenser and far richer Individualism.

Examine the mind of Mr. Ramsay MacDonald and the mind of Mr. Stanley Baldwin, and you see in a moment the most vital characteristic of the present situation. Both men are earnest and unquestioning Christians. Both men are inspired with the idea of lifting up the human race from the squalid and destructive materialism of recent times. Both men are solicitous that such should be the conditions of human life that the soul of man may become naturally conscious of its spiritual nature and its spiritual destiny.

But Mr. MacDonald believes that this end is to be reached by destroying every incentive to individual enterprise which acts upon the cupidity and selfishness of the human heart. His millennium is the condition of the synagogue of the Nazarenes in the first years of the Christian era. We are to have no trade in the country which is not inspired solely by the idea of rendering unselfish social service. We are to have no patriotism which may in any way offend the brethren of other nations. The tremendous differences, the infinite differences, which now exist by reason of climate, blood, and history between nation and nation are to be overcome by a universal acknowledgment that we are all sons of God, and therefore heirs of eternal life. Mr. Ramsay MacDonald, one may say without offence, has never loved his country.

Mr. Baldwin, on the other hand, cherishes the faith of John Milton that the Creator of the universe has a particular mission for the Englishman, and that it will take many centuries before that mission is fulfilled. He believes that individual enterprise is a healthy, and may become a noble force in the affairs of mankind. He believes that men are not born equal, that no mechanical arrangement can make them equal, and that out of the inequality of men arise both the drama of existence and the prosperity of human welfare. To him the man of genius is not an enemy of mediocrity, nor an anti-Christ, but the captain of human progress, the elder brother of those who lag behind. Further, he believes that the whole purpose of creation with man, "a creature most dear to God," is to render him a free being, not an automaton, a free being able to choose right because it is a higher thing than wrong, and to choose self-reliance because it is a nobler thing than servility.

For some distance, with only an occasional quarrel by the way, Mr. Baldwin and Mr. MacDonald can travel very friendlily together; but both of them know very well that presently the road will bifurcate, and that when that point is reached they must inevitably part company. Moreover, both of them know that the road on which they travel is a convenient ambush for assassins. Mr. MacDonald thinks that at any moment Mr. Baldwin may be struck down by a Conservatism impatient of his moderation and suspicious of his sympathy with Labour. Mr. Baldwin thinks that at any moment Mr. MacDonald may be swept away by the brutal forces of anarchy and atheism which are equally impatient of his moderation and suspicious of his sympathy with Conservatism.

It is a part of Mr. Baldwin's work to convince the quiet and just-minded people of this country that while danger exists at every moment the point has not yet been reached where the road of progress bifurcates. He does not believe that any good is to be served by frightening, or attempting to frighten, the common people of the British Islands. He has small faith in political campaigns and mass meetings which make the welkin ring with their cheers. Those things pass and are forgotten. It is an element of his faith in the good judgment of the British people that they tire of spell-binders and fire-eaters, and give their serious attention only to a man who has convinced them of his seriousness and his moral goodness.

He thinks it would be a right thing for Conservatives in the country to fight the soap-box Communist, and to keep fighting him all the time; but he does not think that any high and lofty purpose is to be served by nagging at the present Government in the House of Commons. He is not in the least averse from a fight; indeed, he is always heartened and inspired by the clash of conflict; but it must be a real fight, no sham manœuvre, and a fight in which a man may lose his life with neither shame nor regret. In no other fight will this authentic Englishman draw his sword. He is essentially a captain of the people, not the conspirator of a party.

His indifference to attacks upon his leadership

springs from no immodesty, but from the feeling that
the great body of Conservative opinion wishes him to
carry on. He will be quite ready to go when what is
best in the party points to the door—that door which
leads for him to the blossoms of Worcestershire and the
sight of the ploughman coming over the hill. But, as
for these base and unscrupulous attacks from men of
no moral character, he puts them aside with contempt.
Such men, he tells you with a smile, are the degenerate
descendants of the old robber barons, and if they had
any real pluck they would now be leading murderous
expeditions into heathen territories, or attempting to
usurp the power of the Crown; but, lacking pluck,
they seek to gain their commercial ends by the methods
of footpad and apache. "There has always been that
type of person; politics has always had that species of
assassin." He sees in the Clydesiders this same per-
sistence of type, but with a noble difference. "They
are the old Covenanters; vehement men dominated by
one idea; I like many of them, and all of them, I think,
though they would gladly slay me and my friends,
would not in the least object themselves to be slain for
their cause. They are wrong-headed, but they are not
black-hearted."

It is urged against him by his critics that he is
ignorant of the rules of procedure in the House of
Commons, and does not often enough arouse the enthusiasm of his party by sudden raids into enemy terri-

tory.   He is thought to be a little lethargic and a good deal too easy-going and indulgent.   Even some of those who most reverence him, and indeed have told me warmly that they love him, complain that he does not inspire the party in the House of Commons with that hot and gallant fighting spirit which is essential to a vigorous and conquering Opposition.

In the light of these criticisms I see Mr. Baldwin as something new in the political life of this country.   To no Leader of an Opposition has any Government ever given more opportunities to strike a fatal blow.   At every point—unemployment, housing, and reparations —the Government is vulnerable.   A fool could make them look ridiculous; a bantam weight could knock them out.   If he wished, Mr. Baldwin might very easily establish an enviable reputation as a Rupert of debate.   He might be the hero of a "Scene in the House" every day that House is sitting.   His wit might be the talk of the clubs, and his onslaught the delight of the street.   But he neither taunts nor strikes.   In some ways he appears even anxious to cover up his opponents' mistakes and to help them over difficulties.   What is his purpose?   Is it laziness, or is it guile?   Is it cowardice, or is it a Disraelian strategy?

These questions imply that Mr. Baldwin is a poli-tician of the nature of Mr. Winston Churchill or Mr. Lloyd George.   They might also imply that he is in politics solely to get office, and that he desires office solely to enjoy power. These questions, then, which seem so natural, cannot be answered, because they have no reference at all to Mr. Baldwin's character. To understand why he is not for ever rattling his sabre and hurrahing on his legions one must consider why he is in Parliament, and ponder his definition of a statesman.

From my knowledge of the man I am bold to say that he is in Parliament for no other purpose under heaven than to do his duty as an Englishman, and that his definition of a statesman would be "a politician who tries to do the Will of God."

It is difficult to write of these things. We have all decided not to speak of our innermost feelings, not to open the door to our neighbour and show him where we truly live. We mask our religion. We throw a cloak over our reality. Everything tends to become a pretense. "You ask me if I am going to *The Masquerade?* I am at it: *circumspice.*" Nevertheless one must endeavour to say that the guidance in Stanley Baldwin's life is far other than the guidance of party whips, and that the voice to which he listens most attentively is not the voice of the party organiser.

This man would utterly scorn to strike an opponent merely because he is an opponent. To hearten his followers or to heighten his own reputation as a leader, he would never kick a man who is on the ground. If the

Conservative Party should call for such a leader, he would go into retirement. For him, watching Labour in its appalling difficulties, and heartily desiring the hour for a fair fight and a fight to the death, the main business of his thoughts is to get, not a party victory in the House of Commons, but greater and greater numbers of the working-classes of the country into the ranks of an inspired Conservatism. And he cherishes the hope that it may be in the destinies of Providence that he should win for an enlightened Conservatism this confidence of the self-respecting workers of the country, and that at the head of such a disciplined and self-respecting party he should be able to bring Capital and Labour to a good understanding, and live to see the prosperity of his country established on foundations which nothing can shake—the British Empire the greatest power in the world for peace, justice, and virtue.

In some of the chapters which follow, particularly that which deals with the ideas of Mr. Neville Chamberlain, the reader will be able to see what Mr. Baldwin understands by the phrase an enlightened Conservatism; in this place I have sought only to leave upon his mind the impression which Mr. Baldwin makes upon mine, and upon the minds of those who are nearest to his confidence and best acquainted with his character. It is important, I think, that the country should be thoroughly acquainted with the nature of his mind.

He is a man of the most impressive and beautiful selflessness—a selflessness, as one of his colleagues said to me, almost childlike in its unconscious beauty. He is not a brilliant man, nor is the force of his character to be compared with some of those who are ready to supplant him; but there is nevertheless in the depth and composure of his spiritual life a power which is certainly greater than talent and a fire which, if it misses the magic of genius, at least escapes its instabilities.

He makes mistakes. He misses opportunities. He lacks the commercial cleverness of the professional politician. But he dreams a great dream, follows a true light, and his heart is clean. I do not know any other man in public life more likely to keep the respect of quiet people or to gain the faithful confidence of the steadier elements in the working-classes.

But he is not a good advertiser, and a powerful section of the Press is naturally determined to destroy him; therefore, if Conservatism means to maintain him as the captain of its fortunes, it is essential that the rank and file should take exceeding pains to acquaint democracy with the nature of his qualities and also with the character of his aims.

Loyalty, discipline in the ranks, and a great unselfish purpose animating the whole army, these are essential to Conservatism if it would unmask the real purpose of Labour, and render itself independent of a Press which has become a danger to the country.

SIR ROBERT HORNE

THE RT. HON. SIR ROBERT HORNE, P.C., G.B.E., K.B.E.

Born 1871 in Sterlingshire, Scotland. Educ. in Edinburgh College and in the University of Glasgow. President of the University Conservative Club, 1891. Ewing Fellowship, 1894. Lecturer in University College, North Wales, 1895. Examiner in Aberdeen University, 1896–1900. Member of Scottish bar, 1896. Conservative candidate for Sterling, 1910. Lieut. Col. Royal Engineers and Inspector General of Transportation, 1917. Director of Department of Materials in the Admiralty, 1917. Director of Labor Committee in the Admiralty, 1918. Third Civil Lord of the Admiralty, 1918. Minister of Labor, 1919. President of the Board of Trade, 1920–21. Grand Officer of the Crown of Italy. Director of the Suez Canal Company and of the Great Western R. R. Co. Lord Rector of Aberdeen University, 1921. Member of Parliament for the Hillhead Division of Glasgow, 1918–24. Vice Chairman of Baldwin Ltd., 1871–. Clubs: Carlton, Travellers, Garrick and Conservative.

RT. HON. SIR ROBERT STEVENSON HORNE

II

SIR ROBERT HORNE

Variety is the mother of enjoyment.—DISRAELI.

Go in anywhere, Colonel!   You'll find lovely fighting along the whole line.—PHILIP KEARNY.

IT has been said of Sir Robert Horne that he is a man without enemies. The gaiety of his nature and the sincerity of his mind disarm antagonism. He is Bertie Horne to a vast number of people. Even the Clyde-siders are attracted to him. On one occasion they took his advice concerning a bill and trooped after him into the Division lobby, the chief of them exclaiming, "We have formed a new party, and Sir Robert is our leader!"

He reciprocates this friendly feeling. He is one of those solidly built and big-boned men who rejoice in life and are as mentally alert and as physically active as the lighter or more volatile order of human beings. He makes one think of a runner at the starting-point, on his toes and crouching towards the ground. He laughs with his whole body and smiles with his whole face, but the mind is never unstrung nor the intellect off its guard.   It is characteristic of his personality that with the largest and most generous ideas of hospitality, he does not smoke: smoking, he tells you, is the only virtue he has failed to acquire.   His actions are also characteristic: he walks swiftly, the head carried high, the neck pressed hard against the back of his collar.   The face is large and solid, the brow low and dense, the eyes quizzical, the skin stretched tight over the bone, the mouth humorous.   His reddish hair tends to grow thin, but otherwise there is something boyish and even mischievous in his appearance; 1871, he will tell you, was a good vintage.

There is one man in the House of Commons, I venture to think, who does not like this glad-hearted and brilliant brother Scot, and for whom it would be impossible, on Sir Robert Horne's part, to entertain such kindly and indulgent feelings as characterise his relations with, let us say, Mr. Neil McLean and Mr. J. R. Clynes, or Mr. J. H. Thomas and Mr. Maxton.   The man to whom I refer is the Prime Minister, Mr. Ramsay MacDonald.

This discordance, if I am right in thinking it exists, is not due to any accident of temperament, but is fundamental to the real life of each man.   It is spiritual. Sir Robert Horne is a philosopher, not a demagogue; he is a man of action, not a visionary.   Life has hammered and shaped him into a formidable person. He has toiled, he has suffered, and he has been frustrated in spite of his laughter and his jests. While Mr. Ramsay MacDonald was labouring to acquire the emotional support of democracy, Sir Robert was labouring to equip his mind with knowledge. Born in a Scotch manse, of a family which gave many ministers to the Church of Scotland, and with no financial security of any kind in his youth, no promise of powerful influence in his early manhood, he contrived, by means of scholarships earned entirely by his own intense studies, to complete a brilliant education at the University, to become the friend of those two great brothers John and Edward Caird, and to establish an honourable reputation at the Scottish Bar.

These toilsome days left no black mark on the man's mind. A more cheerful person it would be difficult to find. Even when he is speaking most seriously, and with the whole weight of his personality behind the words, one observes those first movements of laughter which break up the firmness of a face and splinter the hardness of intent eyes into the light of smiles. For the most part his intercourse is full of anecdote, quotation, and a genial persiflage; but occasionally the left eyebrow goes up half an inch above its fellow, the stone-grey eyes search the eyes of his companion, and the pleasant friendly voice becomes stern and destructive. There are certain things he hates. I have heard him find generous excuses for men I heartily dislike and for actions I regard as unpardonable; but I have also heard him deliver judgment on traitors to their country and I am in no doubt as to the power of his scorn.

For the sake of his country, and on the threshold of fortune, Sir Robert abandoned the Bar, came to White-hall, rendered the State great service at a moment of the gravest political crisis, and, when the Conservative Party was defeated at the last election, carried his talents into business and began to build up afresh a new career. He never complained. He is perfectly content with his present lot. He is satisfied because he is enlarging his knowledge.

From his boyhood he has been a Conservative. He is a Conservative now, not by prejudice, but by conviction. His whole intellect has examined, endorsed, and accepted the Conservative thesis. He believes it to be not only the most natural faith for strong and self-reliant men, but the most fruitful and the safest faith for a vast democracy. In his eyes, Socialism is something much more perilous than an example of muddleheadedness; it is one of the most destructive delusions that ever vitiated human judgment. With sympathy and with indulgence he can see men of the type of Mr. J. H. Thomas and Mr. J. R. Clynes exhibiting themselves before the public as apostles of a new age; but I do not think that he has any sympathy with the furtive mind of Mr. Ramsay MacDonald, nor that he looks with anything but the most watchful distrust on the internationalism and communism of that hard and secret brain. Mr. Snowden seems to figure in his judgment as a pedant, like Mr. Sidney Webb; but something surreptitious and evasive in Mr. Ramsay MacDonald, who is by no means popular with his own party, effectually prevents, in my judgment, the approach towards him of any sympathy on the part of Sir Robert Horne.

Of the character and the strategy of Mr. Ramsay MacDonald I shall speak with some fulness in the conclusion to this book; but I should like the reader to keep in his mind, while he follows my exposition of Sir Robert Horne's Conservatism, the thought that it is the masked internationalism and the hidden communism of Mr. Ramsay MacDonald which inspire Sir Robert Horne with the greatest possible antagonism towards the Labour Party.

What is the meaning of Conservatism to this son of a Scotch manse, who has made his own way, through scholarship, to a life of the most vigorous and far-spread activity?

It stands in his judgment for the political expression of that humane sentiment which has always, in a greater or less degree, characterised the social and domestic life of men of our race. It is a continuance and an extension of that neighbourliness which moved the landowner, even when he could not afford to repair his fences, to pension his workpeople and to find cottages for their widows. The old Tory was a man who did things for individual people, tried to make life better for them, kept in friendly touch with them, and whose relations with them improved and deepened as refinement grew and the moral sanctions were more clearly discerned.

These men, let us remember, created the incomparable beauty of the English countryside and were more responsible than any other men in the land for giving to English character that robust sturdiness, that genial good nature, and also that lovable tenderness which have manifested their sterner side on so many battle-fields, in so many encounters on the sea, and also in the heroic work of pioneering through the length and breadth of the British Empire. There was something Shakespearean about those men, and what radiance now persists in our dark and troubled industrial existence shines mainly from their tradition.

In politics, the sentiments of these people expressed themselves in doing things for the people. Their opponents, the Liberals, did not want to do things for the people, but to alter the structure of the State. The Conservatives stood for the common people; the Liberals for the economics of practical manufacturers. The Conservative sentiment of humaneness was outraged by the sight of workhouse children packed in waggons journeying through the countryside to the factories in Lancashire. The Liberals replied that to interfere with economic law amounted to blasphemy, and proceeded to attack the Church. The Conservative grew angry when he heard of women in coalpits, chained to trucks and dragging them through the tunnels; such a thing was monstrous and inhuman in his eyes. The Liberal answered that these things were a part of necessity, and agitated for an extension of the franchise.

All the confusions which we inherit in our national life have descended to us from the days of the Industrial Revolution. That vast change in English life was made at a time when Pitt was absorbed in saving Europe from the tyranny of Napoleon. He and his Tories could not give their attention to the domestic situation, and when Castlereagh and Canning were reaping the harvest of Pitt's genius they found that the sheaves of European victory were thick with English tares. It was not until a great English gentleman, Lord Shaftesbury, lifted up his voice in the cause of suffering and unhappy people that Conservatism roused itself to grapple with the economic chaos. At that first movement of Conservatism towards its historic duty, Liberals of the type of Cobden and Bright raised the standard of non-interference with trade, and all the legislation of Conservatives for a reform of the factories met with the bitterest hostility from Scripture-quoting Liberals. It should never be forgotten by the nation that in the darkest days of the Napoleonic menace the Radicals "tried to magnify Wellington's strategic retreats, especially after Talavera, into routs, and were always hoping something would happen to dash down the fortunes of the Wellesley brothers, even though that something involved the ruin of their country." The same spirit which existed at that time, and is openly confessed to by Creevey, existed during the Crimean War, the South African War, and the war with Germany.

The political duel of Victorian times was between an aristocratic and agricultural Conservatism which championed Labour and heartily disliked and distrusted the commercial middle classes, and a Liberalism which had no feeling of any kind for the unhappy and the poor, but an exuberant enthusiasm for tree trade in labour and raw materials. Conservatism wished to help people and to humanise industrial conditions, but did not wish to surrender its political power. Liberalism believed in giving the people a limited power, but leaving the laws of political economy to be interpreted by the manufacturer in the interest of the trade and commerce of the country.

The historic basis of Conservatism is a close, human, and individual sympathy with Labour; the historic basis of Liberalism is a passion for abstract ideas.

The Conservative was always the practical man in politics. The Liberal was always the doctrinaire. The

Conservative stood for reverence and authority; the Liberal for scepticism and dissent.

Disraeli did nothing new. His work lay in reviving the Conservative tradition. He did not create a Tory democracy; he awakened a Tory party that had fallen asleep and during its sleep had allowed the Liberals to steal its thunders.

Knowledge of these historic facts is necessary to a rightful understanding of the present situation. The Grand Army of Liberalism has disappeared. The Falstaff at present in charge of its tattered banners can no longer raise a ragged regiment to storm either the Church or the House of Lords. It has disappeared because, in attempting to outbid Conservatism, it has itself been outbidden in these days by a new party, the party of Socialism.

And what is Socialism? While denying the individual liberty for which Liberalism stands, it is as doctrinaire in its theory and as little practical in its policy. It, too, has no genuine and individual sympathy for poor people, and it, too, believes that the true reformer is he who effects structural alterations. Liberalism is hoist with its own petard. "You would disestablish the Church," says the Socialist, "you would abolish the House of Lords; you would tax industry in order to befriend the workers in their broken and dispirited old age; such things are fit only for higglers and pedlars; behold, we intend to make a clean sweep of the whole basis on which your crazy structure stands: no more tinkering will be needed, for we are going to sweep away capitalism, we are going to sweep away private enterprise, and we are going to sweep away every vestige of individualism. Mount your soap-box and attempt to outbid us!"

Something of the same taunt is being levelled against Conservatism, yet in kinder tones, for the politician of Labour has affection and respect for the Conservative, but nothing save contempt for the Liberal. "You think," says the Socialist, "that you can improve human life by strengthening all those incentives of individualism which are more responsible than anything else for the hideous dreariness of manu-facturing cities, for the wholesale degradation of human life which you profess to deplore, and for all those incessant wars which are inevitable in a world of selfish greed. Come into the open, and tell the people, who suffer terrible things under the present system, whether you are not the champion of the capitalist and the ground landlord."

The problem must be faced if it is to be solved. To sketch out a rival programme is merely to turn the back upon the difficulty. Sir Robert Horne, for one, is dead against any such procedure. He would not have the Conservative Party appearing in the market-place as a cheapjack of millennium, attempting to outbawl the Socialist. He would rather recall the party to a study of its traditions, and revive in its soul a new enthusiasm for the historic articles of its faith.

The great danger of the present situation, as he sees it, is the success with which Socialism is meeting in its tactic of moderation. It is attempting by moderation and good works to create confidence for itself in the unsuspicious minds of the middle and lower classes, biding its time like a skilful general to strike the blow against a lulled and apathetic democracy which will shatter the present basis of society. It is not a party of moderation; it is a party using moderation for intemperate ends.

Will the people of this country be deceived? If they are, the fault will lie at the door of the Conservative Party. Liberalism has gone down, not fighting, but crying for sixpences from its supporters. Only Conservatism, the historic friend of the poor, the historic champion of English character, the historic builder of the British Empire, stands between an apathetic democracy and those who would ruin it for a doctrine. What is it doing, this great historic party, to fulfil its mission?

Sir Robert Horne would like to see among the rank and file of the party throughout the country the same enthusiasm for Conservative principles as that which sends the volunteer missionary of Socialism into the streets of great cities and even into the villages of the countryside. He does not think it necessary for such apostles to be armed with a programme. He quite agrees that the politician cannot live on negatives, and that to be anti-this and anti-that does not cut much ice; but he holds that an assertion and a re-assertion of Conservative principles is in fact an active and positive effort, and that it is far better to make this assertion than to attempt to outbid in detail the millennial promises of the Socialist. A programme may be stated; it exists in outline at the present moment; but the main business of the Conservative is to convince the individual in every walk of life that Labour is Communism masquerading as a mild Socialism, and a Communism which will do nothing to increase British trade, nothing to develop the British Empire, but, on the contrary, will do everything to reduce this country to the condition of Russia.

To attack Socialism root and branch, in the opinion of Sir Robert Horne, is to make manifest at the same time the policy of the Conservative Party. The Conservative does not love the Russian Bolshevik and the German Communist more than his brothers in Canada and Australia. He does not look with anger and vexation of heart on the activities of the creative mind in commerce. He believes, on the contrary, that unless there is a wide freedom for the exceptional man, and complete confidence for the investing public, the wealth of the country will dwindle, the condition of the poor will become desperate, and all the promise of the

British Empire will depart. He is a man who seeks to multiply wealth until it is sufficient for the needs of the human race, not to divide and subtract the obviously insufficient wealth of the present time. He believes, further, that effort and struggle are essential to the health of the mind, and that a nation of spoonfed, slavish communists, living under the tyranny of an academic bureaucracy, would lose its self-respect, as well as its prosperity, and would soon definitely cease to be British.

Few men in the country could better lead a campaign of this character than Sir Robert Horne. He was in charge of the Ministry of Labour when there were something like 2,000,000 disillusioned, embittered, and unemployed soldiers in the midst of a country exhausted by the nervous strain of the war and impoverished by a merciless taxation. The history of those days has never been written. Sir Robert Horne, I think, is the only man who could write it with full knowledge of the facts. It would be a book to startle many people. He has sometimes spoken to me of those tremendous days. "What issues we had to decide! And how quickly! When I read that Disraeli would spend sometimes two months in preparing a single speech, I am inclined to wonder if we are not separated from that period by centuries instead of decades."

To him also fell the lot of fighting the miners'

strike. He proved himself in that titanic struggle a statesman of the greatest wisdom and the highest courage. He stood firm against all his critics, those of his own household as well as those of the enemy, and he stood firm and unconquerable against the organised forces of the miners. America watched that struggle as well as England, and Sir Robert's victory was hailed over there as the first definite step from the insane finance of war to the only sane finance which could re-establish industry on a normal and healthy basis.

It is important to know that Sir Robert Horne fought that great battle with no enmity in his heart towards the miners. He fought it solely for the sake of the community. He knew that wages had to come down, and that unless manufacturers could obtain coal at a reasonable price there would be no wages at all for men in other trades and for unemployed soldiers returned from the War. It was because he was fighting for the community that he was able to withstand the grim determination of Mr. Robert Smillie, the fidgeting statistics of Mr. Frank Hodges, and the clamour of nervous politicians for peace at any price.

The parish of Sir Robert Horne's birthplace was the centre of a mining community and he brought to the task of negotiation a complete and intimate knowledge not only of the conditions under which miners work, but also of those in which they live.

When he was being accused sometimes of callousness

and total ignorance of the miners' lot, he was the last
to be unmindful of the hard and sordid conditions
in which so many colliers are condemned to spend
their days. His heart is not worn on his sleeve; he
has no such talent for emotional appeals as Mr. Robert
Smillie possesses; but he can find many better excuses
for the violence and the bitterness of the poor ignorant
collier and his overburdened wife than for the affected
sympathy with which the agitator approaches them in
order to exploit their personal sorrows for his own
political ends.

Much of the talk at the manse concerned colliers.
His father was a man of wide sympathies and hard
horse sense, and set himself to see what could be done
for the improvement of the miners' lot. As far back
as the 'seventies the old minister pointed out that the
volumes of steam for ever being wasted at the pithead
might be turned to the labour of heating baths and
drying clothes for the miners, so that they could return
to their cottages clean and refreshed after the day's
work. It was an unlucky chance for Mr. Robert
Smillie and Mr. Frank Hodges, both able men for whom
Sir Robert has respect, that in the days of the greatest
strike on record they had to deal with a man, not only
strong in the conviction that it was his bounden duty
to serve the community and not truckle to a section, but
a man who knew almost as much about the life of a
collier as they themselves.

That such a man is a tower of strength to Conservatism needs no argument. The interesting question is whether he can yet afford to give up the time which is necessary for the pursuit of politics. He is a director of the Suez Canal, of Lloyds Bank, of the Commercial Union Assurance Company, and vice-chairman of Baldwin's. His personal correspondence is world-wide. It occupies two hours of every day before he gets to his administrative duties. And it is absorbingly interesting.

He has been a professor of philosophy and could have been happy enough lecturing on Aristotle and Kant for the rest of his days. He has been an extremely successful advocate at the Scottish Bar, and could have been well content to follow that career to its honourable and dignified conclusion. He has been a minister of state, and at this moment has as large a following in the House of Commons as almost any other man. But the splendid life of creative commerce—commerce which reaches out to all nations and permeates in a thousand ways the destinies of the human race—offers opportunities to his mind for dreams and for action which he finds it hard to refuse.

Nevertheless the need to unmask the dishonest moderation of the Labour Government, and to fight conspiring Socialism with all the energy and trained thinking power of the nation, presses on his mind. He is pulled in this direction and in that. His great physical strength, his inexhaustible nervous energy, and the extraordinary rapidity with which his mind works, enable him for the present to take his part in both fields of action with conspicuous success. But the day cannot be far when he will have to decide for one or the other, and though his patriotism is strong and his love of politics is powerful enough, I am inclined to think that for the present at least he will decide for commerce. One thing only would be strong enough to change this current in his life, and that would be any sign of weakening or weariness in the ranks of Conservatism.

MR. EDWARD WOOD

THE RT. HON. EDWARD FREDERICK
LINDLEY WOOD

Born in Ripon, Yorks, April 16, 1881. Son and heir of the Viscount Halifax. Educ.: Eton and Christ Church, Oxford. Fellow of All Souls, Oxford. Under-secretary for the Colonies, 1921–22. President of the Board of Education, 1922–24. M.P., 1910–24. Major in the Yorkshire Dragoons. Clubs: Carlton, Brooks's.

RT. HON. E. F. L. WOOD, P.C.

III

MR. EDWARD WOOD

He was what a man should be to a woman ever; gentle, and yet a guide.—DISRAELI.

Conservatism has the colleges, the castles, the gardens, the traditions, the associations, the fine names, the better manners, the poetry; Dissent has the dusky brick chapels in provincial by-streets, the names out of Dickens, the uncertain tenure of the h *and the poor* mens sibi conscia recti. *Differences which in other countries are slight and varying, almost metaphysical, as one may say, are marked in England by a gulf.*—HENRY JAMES.

. . . he was one of those who cannot but be in earnest; whom nature herself has appointed to be sincere.—CARLYLE·

WHEN I say to people that Edward Wood seems to me the highest kind of Englishman now in politics, many of them look surprised and perplexed. "Edward Wood?" they question; and one can see in their eyes the effort of the memory to attach this name to some sensational event in Parliament or some haunting paragraph in the newspapers. "He is the son of Lord

49

Halifax," I explain. The trouble clears from their faces. "Oh, yes; of course; that extreme High Church-man." "He was Minister for Education in the late Government," I continue. The trouble returns. "Oh, was he!" they say, and dismiss Mr. Wood as a nonentity, and me as a pedant or a poseur.

But I have never had this opinion of Edward Wood challenged in the House of Commons. Men of all parties recognise in his personality something which is admirable, something which distinguishes him from other men. Even those who do not share his political opinions readily pay their tribute to the range of his intellect and the graciousness of his character; more remarkable still, even those whose intellectual qualities are the equal of his, but whose moral qualities have degenerated in contact with the sordid atmosphere of politics, never speak of him with an affected amuse-ment as a religious bigot or a narrow-minded moralist; in the remarks of these latter politicians I often detect a tone of rather wistful regret, as if they were conscious in themselves of a loss for which the world they have gained has by no means compensated.

I call Edward Wood the highest kind of Englishman now in politics for the following reasons. He is a man whose life and doctrine are in complete harmony with a very lofty moral principle, but who has no harsh judg-ment for men who err and go astray. He is a scholar of real distinction, but his sympathies with ignorant and

half-educated mankind are both generous and affectionate. He has a most gentle and attractive sense of
humour, but there is no derision in his words, and no
unkindness in his smile. He is profoundly convinced
of the truth of one form of the Christian religion, but
he is as profoundly interested in the good work of
men who represent quite different forms of that religion.
He is wise, reflective, careful of his words, and unemotional in his public utterances, but he has a warm and
cheerful admiration for the effective gab of a genuine
spell-binder. He believes without one shadow of doubt
that Conservatism is the truest and most enduring form
of politics, but he can see the good that is in Labour,
and in the sorrows and sufferings of the depressed
classes he can perceive at least some excuse for the
wild words of the extremists.

Like his friend Algernon FitzRoy, Edward Wood,
who is only forty-three years of age, is six feet three
inches in height, but holds himself with none of the
rigidity of the Life Guardsman. It is difficult to think
of him as a major in the Yorkshire Dragoons, or as
hunting a pack of harriers at his home, or going out
across the moors with a gun and a dog.

He has something of the priest-like, boyish look of
the Cecils, and is of a rather dusty and untidy appearance, as though he lived chiefly among books and was
entirely careless of practical matters. Under a strong
forehead the large eyes are set deeply in the face and

look out upon life very quietly and entirely unexcitedly, with as much humour as sweetness, as much tolerance as earnestness, as much kindness as seriousness. The large and flexible mouth which is above all other things critical, expresses also good humour and friendship; never does it harden into severity or become firm and oppugnant with self-aggression. The face is self-evidently that of a grave, scholarly, and kindly man, whose wisdom is gentle, and whose sympathies are sincere.

Before the Conservative Government fell, and before Labour had given any indication that it would use moderate courses if it came into power, I was one night talking to Mr. Wood in his private room at the House of Commons about the manners and methods of the Labour Opposition. He said to me then: "Labour at present seems wanting in appreciation of the values of loyalty and discipline. Some of them say to me quite openly, 'Our troubles will begin when we get into power,' and 'Ramsay is the only man who can hold our crowd together.' Many of them are disorderly. Many seem to me essentially violent-minded. I do not think they find it easy to see any great question in its true proportions. Relativity would appear to have no meaning for them!"

But he added to these remarks, which were uttered without any unkindness at all, "Nevertheless, I am very glad that the point of view which these men represent is articulate in Parliament. Our debates are richer for their presence. Not all of us are as near to the sufferings of the working-classes as they are. Sometimes I think we are like people listening to a band with wool in our ears; we hear, but the music comes to us muffled, seems to us remote, and does not really penetrate to our souls. These men, however misguided they may be in their opinions, and however violent they may be in publicly expressing them, do, all the same, bring home to the House of Commons the gravity of our social problems and the importance of getting fundamental things right.

"For example, much of the money we spend on education, believing that we solve the greatest of our political problems by this expenditure, is wasted. We have come to see that education is only one instrument of reform, and that it must be used in conjunction with housing reform if it is to give us a higher order of citizen. And we have also come to see that it must be more closely linked up with employment. This is to say, we shall never get value for the money we spend on education until the people live in better houses and are assured of regular employment. The whole atmosphere of their lives must be changed."

On that same occasion he told me that he had no fear of a Labour Government. The House of Commons, he said, had taught him that in all men there is something good, just, and straight. In spite of many symptoms of materialism in the present generation, he believes that goodness is still the mark to which humanity is pressing. Among the Labour men he told me he had found few who thought more of cleverness than of character. However wildly they may express themselves in public speeches the majority of them acknowledge goodness as the highest thing in human life.

"There is something genial, too," he said, "about the judgments of the best of them. They seem to think, for example, that Lloyd George is a good argument for the doctrine of purgatory; he is not fit for the society of the elect, but not quite bad enough to burn permanently!"

At the present time Mr. Wood regards Labour more with pity than with anger. Its difficulties are great; in a few months they may be prodigious. He watches Mr. Ramsay MacDonald with a certain amount of sympathy. But he thinks that Conservatism is justified in criticising Labour with severity—and he is quite sure that the country will not recover from its present dangerous condition of uncertainty and drift until a strong and powerful Government is formed determined to rule the country and develop the Empire on the principles of Conservatism.

His definition of Conservatism is simple and convincing. It stands in his mind for an evolution of the social order as thorough and as peaceful as the evolution of nature. It is, moreover, not a mechanical nor a materialistic evolution, but a moral and spiritual evolution. The end of everything it does is the moral and spiritual nature of man. It is not a policy of mere expediency, but a definite thesis of life in action. It believes in confidence and security because trade cannot flourish without those conditions; and it desires trade to flourish, not for the enrichment of manufacturers and speculators, but because a flourishing trade is necessary for the revenues of the State and the personal welfare of the population; and it seeks revenues for the State and the personal welfare of the population because these things are necessary to the evolution of man's moral and spiritual nature.

There is now, he thinks, no stationary party in the State. "After the experiences of the last five years," he said in 1919, "men no longer fear new departures any more than one who has been torpedoed in mid-Atlantic would shrink from being capsized on his garden pond." Men in general, he thinks, now recognise that stagnation is not stability, and that "every minute is a journey." The dispute between them is over the character of movement. What movement in politics is towards better things, and what movement is either a movement aside or a movement backward? Socialism, in his view, is a movement clearly backward, for it involves the suppression of individuality, the curtailment of personal freedom, and the sacrifice of a great and noble body of national tradition on the jerry-built altar of an utterly untried Internationalism.

Life as he sees it is a continuous struggle between the soul and the law, or, politically speaking, between the individual and the State. The object of a wise political system must be to strike a true balance between the personal rights of the individual and those of the society of which he is a member. A State cannot be healthy and progressive unless it provides full scope for individual enterprise and individual development; at the same time, an individual who denounced the right of the State to interfere with his liberty would soon fall into moral anarchy. A balance must be struck. The various loyalties of individual life must be linked up and harnessed to a greater loyalty on which ultimately they all depend. These lesser loyalties, he says, valuable as they are as the mainspring of much that is best in human life, become disruptive unless, consciously or unconsciously, they can find a contribution to make to some organism larger than their own.

"In the affairs of the next world the pure individual becomes the gloomy Calvinist, intent only on the importance of saving his own soul. In the affairs of this he becomes the greedy profiteer, intent only on increasing his bank balance without reference to the welfare of his fellows."

The Conservative does not regard the unusual man as an enemy of the State, but as a useful person whose activities must be watched and whose profits may rightfully be taxed for the advantage of his less gifted fellows. He will do nothing to hamper the talents and energy of the unusual man, but at the same time he will not permit any exceptional person, however beneficent his activities, to use his powers in an unsocial manner.

The Conservative does not look upon the Empire either as an encumbrance to the British Isles or as a challenge to other nations. He regards it as a responsibility and as an opportunity. He believes that one of his chief duties to the present generation, and one of the greatest of his responsibilities to those who come after him, is a wise and just development of his tremendous estate. He is convinced that the Empire promises better social conditions at home, a greater and healthier race of English-speaking people for the future, and also by far the most powerful influence for world peace.

No student of history, Mr. Wood has said, can fail to observe the regularity with which, at intervals of a century, the duty has been thrust upon the British race of acting as protagonists in the defence of Europe against one form of tyranny after another. We can hardly believe, he says, that the historical film, of which, so far, the main scenes have been 1588, 1700, 1800, 1914, has been the product of anything but an overriding purpose, of which the final outcome is yet to be seen.

"That the British race in 1914 should have been empowered to play its part in the world struggle must compel the reverent mind to acknowledge with gratitude the heritage of the past that has been the instrument of the present achievement. In this spirit we shall surely seek to preserve all the best of what is old, in order that we may, in years to come, better discharge the duties of the national trusteeship which world events have laid upon us."

This attitude towards the Empire, and towards the moral character of the English people, is characteristic of modern Conservatism. It is an attitude of great firmness, strong courage, and no boastfulness. Nothing in the performances of the Labour Government has so disappointed and troubled Mr. Wood as its attitude towards the Empire. He sees now that Labour, however good its domestic and its foreign intentions, can easily inflict great damage upon this most precious and sacred achievement of British genius. He deeply deplores the break into our inter-imperial relations which Labour has so rudely and so roughly made. He has all the intellectual contempt of a man whose whole life is ruled by great principles, for politicians whose minds are ruled by a shibboleth. He cannot easily imagine how a man of Mr. Ramsay MacDonald's vision is unable to see the benefit to our working-classes of developing the British Empire, nor can he understand how a party, representative of Labour, is unable to see what great danger

they run in flouting the wishes of our Dominions.
The principle of generous co-operation, in his judg-
ment, is vital to the maintenance of the unity of the
Empire.

It is the essence of Conservatism, he says, to assert
the essential unity of all classes and interests, to break
down every barrier of prejudice and ignorance which
prevent comradeship, and to denounce the odious spirit
of class-hatred and sectional antagonism which is working in the country to destroy the freedom of the
individual and the unity of both the nation and the
Empire.

He believes that Conservatism may do much to bring
employer and employed in closer and more har-
monious relations, and that by a comprehensive
scheme of insurance the Conservatives may do a great
deal to relieve the workman of his more pressing
anxieties. He believes that these things can be accomplished by wise and prudent Acts of Parliament, but
he believes that even more important than Acts of
Parliament is a revival of the Conservative spirit in the
nation. From such a revival he looks to see in the
national life a real sense of unity and comradeship, a
real feeling of friendliness and co-operation, a real
conviction that we are a great nation discharging
great duties and bound by great responsibilities.

I once talked to him about the place of religion in
politics. He thinks that, for obvious reasons, Chris-

tianity can never be made the touchstone of a detailed
political policy, but believes that as an attitude
towards the problems of the world it is essential to
right action. The attitude of religion in an employer
makes a good employer, and in a workman a good workman. It is an attitude entirely opposed to greed and
dishonesty; it consecrates energy and sanctifies ambition; it robs commercialism of its ugliness and vul-
garity; it gives grace and beauty to every aspect of
everyday life.

Christianity, he thinks, thus can, and ought to,
exercise a powerful influence on politics; but it not
infrequently fails through a confusion in the minds
of religious leaders between motive and action. The
first can be brought to a spiritual test; the second must
be judged by whether or not it is well calculated to
achieve the desired result. It is clearly the function
of the spiritual leader at all times to insist upon the
moral responsibility of wealth in the face of poverty
or want; but there is no reason to suppose that he
will be a better judge than the statesman of the
wisdom of particular proposals by which the State may
secure that this responsibility is discharged. Thus
to Lazarus the Church may justly say that she offers
him an inward peace and a certain hope which will
enable him to triumph over the social conditions of
his material life; but she must also say to Dives,
"What are you doing to help your brother Lazarus?

How are you using the riches and the powers which are entrusted to you only for a little while?" Too many clergymen, when they see the necessity for this admonition, rush into Socialistic excess, and denouncing Dives with ferocious hatred proclaim an economic gospel which would be disastrous to Lazarus. They do not see that the virtue of the Christian attitude consists in its gentleness and compassion. Hatred is foreign to it. " . . . Though I bestow all my goods to feed the poor, and though I give my body to be burned, and have not love, it profiteth me nothing."

Edward Wood is greatly beloved and trusted by the people among whom he lives, and from his close, personal, and affectionate knowledge of his countrymen he is convinced that the day has not gone past, in spite of all the propaganda of atheism and hate carried on so ceaselessly by Communists, when the people of England can be appealed to in the name of religion and virtue. His faith in their good sense is strong and deep. His admiration for their moral qualities is boundless. A finer people, he holds, is not to be found anywhere under the sun; and to mislead such a people seems to him one of the greatest of sins.

He longs for a better world, and he prays for it. The unhappiness of many poor people, the divisions and separations of our social and political sectarianism, distress him and pain him, but never deject him. He holds firmly to his faith that love and good sense can

deliver man from all the delusions of materialism, and
that a day will come when an England conscious of
comradeship, and a British Empire conscious of unity,
will lead the world into the way of peace.

His great affection for Robert Cecil, apart altogether from his own religious impulse, makes him a
warm friend of the League of Nations; but he is practical and far-seeing, and he would not go the length
in this matter which many of our idealists have already
gone.

"Sometimes," he once said to me, "I wonder where
one can look for a common centre for the world's
loyalty. There was a time when every European
nation acknowledged a common centre for its loyalties
in the Church, and a world peace did not come even
then; now, not only has that common centre ceased to
exist for mankind, but there has been a powerful revival
of nationalism and racialism, and it looks as if we are on
the eve of a new fierceness in commercial competition.
It would be foolish, I think, to expect for some time
any absolute security for a long peace from the League
of Nations. Humanity, one supposes, has far to go
before War can be abolished. But the influence of a
powerful British Empire, in friendly relation with the
United States of America, may at least keep War at bay
until the democracies of the world are on higher
spiritual ground."

Peace is a word not very often on his lips, though

it is the secret of his own heart. But in everything he says one perceives that he is trying to find for mankind a way out of complexity, antagonism, strife, hatred, and confused thinking, so that they may be able to enjoy in their souls those invisible and intangible things of the spirit which are the bread of real life.

"To know Edward," one of his friends said to me the other day, "you must see him among his own people at Garrowby, and get him out on the wolds talking of the things that really count." It must be difficult for such a man, I think, to breathe freely in Westminster or to hold his faith unshaken in London. But few men at Westminster or in London have ever given me so sure a feeling that faith is stronger than circumstance.

MR. NEVILLE CHAMBERLAIN

THE RT. HON. ARTHUR NEVILLE CHAMBER-LAIN

Born 1869. Son of the Rt. Hon. Joseph Chamberlain. Educ.: Rugby, Mason College, Birmingham; Birmingham City Council and Chairman of Town Planning Committee, 1911. Alderman, 1914. Member of the Central Controlling Board for the Liquor Traffic, 1915. Lord Mayor, 1915–16. Director General of National Service, 1916–17. Postmaster General, 1922–23; Paymaster General, 1923. Minister of Health, 1923–24 (in the Baldwin Administration). M.P. for the Ladywood Division of Birmingham since 1918.

© Farrington

COL. SIR NEVILLE CHAMBERLAIN, K.C.B.

IV

MR. NEVILLE CHAMBERLAIN

This city and this country has brought forth many mayors
To sit in state and give forth laws out of their old oak chairs.
          —WILLIAM BLAKE.

To tax the community for the advantage of a class is not
protection; it is plunder, and I disclaim it; but I ask you to
protect the rights and interests of labour generally.—DISRAELI.

A well-employed and prosperous community can buy and
consume. An ill-employed community cannot buy and con-
sume. This is the solution of the whole matter; and the
whole science of political economy has not one truth of half so
much importance as this.—DANIEL WEBSTER.

IN spite of a moustache and no monocle, Mr. Neville
Chamberlain bears a much closer resemblance than
his brother Austen to their famous father, of whom,
like his brother, he is reverentially proud and a most
faithful apostle. The mental resemblance, I think, is
even greater.

One is conscious in him of that reined-in passion
and that restive but controlled scorn of muddy-minded-

67

ness which made private conversation with Joseph Chamberlain so memorable an experience. He has something of the same physical delicacy, something of the same look of fragility, and the dark eyes burn in the ivory-coloured face with something of the same feverish brightness. Taller than his father, more upright and alert, with swifter gestures and a greater direction of mind, the voice has nevertheless that rather husky weariness of tone, however vivid his sentences, which marked the utterance of his father in private discourse, and gave almost a note of pathos to the confidences of his later years.

In one respect I think Mr. Neville Chamberlain excels the virtues of his father, and that the tidiness of his mind. Inflamed as he is by a consuming passion for the British Empire, he is careful all the same to get his political ideas into good order, and to subject every one of his thoughts to a rigorous analysis. Everything in his mind is classified and docketed. His expositions are marked by a convincing lucidity. A thread of logic runs through every sentence to the appropriate conclusion. I have never known him use an incongruous word or in the heat of controversy to loosen his control of his argument. He is a man who has prepared himself for every battle in which he is likely to be involved.

There is something romantic in his sudden appearance on the political stage. The superstitious might suppose that the spirit of his father had intervened to call him from the field of local government to the high places of imperial statesmanship. His coming to Westminster has made a difference, and may well make a greater difference still. Perhaps there is no one now in Parliament, with the exception of Sir Philip Lloyd-Greame, so qualified as he is to convince the country of the wisdom and the promise of his father's ideas; and yet, until the late days of the War, the Empire was scarcely aware of his existence. If he keeps his health, and is encouraged and supported by his colleagues, he may do much during the next few years to revive within the Conservative Party those large notions of our imperial future and those courageous ideas of social reform which both in Disraeli and in Joseph Chamberlain sounded the true note of the Conservative tradition.

He holds that the working-classes of the country are responsive to the imperial sentiment. The imperial relationship, he will tell you, is as real to the poor man as to the rich. The poor man may not have the same exalted vision of the imperial destiny as the educated and the travelled man, but he does feel in his blood that the British Empire is something to be proud of, and he can be made to see that his own happiness and the improvement of his own English circumstances are bound up with the prosperity of the Empire.

It is the first business of the Conservative, he says, to begin his approaches to the confidence of the working-classes on imperial grounds. Let the Conservative not be afraid of the gibe that he uses the Empire in order to distract the workman's attention from the domestic situation; nor let him wince at the accusation of Jingoism. If he is a well-instructed man, if he is a genuine apostle of the imperial destiny, he will know how to turn these ancient taunts to the advantage of his cause. Let him, then, explain at the outset of his approach that he has come to talk to the workman about business, and business which touches his life, and affects his happiness at every point, and then let him proceed to develop his imperial argument.

Take the case of Canada. The people of this country do not yet realise the marvel of our commercial intercourse with that great Dominion. We are separated from it by thousands of miles of ocean. A crate of goods from Sheffield to some of the towns in the Middle West is man-handled again and again, and may take weeks to reach its final destination. The same class of goods might be despatched by rail or motor-lorry from an American city just across the border and be delivered to its consignee in a few hours.

Why is it that the Canadians prefer to trade with us, giving themselves the further trouble entailed by our different currencies? Is there not here a ground of reasonable appeal to the sentiments of our British working-classes? Mr. Chamberlain has travelled in Canada, has addressed great meetings there, and has studied the facts of our commercial dealings with Canadian people. "I can describe the wonder of our trade with Canada," he says, "as nothing less wonderful than making water flow uphill. It is a thousand times more natural, and more reasonable, that Canada should buy what she wants from the Americans, who are most willing to take her wheat; but she goes out of her way to do the unnatural and unreasonable thing, because in her heart she cherishes a sentiment for the British Islands, and because with all her soul she believes in the future destiny of the British Empire. If the people of Canada, the vast majority of them sprung from our working-classes, entertain these sentiments, why should we despair of getting our own working-classes to entertain sentiments of a reciprocating kind?"

He thinks that our working-classes have not yet grasped the significance of colonial preference. In one year the Dominions gave us a preference of over £11,000,000. What does that mean? It means that our people across the sea paid to our people here at home £11,000,000 more than the foreigner would have charged, in order to make sure that they had British goods, which amounted to hundreds of millions of pounds in value.

Does this attitude of the Dominions towards the home country mean nothing to our working-classes?

Cannot they see that it is a good thing for them to have their kinsmen's faces, and not their backs, turned towards the British Islands? Do they not wish to take their part in building up the wealth, power, and domestic happiness of the British Empire? If the Socialist can appeal to them in the name of Russia, surely the Conservative may appeal to them in the name of the British Empire.

Mr. Chamberlain has explained to me why he looks towards the Empire as the main line of our forward march. He desires to see the Empire become greater, more glorious, richer, and more united, because he believes that it is a good thing for the world as a whole that there should be this tremendous commonwealth of freedom-loving and law-abiding nations in its midst, and because England, with no empire, would play only a very poor second fiddle to the United States in the higher tasks of civilisation. If we continue to grow great and strong, he argues, America will respect us, for quite rightly she respects only those countries which are not afraid of greatness; and if she respects us, she will not only co-operate with us in preserving the peace of the world and promoting the best kind of civilisation, but she will be content, helping us generously, to let our people do the main work of world-civilisation for which they have manifested so commanding a genius.

This is one of his reasons for taking the imperial path.

He believes in the British Empire as the greatest conceivable power for good in the general welfare of mankind.

But he has another reason for taking that path, and for taking it at this present moment with all the earnestness and eagerness of his intense nature.

He is a social reformer. He would call himself a Radical, and would not be greatly discomposed if someone called him a Socialist. He believes that every generation is an opportunity for making things better, and that there are conditions in this country crying aloud for reform. In order to make things better for English democracy and to reform those social conditions which impoverish our spiritual life and debilitate our physical life, he wants money, all the money he can get, and in the development of the British Empire he sees the quickest way of obtaining these communal supplies.

"Without a growing trade," he said to me, "there can be no money for social reform. The purse of the State, into which the Socialist thinks he can go on dipping his hand for ever, is filled only by industry. The State spends: it does not earn. Every activity in this nation—religion, science, art, literature, philanthropy—draws its revenue from the co-operating toil of capital and labour. Until democracy grasps this elemental fact of economics, it cannot have even the social reforms it deserves, much less the millennial perfection promised to it by the cranks of politics."

He argues that if we promote imperial consciousness in our democracy, we shall do something to bring Capital and Labour together, and much to increase the prosperity of the country. The Dominions will take our surplus population as well as our manufactures, and, growing swiftly into great nations, will be able to send us everything we need in the way of grain, fruit, and raw materials. Thus, out of the bounding prosperity of British trade, the statesman of Conservatism will obtain his revenues for social reform.

It is interesting to know Mr. Chamberlain's idea of social reform. He begins with Health. The first thing to do, he says, is to improve the physical health of the individual citizen. This enables a man to do his best, and puts him in the way of helping himself. "No social reform that does not do that," he says, "interests me a straw. I want to see our people in such a position that they can do things for themselves."

Health means Housing. He desires the Conservative Party to play a courageous part in housing reform. The citizen should be both encouraged and financially assisted to buy his own freehold. No barriers could so powerfully oppose the flood of communal anarchy as those built by a healthy and a sane democracy of well-housed freeholders out of their own domestic well-being. When he was elected to serve on the Birmingham City Council, the first committees he chose to join were those concerned with health and housing, and he has never lost his enthusiasm for the work accomplished in those years. Much can be done by town-planning, he is convinced, to improve the domestic circumstances, often cruel and always uninspiring, of the working-classes. The State must help, it must help all it can, but its help must take the form of sharing with the individual citizen the cost of his improved circumstances and his greater happiness.

"Fundamental to my politics," he says, "is the conviction that it is the duty of a great State to help its individual citizens to help themselves; and fundamental to all my thinking is the knowledge, gained from experience and observation, that anything which tends to slacken the fibres of self-help and to dope the natural self-respect of a self-relying man is bad for that man, physically and morally, and bad for the State."

There is scarcely a reform, outside the absurdities of Communism, which he is not willing to discuss. His acid test for all the suggestions of the Socialist is the cost involved by the reform and its effect on the trade of the country. He never denounces a man as a Socialist. He examines his ideas. And if the idea is good and reasonable, he asks the Socialist two questions concerning it: How much will it cost?— and, Can the workman afford it?

An example of what I mean may be seen in his treatment of Old Age Pensions. He would limit the benefits only by the cost of the workman's payments, and their effect on the industry in which he is engaged. He would like to see the pension raised to 25s. a week, and come into operation at the age of 65. This can be done with the co-operation of the State if the workman is willing to make a slightly greater sacrifice of his wages. Such a reform, he argues, would carry many advantages. It would remove from the minds of millions the shadow of a sad and sordid fear. It would spread over the whole body of the nation a more vivid notion of the satisfactions of thrift. And it would enable men to enjoy their old age in comfort and peace, while at the same time the younger men came sooner into their kingdom.

He would gladly include widows' pensions in this reform, and he would certainly make these increased pensions utterly independent of the private savings of the insured. He would be concerned only about cost. He would say to the workman, "If you are willing to do your share, the State will do its share. Work it out for yourselves. Consider the blessings and calculate the cost."

He has every reason to believe that the working-classes of the country would willingly put by money for such an advantage, and is convinced that they would cheerfully join with the State in buying their own houses. When he was Lord Mayor of Birmingham he started a Municipal Bank in that city. He was ridiculed and opposed. At the end of the War—and the Act of Parliament only permitted the existence of such banks for the duration of the War—the funds amounted to £300,000. At the end of the War the Corporation took the bank over as a purely local enterprise, and to-day its funds exceed £4,000,000.

During his mayoralty a deputation from the local Trades and Labour Council approached him on the subject of the city's milk supply. He did not refuse to see them. On the contrary, he cordially invited them to lay their views before him. They said that the milk supplied to the city was insufficient in quantity, inferior in quality, and that in price it was prohibitive for many poor mothers with young children.

He asked them for their remedy. They replied "Municipalisation." He asked what they understood by that term. They could not tell him. He asked whether they meant that the City should act as retailer of the milk or wholesaler, or both, or whether they suggested that the city should begin with the cow. They could not tell him. They had not thought the matter out.

Instead of dismissing them with derision, he informed them that he would appoint a commission to go into the matter. He invited them to choose a member for this commission, and he himself nominated the town clerk, who was a first-rate person, and an accountant, who was also a first-rate person.

Before the commission could report, Mr. Chamberlain was dragged off to London on one of Mr. Lloyd George's sudden stunts, and had to break his ties with Birmingham. But it is not at all unlikely that he would have used all his powers and influence, if he had remained in office as Mayor, to give effect to the recommendations of the report, which set forth a bold scheme for the municipalisation of an important part of the trade.

Many Conservatives make a fatal mistake, he thinks, in scouting socialistic suggestions, instead of patiently and scientifically examining them. There is already much Socialism in action and there was more during the War, and the War might have been over sooner if that Socialism had been greater—so great, for example, as to make strikes impossible. In any case, it is quite certain that the future of legislation will see an increasing co-operation between the State and the individual, and the Conservative should gratefully welcome this humane movement and keep it in the healthful channel of self-reliance and self-help.

In what manner does he differ from the more moderate representatives of Labour? He sympathises with many of their ideas, and along a part of their road is ready to march with them; and yet few men in the Conservative ranks are more vigorous and implacable in their political attacks than this well-qualified apostle of social reform.

The reason is extremely interesting. Mr. Neville Chamberlain finds that these men, who appear to be so genial and friendly in the House of Commons, are so used to associating the Empire with Jingoism and Militarism that their first instinct is to reject any proposal which would appear to favour the Empire at the expense of the foreigner. They are not haters of the Empire, but they are devoid of imperial consciousness. They are such enthusiasts for international brotherhood that the imperial brotherhood seems to them a parochial matter. Little Johnny Head-In-Air never went to his doom more oblivious of the solid ground under his feet than these visionaries of millennium.

The McKenna duties were doing no harm to anybody. In the opinion of many able men and many practical people they were of very great advantage to the trade of the country. To leave them as they were would have inflicted not a farthing's worth of inconvenience on any single member of the British nation. To remove them will be quite certain to inflict considerable hardship on the trade of this country. But Mr. Snowden said they must go, and the Labour Party supported him.

If we put ourselves in the place of these men, we shall see how right they are to suspect the Empire, for it is a symbol of successful political power, and a political power built upon the ancient foundations of private enterprise.

Is it to be expected that the wild men of Socialism, who rave against the iniquities of capitalism, will lift a finger to prosper British trade, or hold their hands when they see an opportunity of doing it a bad turn?

Do they desire the prosperity of British trade, or its bankruptcy? Do they desire the unity of the British Empire, or its downfall? The more honest of them make no bones about the matter. They are out to smash the entire fabric of our British civilisation.

I am told that there are Socialists in this country who make it a practice to spit whenever the British Empire is mentioned, and whose intense loathing for the Union Jack can only be restrained from an obscene and blasphemous utterance by hastily pressing into their hands a Red Flag and calling upon them to give three cheers for Lenin and Trotzky. Such men may now be regarded by Mr. MacDonald as a great nuisance, but he will not deny, I think, that his own ultimate political opinions differ from theirs only in the manner of their expression. His motives, I am sure, are entirely different from theirs, but he does share with them a violent antipathy to patriotism and he is as deeply committed as they are to a form of internationalism which confesses that the British Empire is the greatest obstacle to the realisation of its dreams.

It is a strange situation. The British people are governed by a body of men whose ultimate and publicly avowed aim involves the total destruction of their wealth, the total loss of their personal liberties, and the total surrender of their national independence. Therefore the British people are governed by a body of men who will do nothing to increase the prosperity of their trade, nothing to strengthen and consolidate their mighty estates across the sea, and nothing to give them even a just advantage over other nations. It is almost as if we had chosen an enemy to rule over us.

In this light Mr. Neville Chamberlain sees the present problem. He is in Parliament as a representative of all those heroic virtues which have made us a great people, and he is determined, so far as his health and opportunities permit, to wage continued war upon the anti-imperial representatives of international communism. With little of the address and cunning of the old Parliamentary hand, he nevertheless carries in his logical mind a profound knowledge of the art of government, and in his honest heart a deep passion for the British Empire, which render him one of the most forceful and fighting leaders of modern and democratic Conservatism.

Something is lacking in his personality. He does not inspire that grateful affection in the rank and file which is the mark of a powerful leader. Men admire and applaud him, but are not conscious towards him of any loyal enthusiasm. One of his best friends, who greatly admires his intellectual grasp of political problems, said to me, "Neville is a man to die with, but not a man to die for."

All the same, certain good judges see in him a man who is destined to play a noble part in the great struggle which is fast approaching. Lord Grenfell, the venerable Field-Marshal, told me the other day that he never fails to make his way to the Peers' Gallery in the House of Commons when Neville Chamberlain is speaking. "I knew his father intimately," he said; "Neville has many of his qualities. A fine fellow—a very fine fellow."

THE
DUKE OF NORTHUMBERLAND

DUKE OF NORTHUMBERLAND, 8TH DUKE

ALAN IAN PERCY

Born April 17, 1880; eldest surviving son of 7th Duke of Northumberland and Lady Edith Campbell, daughter of 8th Duke of Argyll.

Brev. Lieut. Col., formerly Captain Grenadier Guards. Served South Africa, 1901-2 (Queen's medal, 4 clasps); Soudan, 1908 (Egyptian medal and clasp); European War, 1914-16 (despatches).

THE DUKE OF NORTHUMBERLAND

V

THE DUKE OF NORTHUMBERLAND

Enthusiasm is grave, inward, self-controlled; mere excitement—outward, fantastic, hysterical, and passing in a moment from tears to laughter.—JOHN STERLING.

Madame de Staël says, that the English irritated Napoleon mainly because they have found out how to unite success with honesty.—EMERSON.

There is not less treasure in the world because we use paper currency; and there is not less passion than of old though it is bon ton to be tranquil.—DISRAELI.

IN the eyes of a good many people, "light half-believers of their casual creeds," the Duke of Northumberland figures as a fanatic pure and simple. It is a title not easily to be earned in these days; harder still to be maintained. One who is a genuine fanatic, more especially if born in the purple, deserves our notice and commands our curiosity.

With no moustache, and with a monk's cowl drawn forward over his head, the Duke would bear a remarkable likeness to Fra Bartolommeo's well-known profile of Savonarola. There is great intensity in the brows which seem to be sharpened like a pencil, and in the precise, penetrating, small eyes. The forehead slides forward as if in haste to reach the point of the prominent nose, and from the point of the prominent nose the face slides backward to the neck, tucking itself in, as it were, to leave the beak-like nose full freedom for attack. It is the eagle-like face of an enthusiast; but the bright red hair is clipped close and smoothly groomed to the head, the narrow line of red moustache is trimness itself, the eyes smile very cheerfully, the slightly husky voice is friendly, and not without a tone of amusement, and there is a complete absence of gesture or unrest, or indeed of eagerness of any kind, in the carriage and manner of the body. One thinks of the Duke as an enthusiast, indeed; but as a fanatic tamed and socialised by the traditions of an ancient northern people. He sets one wondering how Savonarola would have fared if he had been to Eton and soldiered in the Grenadier Guards.

Much is to be learned, I think, from a study of the Duke's mind. Indeed, I know of few men in the Conservative Party who can teach the country in one respect a more useful lesson. Narrowness of mind is not always a defect. At least it excludes many wandering and foolish notions which may lead a man, priding himself on his breadth of mind, into the way of destruction. A right kind of narrowness means concentration,

driving power, economy of time and effort. It need
not be pedantic and it certainly need not be crazy. A
right kind of narrowness means an undistracted vision
and a decisive judgment.

The Duke is called a fanatic because he thinks like
a mathematician. That is to say, all his thinking is
governed by certain definite postulates. In his mind
there are a number of fixed principles, and his opinions
have to answer to those principles before they become
a part of his life and doctrine. He does not think in
the air. He does not chase rainbows. He has never
once in all his life taken a Sentimental Journey or
gone wool-gathering on the eccentric hills of caprice.
Life is for him neither a hectic adventure nor a chemist's
laboratory. Enough is already known of its unbreakable and unaltering laws, he considers, to tell any sane
man how he should live and what he should think.
The more it changes the more it remains the same
thing.

You may see how fixed principles govern his mind
if you consider those of his political opinions which
are usually cited, or were cited, to prove him a mere
fanatic.

He has always opposed himself to Irish self-government. Even when a great body of Conservative
opinion was inclined to repent of the party's antagonism to Mr. Gladstone's proposal, the Duke stood absolutely firm in his opposition to any substantial grant

of Home Rule. In this matter, and at that time, it certainly looked as if the Duke was opposing himself to wise and rational progress. He was called a Die-Hard, and earned the annoyed contempt of a great number of intellectual people in all parties.

But the Duke's opposition to Irish self-government was dictated by a fixed principle. He said that in all those things which are essential to good government, the Irish are an inferior race. He said that no evidence existed to prove that they could rule Ireland either well or wisely, and that there was sufficient evidence to convince any impartial mind that they would use Home Rule to attack England and disrupt the Empire.

At that period these views were unpopular. I confess that my own sympathies were with the South of Ireland, which I regarded as a sad but beautiful country filled with a most simple and charming people; while for the hard and industrial North I had little or no sympathy and a good deal of dislike.

But the history of Ireland since those days has surely justified the Duke, and discomfited those of us who regarded him as a fanatic. It is not the history of a civilised country. It is a history of a lawless people. It is a history which would shock even the inhabitants of the Balkans. Perhaps only Turkey could read that history without amazement and shame. And, so far as I can learn, worse is yet to come. Large bodies of the people, who have broken away from the control of the priests, and who are committing sacrilege with a kind of fiendish pleasure, are now working hand and glove with Russia, and have no other passion in their minds than a blind lust for bloodshed and destruction.

It would seem that daily work, thrift, domestic happiness, and kindly intercourse with his neighbours, have no satisfaction for the modern Irishman. Conspiracy is in his blood. The excitements of intrigue, the adventures of secret societies, the dark passion that gives to the assassin a depraved joy, are to him a kind of political vodka. He is not so much a drunkard as a dipsomaniac. It looks as if he could not think of life except as an opportunity for working in the dark against all causes that love the light.

The Duke may be right or he may be wrong in thinking that, for Ireland's own sake, we shall soon have to go into that sorrowful country once again, and there re-establish the structure of civilised government; but even the most embittered of his critics will surely agree that the Irish situation grows worse and not better, that in the lifetime of no grown man is it likely that there will be peace and security in our sister isle.

In the region of our imperial responsibilities the Duke sees everywhere signs of a weakening grasp and myopic vision. To this sworn enemy of political sentimentalism it seems that the present generation is attempting to do by compromise and surrender what our fathers did by strength and courage. He does not believe that Eastern people respect compromise and surrender; he does believe that they understand strength and courage. In his view we are in India, not only for the good of Hindus and Moslems, but for the good of the whole world. The Pax Britannica is a Pax Mundi. So long as we are not stricken by craven fears of being great, and so long as we never surrender the higher moral code of our race to the lower moral codes of inferior races, we shall be exercising an influence in the world against treachery, retrogression, and war; and we shall also be doing something to commend a higher moral standard in public affairs and a more uncompromising form of honesty in private affairs, to races who still regard nepotism as a religious virtue, and trickery, cunning, and chicane as personal accomplishments.

Now, take the case of Russia. The Duke has always held that it is beneath the dignity of a great civilised nation to attempt to enter into any contract of any kind with a people which has publicly denounced, and bloodily destroyed, the foundational things of mankind's moral security. He has also said that such an attempt is impractical. For these opinions, again, he has been most violently abused. The gentlemen who call themselves progressives and intellectuals dismiss

him, with the easy and impertinent contempt of their
order, as a poor ignorant reactionary. But, as I write,
it would look as if the Russian Conference is breaking
down. At any rate, I can discover no note of triumph
in Mr. Ramsay MacDonald's references to these painful
and long drawn negotiations, while surely the answers
of Mr. Arthur Ponsonby to questions in the House of
Commons suggest that he is not as happy as his friends
could wish.

Here again it is a matter of principle outliving easy
sentiment. Principle tells a man that he ought not to
shake hands with murder or enter into a friendly
undertaking with robbery. It tells him that atheism
is the most deadly disease that can attack the mind of
man, and that he who would compromise with so
destructive and contagious an affliction is not only a
fool but a criminal. These things are not loose hypoth-
eses buzzing occasionally, like bees, in the Duke's
bonnet. They are facts, realities, absolutes. He
would not admit into his house a scoundrel not to be
trusted with the silver, or a homicidal maniac not to be
trusted with the children. Nor would he enter
into business relations with a man who refused to
acknowledge those moral sanctions which are taken for
granted by civilised men. It is not a matter of expediency, but a matter of principle. You may drink
beer for fun, but not strychnine; you may play with
fire, if you are careful, but not with T.N.T.

Then there is the case of Germany. The Duke went from Eton and Christchurch, Oxford, into the Grenadier Guards. He was not content to take for the motto of his life the famous line from *The Immortal Hour*, "How beautiful they are, the lordly ones," but gave himself up to a serious study of strategy. He went out to South Africa and to Egypt, and joined the staff of Earl Grey in Canada. It speaks volumes, I think, for the self-determination of his character that loving Albert Grey as he did he was able to resist enthusiasm for that most charming person's numerous ideals. Always he was observing and studying the hard facts of life. A turning-point came in his career when he met Sir Henry Wilson. A friendship grew up between the two men, a friendship founded on intellectual sympathy, and together they made a close and exhaustive study of the European situation.

The Duke became convinced that Germany meant war. He had the boldness to announce the fact in a series of articles. He associated himself with Lord Roberts. He hammered on every door that he could reach, both public and private, and never ceased from a vigorous effort to awaken the nation from its sleep. Again I confess that I was against him, believing that the better elements in Germany might save the situation. I read Mr. H. W. Massingham's articles with high approval. I believed that he knew more than most men on this matter, and I was content to take him for

THE DUCHESS OF NORTHUMBERLAND

my guide. Lord Haldane's attitude seemed to me the right one; prepare for War, say nothing to influence the militarists in Germany, cultivate the good opinion of the peace party.

But, looking back with all the long experience of German mentality since 1918 to guide us, must one not say that the Duke had good reason for warning us, and must one not think that he is perhaps more right than our sentimentalists at the present moment in telling us that the German has not repented, and will strike first at France and then at us on the first opportunity? Again he is guided by principle. The character of the average German fills him with mistrust. He sees in him none of those attributes which are taken for granted in a gentleman. Watch him; but do not treat him as an equal.

The Duke has many good reasons for feeling that he was right in this matter of the German menace; but the intelligentsia still call him a fanatic. Does Mr. Massingham, looking back over the last dozen years, feel that he was a safe guide for the nation? But no one calls Mr. Massingham a fanatic.

Let us now come to the question of our own politics. The Duke opposes himself to Labour because he believes present representatives of that Party are merely the advance guard of an army inspired by the hateful and bestial principles of Bolshevism. No one would say that Mr. MacDonald is a repulsive object, like Trotzky, or that Mr. Clynes is a merciless and odious monster, like Lenin; but not many people say so boldly as the Duke that such men as these are the worst possible enemies of the State because they are, knowingly or unknowingly, the agents of a Bolshevist despotism.

He refuses to regard the Labour Party as a party of moderation. He refuses to regard them even as a party of honest men. His principles tell him that if a man loved his country he could not conceivably attach himself to the Second International—he could not conceivably think of making the interest of his country subordinate to the Communists of Hamburg. The Duke will not listen to any sentimental version of Labour's aims and policy; or, rather, he will listen, for he is the least arrogant or noisy of men, and listen with a smile, for he can appreciate the comedy of our rather down-at-heel idealism; but for every kind thing you may have to say of Labour's intention he will quote you a dozen of their official utterances showing that their ultimate object is the destruction of the present basis of society.

Once more: fixed principles effectually prevent him from looking upon the struggling forces of Labour with a kind and sentimentalising eye. These men are enemies of the social order. They hate the things that he loves. They would destroy the things which he regards as foundational to the greatness of England.

The more moderate and accommodating they would

make themselves appear, the greater is his contempt
for them. They are dishonest. They dare not speak
the thing which is in their hearts.

I spoke to him one day of letters I received from
miners all over the country condemning him on account
of the huge income he is supposed to enjoy from royalties on coal. I asked him how far that income was
affected by taxation. His answer was characteristic
of the man. "I receive," he told me, "half-a-crown
in every pound of those royalties. The other seven
half-crowns are taken by taxation. But I am not in
the least ashamed of receiving mining royalties. I
am as much entitled to those royalties as the trades
unions are entitled to the interest they receive on their
capital investments. They are as much my private
property as Mr. Ramsay MacDonald's Privy Coun-
cillor's uniform is his property. My ancestors bought
the land I hold. One of them paid as much as £180,000
in old days for a strip of land by the Tyne. At that
time it was a highly speculative investment. It
was not known whether coal was there in workable
quantities. His speculation was of great advantage to
the industry, because he bought up the copyholders and
small proprietors who had no interest in the minerals.
In fact he took great risks in the public welfare as well
as in his own. Why were he and his heirs not entitled
to as much profit as any other fortunate shareholder? I
admit the right of the State to tax me. I contest the

right of the State to tax me unfairly. And I entirely repudiate the right of the State to filch my land from me. If I may not keep my land, why should Mr. J. H. Thomas be allowed to keep his car, or Mr. Philip Snowden the watch in his pocket?"

His indictment of Liberalism is a severe one. "When the Radicals," he once said to me, "gave up academic Liberalism, because it did not pay, and began promising the workers all sorts of blessings, for the sake of votes, old-fashioned Liberalism was brought to bed and delivered of this dreadful, bastardly, and un-English offspring, Socialism. Liberals are to blame for everything. To form an alliance with such people would be fatal to Conservatism. There is one course open to them: publicly to renounce their opinions and to enter the Conservative Party as converted men."

His dislike of Mr. Lloyd George is purely a matter of principle. He acknowledges the man's charm, and can see even the humour of that astonishing career; but his contempt for his political life is vigorous and intense. He is not among those who feel gratitude for Mr. Lloyd George's part in the War. As a close friend of Sir William Robertson, and a member of his staff, the Duke has reason to think that Mr. Lloyd George was an entirely fatal influence in those days of crisis—crisis for which he had done nothing whatsoever to prepare.

When the Russian Revolution came, he tells me,

Robertson saw at once the inevitable effect. Russia would be out of the War; the Germans would concentrate many of their eastern troops on the western front. Robertson urged in the summer of 1917 the recall of all available British troops from eastern theatres, in order to be ready for a German onslaught in the spring of 1918. Lloyd George, at this time, was all for winning the War in any other theatre except that of the western front. He flatly refused Robertson's request, saying that we were "over-insured on the western front." He actually wanted to take five divisions from France and hurl them at some of our enemies in the East. In this matter at least Robertson beat him and saved the country. In the spring of 1918 the Germans made a tremendous concentration on the western front. They smashed through our lines, and were within an ace of reaching the Channel ports. But for those five British divisions in France nothing, humanly speaking, could have saved the world from a German victory. With the help of five British divisions from the eastern front our line would have held and the Germans might have surrendered in March.

In this, in everything, the Duke is guided by principle. He suspects a man who is for ever changing his opinions. He has no faith in the amateur reformer, no sympathy with any form of quack. His views are simple and strong. Foundational to all clear thinking is a moral character unshakeably convinced of the eternal difference between right and wrong. Foundational to all wise politics is a moral character trained to know the difference between what is practical and wise, and what is impractical and disastrous. A nation that is governed by wise, practical, and honest men may survive the obvious perils which beset democracy; any nation governed by foolish, impractical, and dishonest men, sooner or later, is bound to perish.

One of my friends, who is still an ardent Liberal, tells me that the Duke is the worst enemy of the League of Nations in this country. He is inclined to agree with what I have said of the Duke's rightness in the matter of Ireland, Germany, and Russia, but he is fiercely convinced that the Duke is monstrously wrong in the matter of the League. My answer does not shake him. I tell him that the Duke does not love war and does not hate peace, but will not consent to put the destinies of this country into the hands of a committee, representative of many races, who certainly do not share our English view of moral character, and some of whom, obviously, have not yet reached our degree of civilisation. He replies to this that the Duke's assumption of moral superiority is offensive to other nations, and that nothing is so likely to revive the horror of War as a spirit which rejects the most sensible avenue to peace. I say that the Duke does not consider this League of Nations avenue to be a sensible road to peace. He replies emphatically, "It is; and the Duke is a reactionary of the worst possible kind." So end many similar discussions.

My own view is that it is not so much the opinions of the Duke which antagonise certain minds, such as that of my friend, as a certain hardness with which he expresses them, and which conveys the impression that he is lacking in human sympathy, as it were a Calvinist of politics.

But this impression is not a true one. The Duke is not a sentimentalist, but he is not an iceberg. He is a kindly enough man, free from all vanity and arrogance, who is fond of shooting, hunts a pack of hounds at Alnwick, loves to be with his children at Albury, is devoted to a very beautiful wife, although he cannot yet bring himself to share her enthusiasm for golf—and is as little in London as his business will allow. Only a few years over forty, devoted to hard work, fearless in confronting an opponent, and inspired in everything he does by an unquestionable earnestness, he may, in spite of a certain scepticism towards the capacity of social reform to make things better, render the country useful service in the next decade, which looks as though it may be one of no little trial.

His warm regard for Mr. Baldwin, who is a firm believer in social reform, strikes me as a pleasant note in his character; it is as if a part of his happy domesticity had crept into the severe region of his uncompromising politics.

SIR PHILIP LLOYD-GREAME

THE RT. HON. SIR PHILIP LLOYD-GREAME, K.B.E.

Born in Bridlington, 1884. Educ.: Winchester, University College, Oxford. Called to the Bar, 1908. Army service, 1914–17. Secretary of Ministry of National Service, 1917–18. Secretary of Board of Trade, 1920–21. Secretary of Overseas Trade Department, 1921–22. Chairman of Permanent Labour Committee of War Cabinet, 1918. Member of Select Committee on National Expenditure, and of Select Committee on prices and profits, 1919. President of the Board of Trade (in the Baldwin Administration), 1922–24. M.P. for the Hendon Division of Middlesex, 1918–. Clubs: Carlton, Oxford and Cambridge

RT. HON. SIR PHILIP LLOYD GREAME

VI

SIR PHILIP LLOYD-GREAME

*O Thou who of thy free grace didst build up this Brittannick
Empire to a glorious and enviable height, with all her daughter
islands about her, stay us in this felicitie.*—JOHN MILTON.

*Individuals may form communities, but it is institutions
alone that can create a nation.*—DISRAELI.

*I am sure that without departing from the settled fiscal
policy of this country of not imposing duties either on essential
raw materials or essential foodstuffs, it is quite possible for
you to give the Dominions such additional preference on a
number of articles that there will be a tremendous development
of Empire resources.*—GENERAL SMUTS.

LORD RANDOLPH CHURCHILL was a power in the country before he had done anything to deserve the attention
of the historian. He knew that if he would catch the
eye of the nation he must stand sheer out from the ruck.
But in those days, the picturesque days of politics, it
was not difficult to become a public figure. A collar
could decide a destiny and a buttonhole assure a
career

I am inclined to think that if Sir Philip Lloyd-Greame had been functioning as a politician in the years immediately preceding his birth he would have sported a conspicuous waistcoat or cultivated a mysterious manner, and so, with the help of cartoonist and caricaturist, might have been something of a national figure in the late seventies.   But he was only forty years of age the other day, and belongs, therefore, to a generation of men who would rather die unknelled, uncoffined, and unknown, than challenge the prevailing fashion in clothes or practice a manner which might distinguish them in any way from the blurred ranks of average mortality.

He is either much more modest than his predecessors or a great deal less imaginative.   On the whole I am disposed to think that the nation loses by such behaviour in Sir Philip Lloyd-Greame, for I think it may easily be proved that he, who is at present so little known to democracy, could render the State infinitely more solid service, than let us say, Mr. Jack Jones of Silvertown, "a gentleman," to quote the words of Dizzy, "whom I will not call distinguished, for that would be prostituting an epithet—and whom I will not call notorious, for that might be offensive—and whom I therefore describe as well known."

Philip Lloyd-Greame is unquestionably one of the ablest men now in Parliament, and one of the most eager and energetic.   He has the economic facts of the

British Empire at his fingers' ends, and his brain is a
series of pigeon-holes stuffed with the documents of
world trade. Like all true experts he is an enthusiast.
His mind seems to rejoice in the smoothness and pre-
cision with which it works, in the unerring deductions
it makes from the facts it has so thoroughly accumulated, and in the lucidity of the language with which he
can state an unanswerable argument or conclude an
appeal to the intelligence of reasonable men. He is one
of the few ex-ministers, by the way, who can use a
pen with some degree of distinction.

But he comes of an ancient Yorkshire family, a
county which is perhaps more set against the eccentrici-
ties of swagger than most other divisions of England,
and he went to Winchester, where modesty and sim-
plicity are a part of religion, and on to Oxford, where
a Yorkshire gentleman and a Winchester scholar may
just manage to escape the contagion of the Oxford
manner. His family had decided that he should go
into the diplomatic service, but at Oxford he contracted
such a passion for the cockpit of politics that he found
himself unable to contemplate with any ease of mind a
career spent on its decorous fringes.

He therefore decided to train his mind for politics
by going to the Bar, but only for a time, and while at
the Bar, anxious to make himself the master of one
particular subject of litigation, he went to a Yorkshire
coalfield and for some months descended the pits and

studied the collier at close quarters. The War inter-
rupted this peaceful but energetic career. He went out
to France, rose to be a major, won the Military Cross,
and was invalided home. By a lucky chance the
national service assigned to him in Whitehall brought
him under the notice of Mr. Bonar Law and Sir Auck-
land Geddes. He rose quickly to an administrative
eminence, a seat was found for him at Hendon, he
became successively Parliamentary Secretary to the
Board of Trade, Secretary to the Department of Overseas Trade, and then President of the Board of Trade.
In 1923 he set the stamp of his personality on the great
Imperial Economic Conference, which in days to come
may seem to the judicious historian a turning-point in
British destiny.

There is something in the appearance of this industrious man which helps one to understand the workings
of his mind. He is tall and powerful, but with a slight
stoop of head and shoulders. He is boyish-looking,
but prematurely bald over the forehead. His clean-cut
and well-bronzed face is chiefly noticeable from the
structural point of view for a jowl which a prize-fighter
would regard as a stroke of genius; but the blue eyes
are so kindly, and the mouth is so bent on smiles, that
the strong jaw seems to be thrown away upon him. In
brief, here is the face of a man who might remove
mountains, but for an occasional whimsicality which
sets him laughing at ant-heaps. He is an Edward

Carson with a sense of humour, or a Birrell with a stern
ambition. Whether we are to say that the strong jaw
underpins a top-story otherwise too shaky for the
accommodation of great purposes, or that a friendly
and playful mind has effectually prevented the strong
jaw from carrying him into the excesses of fanaticism,
depends upon our view of life and the best way of
getting things done. A sense of humour would have
destroyed St. Paul; but it might have saved Charles
the First.

I think my personal regard for Lloyd-Greame does
not mislead my judgment far afield from the truth of
his personality when I say that he is a great man in the
making, and that all the elements of greatness in his
mind are somewhat hampered by that same modesty of
character and sweetness of feeling which hinder his
friend Edward Wood from making a firm mark on the
history of the present time. I regard him as a man of
the very highest promise, and one who may yet do as
much for the prosperity of the British Empire as any
man now living; but although he is a young man with
thirty years of work ahead of him, I am sometimes disposed to doubt whether his very thesis of Conservatism
is not bound to hold him back from playing the conspicuous part he ought to play in the destinies of our
generation.

That thesis is well worth the attention of the public.
Sir Philip once said to me that he differentiated the atti-

tude of the Socialist from that of the Conservative in this fashion. The Socialist tries to find a common syndical unit in all the factories of a given trade, the Unionist sees that there is a closer and broader union in the different trades in a particular place. There is a more natural bond, and a more useful bond, between, let us say, the butcher, the baker, the schoolmaster, and the parson of one town than between all the butchers scattered through England.

"I do not particularly like the term Conservative," he said to me; "I much prefer the term Unionist. Unionism seems to me an admirable word for expressing the faith and the ideals of those Conservatives who believe in growth and development. It has also an evolutionary content. Civilisation has surely proceeded so far on Unionist principles. People have combined and worked together in the past for the sake of a trade, an art, a religion, and a community. They have proceeded from a tribal unity, or a guild unity, or a civic unity, to the larger unity of country and race. Is it not, therefore, a reasonable anticipation of history to suppose that the British people, who have always had this sense of unity in their blood, should go on to mak an absolute unity of the Empire, through which, and perhaps preceded by a unity of all English-speaking people, mankind may come into the possession of a warless world unity?"

Now, it is important to know that Sir Philip's idea of

Unionism is based upon the subordination of all selfish instincts in the individual. To him the British Empire is so conspicuously a magnificent creation of British character that he cannot conceive of any pigmy individual having the impudence to regard it as an opportunity for showing off his own talent or filling his own purse.

Loyalty, he seems to think, is surely the beginning of education. We set out with loyalty to our family: we must do nothing to disgrace it. We go on to acquire school loyalty, and learn that lesson in the playing field as well as in the classroom and the dormitory. We go on again to acquire loyalty to our university, and associate ourselves with all its past history and all its efforts to hold its place in the world as a centre of learning and a nursery of clean games and manly sports. In all this there is a call to unselfishness. We are not to think of ourselves. We are not to shove and jostle for a first place. Our bounden duty is to play for the side. Our one justification for tremendous effort is the spirit of team work. And so, as he sees it, the Unionist Party calls for men who are willing to subordinate selfish ambition, and to tread under their feet any base inclination towards self-aggrandisement, and who will band themselves together as a team, gladly and with all their hearts, to achieve a purpose quite transcending any conceivable personal ambition—namely, the unity of the British Empire.

In conversation he is apt to walk up and down his room, his head bent forward, his steps quick and decisive, his gestures few but restless, the voice rising and becoming slightly nasal when he desires to emphasise a particular word. It is easy to see that here is a man absorbed in hard work, and work of such a character that he could no more lay it aside for a selfish ambition than he could stoop to entertain the suggestion of conspirators. He is pre-eminently the best kind of public-school boy turned politician, and the best kind of politician turned idealist. Truly I do not think that he ever sits back in his chair to consider his own career, or throws aside his papers, which are as well-ordered as they are numerous, to calculate his next office. When he has finished his work his natural impulse is to take his gun or his golf-clubs and get into the open air.

Happy in his domestic circumstances, distracted by no temptations, demoralised by no weakness of character, he gives himself, with all the clean and cheerful heart of a boy, to the thing that he loves and to the star that he follows—the greatness, the glory, and the beauty of the British Empire.

He is a Unionist because the Unionist Party in his eyes is the only political body in the state animated by a fully-awakened imperial consciousness. For this reason he is a party man. He believes that in fighting for Unionism he is fighting for England, and he fights with the joy and satisfaction of a man who feels in every vein of his body that he is on the right side and the winning side, the side that is least disgraced by personal ambitions, least dismembered by personal intrigues, least haunted by doubts that the cause is not the cause of England and Empire—and this, not necessarily because it is made up of better or nobler men, but because its purpose is so commandingly the purpose of right reason and the Will of God.

His theory of politics may be expressed in the phrase "social reform linked up with a sound economic policy." First the sound economic policy, and then as much social reform as the revenues of the policy can supply. Therefore he lays his first emphasis on Imperial development, and this he would seek in co-operation with the Dominions and the Colonies by every practical means: Preference; Credit; Communications; Settlement. He was accused by one of the Dominion Prime Ministers of coining the term "mutuality" to describe the economic relations which should exist within the Empire; he replied that if a word did not exist which accurately described this conception, it was certainly high time that one did.

"Does the nation," he asks, "realise the situation? Since the last census our population has increased by one million and three-quarters. Our overseas trade was last year less than three-quarters of its pre-war volume. All around us are nations who enormously

increased during the War their manufacturing efficiency, and who are less willing to take our manufactures, and more able to compete with them in the
markets of the world. The world is poorer: the competition is keener. A million and more of our people are
out of work. That is the situation. Those are the
facts. And the Labour Government goes out of its
way to flout the British Dominions, who can help us
so powerfully to recover and to extend our pre-War
prosperity!"

He bids the Socialists and the Liberals to study the
history of the United States during the last three generations, and, comparing the resources of that great
federation with our own, to ask themselves whether it
is possible to doubt that the British Empire can achieve
a prosperity as great and a strength as formidable.

"One of the most hopeless features of our democracy
since the War," he declares, "is that the more onerous
our burdens become the more fiercely does it fore-
gather round the parish pump."

When people complain to him of the cost of living,
he replies, "I do not wonder that you feel hopeless, for
you are conceiving of your country as an island province
and not as a self-supporting Empire. Lift up your eyes
unto the hills whence cometh your salvation."

He comes back again and again to his master idea of
Unity. "Why can't our people see that their strength
lies in three central unities: the union of classes, the

union of town and country, the union of Empire?
There is also a threefold community of interest:
family life, local life, national life. These ideas are
the creation of natural instincts, fortified by the wise
experience of our progress in civilisation. Surely
democracy can be made to see that here is the natural
path of evolution."

He lays as great an emphasis as Disraeli did on the
infinite value of Parliamentary Government. "Communists are ceaselessly propagating the idea that all our
institutions are the artful contrivances of capitalism
to keep the people in subjection. It is a real part of
Unionist loyalty to explain to democracy the value of
its institutions. They were fought for and won by
men who have loved liberty and hated despotism. Many
of our greatest ancestors gave their lives in that
immortal struggle for the constitutional liberties of
England. Did they fight for a fudge? Did they die
for a sham? All our Dominions have welcomed the
grant of Parliamentary Government. Are they fools?
Every democratic nation has copied us. Are they deluded? The whole intellectual world has paid tribute to
England's genius in creating these great constitutional
forms. Is it mistaken?"

Then he swings round to the revolutionary alternative. Class hatred: the clash of sectional interests: the
tyranny of a determined minority: the suppression of
free speech: the extermination of all personal liberties:

the disruption of the Empire: chaos—economic and moral.

"Who can doubt," he asks, "if the case is well put, on which side Englishmen will elect to stand?"

Nothing can shake his faith, and in this matter he speaks as an expert, that the physical and moral resources of the Empire are inexhaustible. If we choose, but only if we choose, we can multiply our wealth and our power a hundredfold. The matter rests entirely with us. The Dominions are willing to do their part. They are ready to make sacrifices in order to attain this great end of Imperial unity; they will take our people, if we will take their products in preference to the products of alien peoples; and if they take our people, who cannot here find work, those people, growing in strength and prosperity, will develop the inexhaustible riches of the British Empire and solve every economic problem that now threatens England with poverty and weakness.

Will our people adopt this Imperial outlook, or will they see the world with the eyes of a provincial? Will they say, "The Empire my country, England my home," or will they say "To hell with the Empire" and go on butting their heads against the hard wall of economic law?

Sir Philip is not so absorbed in this Imperial ideal as to keep his back turned on social reform. Long ago, in the years before the War, he had worked out, in

company with other keen Unionists, an excellent scheme
for the reform of the agricultural labourer's social
conditions. He is an advocate for a wise extension of
our pensions system. He is convinced, too, that
housing reform is a most urgent duty of the Conservative Party, and that much may be done to improve the
physical conditions and the mental outlook of the urban
worker by extending the principles of co-partnership.
He insists, too, that the worker in a factory might
become much more interested in its fortunes if the
managers took him more into their confidence. A man
must have joy in his work. The craftsman of an earlier
age fashioned a complete thing under his hand. To-day,
inevitably, a man works as a cog in a great machine.
How much greater the need, then, to arouse his interest
in the whole field, in a small corner of which he works.
As an example, the managers of a factory might do
something to stimulate the interest of their workers
merely by introducing cinematographic pictures of the
Dominions and the foreign countries to which their
manufactures are consigned. Nothing should be
neglected to awaken the interest and stimulate the intelligence of factory workers. In all this he is moved
by the human sympathy which is never an affectation
in a countryman, and by a certain quality of imagination which distinguishes all forward-looking men. He
does not despair of the idea that industry may be
humanised.

But his value to the country lies mainly in his great and sure grasp of economic facts, in his profound knowledge of the world's industrial situation. Let me, then, conclude with a summary of his views on this matter, which, of all others, presses most hardly now on the attention of serious men. These views he has expressed with excellent clearness in an address given to the Royal Colonial Institute in 1922, an address, I should have thought, which Unionist headquarters might well use as one of the chief of its pamphlets.

The foundations of Modern England were laid during the struggle with Napoleon. From the year 1800 to the year 1825, England carried a tremendous burden of taxation and passed from the state of exporting corn to importing it. All the same in 1820 only 4 per cent. of our population depended on breadstuffs from overseas.

From 1825 until 1850 England forged ahead of other nations on the road of industrialism, which she had been the first to take. At the end of this period she produced 60 per cent. of the world's output of pig-iron. Her exports nearly doubled. The holding of the Great Exhibition in 1851 was an advertisement of insular success.

From 1850 till 1875 the world was England's oyster. Her production of coal rose from fifty-six million tons to one hundred and thirty-two million tons. The introduction of the Bessemer process gave her a new industry in the large-scale production of steel. The rapid accumulation of capital led to foreign investments, chiefly in the United States and the Dominions, which facilitated the importation of England's necessities, and enormously increased the capital wealth of the island. Exports increased from ninety-seven million pounds in 1854 to two hundred and twenty-three million pounds in 1875.

From 1875 to 1900 a radical change occurred in the national fortunes. France had been England's only serious competitor in world trade. Now there came first Germany and then the United States. From 1880 to 1900 Great Britain definitely lost her leadership in several basic industries. "The increasing severity of this competition," a Royal Commission reported, "both in our home and in neutral markets, is especially noticeable in the case of Germany. In every quarter of the world, the perseverance and enterprise of the Germans are making themselves felt. In the actual production of commodities we have now few, if any, advantages over them, and in a knowledge of the markets of the world, a desire to accommodate themselves to local tastes and idiosyncrasies, a determination to obtain a footing wherever they can and a tenacity in maintaining it, they appear to be gaining ground on us." Our population increased by 8,000,000. The export of articles wholly or mainly manufactured in these islands increased from £136.2 millions in 1870 to only £138.6

millions in 1900. During this difficult period it was only the custom of our Dominions which saved us from ruin.

From 1900 to 1913 there was a marvellous recovery in British trade. Canada's consumption of our goods more than doubled; New Zealand's increased by 97 per cent.; South Africa's by 70 per cent.; Australia's by 60 per cent. At the same time our exports to India and Ceylon rose to 130 per cent. Moreover a general prosperity throughout the whole world enabled the British manufacturers to work with confidence and security.

Since the war there has been a grave economic disturbance throughout the world, accompanied by higher tariff walls, the complexities of depreciated currencies, and considerable unrest among the wage-earning classes. To regain what we have lost, to press forward to greater fortune still, it is essential that we should develop the resources of our own Empire, and throw the whole weight of our influence into the scale of world peace.

Sir Philip Lloyd-Greame is in essence neither a Protectionist nor a Free Trader. He regards fiscal policy as a matter of practical expediency to be adapted to the varying circumstances of different industries at different times. To protect an inefficient industry is a form of ca' canny, and utterly indefensible at any time. The industry that is inefficient, demands not a bolster under its head but a pillow over its face. But there is no man in the country who feels more earnestly than he does that unless we set ourselves with genuine enthusiasm and absolute faith to develop the vast resources of the Empire, we cannot hope to weather the industrial storm and stress of the next twenty years.

Politics is not a game to this man, but a passion; and the passion is engendered by a religion which inspires every moment of his industrious days—the religion of the destiny of the British Empire. To make our island democracy understand the difference between insular Protection and Imperial Development, to get the British Press to hammer the facts of the economic situation into the public consciousness, and to persuade every Conservative in the country that the supreme appeal he must make to the people is the Imperial appeal—this, I think, is the one driving political ambition in the mind of Lloyd-Greame.

SIR DOUGLAS HOGG

THE RT. HON. SIR DOUGLAS McGAREL HOGG

Born 1872. Educ.: Eton. Sugar Planter in West Indies and British Guiana in the firm of Hogg, Curtis, Campbell & Co. Served in South African War with Yeomanry (medal). Called to the Bar in 1922. Vice President of the Polytechnic, founded by his father, the late Quintin Hogg. Captain of the County of London Volunteer Regiment, 1914–19. Director of the Legal Insurance Company, 1920–22. Director General, 1922–. M.P. for Marylebone, 1922–. Clubs: Athenæum, Carlton.

RT. HON. SIR DOUGLAS McGAREL HOGG, P.C.

VII

SIR DOUGLAS HOGG

*The great charm, however, of English scenery is the moral feeling that seems to pervade it. It is associated in the mind with ideas of order; of quiet, of sober, well-established principles, of hoary usage and reverend custom. Everything seems to be the growth of ages of regular and peaceful existence.—*Washington Irving.

*The wealth of England is not merely material wealth—it does not merely consist in the number of acres we have tilled and cultivated, nor in our havens filled with shipping, nor in our unrivalled factories, nor in the intrepid industry of our mines. Not these merely form the principal wealth of our country; we have a more precious treasure, and that is the character of the people.—*Disraeli.

IF Sir Douglas Hogg had possessed twenty years ago Mr. Winston Churchill's appetite for public life, he would now be a Gargantuan figure. He has all the qualities of a great fighting politician. Many men less gifted in this respect are now either the cynosure of every political eye or the cockshy of every political missile. Sir Douglas Hogg, however, is assailed by no enemies, huzzaed by no followers, and the mob of all classes is almost unaware of his existence.

Nothing could be so likely to take away his breath as either to hear his name in a pantomine or to see his face in a cartoon. It would be as if Mr. George Moore heard himself quoted in St. Paul's Cathedral by Dr. Inge, or Mr. Bernard Shaw found one day no mention of his opinions in the daily paper.

It is a rather curious political case. I think it would be true to say that his intellect has a punch in it, but not his personality. It is the first of Carpentier, but the soul of Joe Beckett. One feels that if his intellectual equipment had been at the disposal of any ambitious politician it could not have failed to make its mark, and perhaps a permanent mark, on contemporary politics. What makes the matter even more curious is the fact that Sir Douglas Hogg cares very deeply about a number of things which he regards as essential to the greatness of his country, which things he also regards as standing in no little peril at the present time. Perhaps he has left the matter too long. He entered Parliament when the creative instinct was inclined toward ca' canny, and the fighting instinct was too tempered by geniality to care about black eyes and battered noses. Moreover, he has scarcely an equal at the Bar, and is devoted heart and soul to his profession.

He is the son of Quintin Hogg, whose name will always be associated with an ugly building, a comic word, and a most splendid philanthropic undertaking. At the outset of that romantic career at the Polytechnic in Regent Street, Mr. Quintin Hogg, who was an aristocrat, cherished the impassioned faith of Victorian Radicalism. He denied his own prejudices, swept his natural traditions aside, plunged into the slums of modern industrialism, rescued, cared for, encouraged, and saved in the name and power of Christ, hundreds of poor boys, and at his own dinner-table proclaimed a political faith which, mild as it was, would have frightened two-thirds of his subscribers out of their wits.

If the father had been a Tory, Douglas might have begun life as a follower of Gladstone. He tells me that in those days he was always wanting to fight the other side, and that his critical faculties were never so incensed as when he encountered enthusiasm. His father's enthusiasm for Mr. Gladstone carried the inference that Disraeli was a miserable charlatan and Salisbury a mere lath painted to look like iron. This was a deal too much for a young Etonian who dearly loved an argument and was youthfully averse from anything in the nature of exaggeration. He studied the works of Disraeli, he bestowed some attention on current politics, and he announced that he was a Conservative.

In those days he had every reason to style himself a Tory democrat, for his holidays were largely spent in the closest and most familiar intimacy with some of the hardest nuts from London slums. The Polytechnic dealt at that time in roughs, and the London roughs at that time, most of them crop-headed, slit-eyed and flat-nosed, were of a very different moral texture from the pale-faced and loose-lipped young men of the present slums, whose long hair flops over the back of the head and gives them the decadent appearance of convalescing æsthetes. Douglas Hogg played foot-ball with these formidable roughs, and met them intellectually in the Debating Society of the Poly-technic. The Debating Society had its Government and its Opposition, and in this Polytechnic Parliament young Hogg was for some time Her Majesty's Secre-tary of State for the Colonies. His friendship with many of the roughs was close and in some cases inti-mate. He has a gladness of nature and a sincerity of mind which are attractive.

He was at the Bar, making his way to success like a tug with its syren in full blast, when his father came under the influence of Mr. Joseph Chamberlain, and straightaway the founder of the Polytechnic began to see the British Empire with the oriental imagination of Dizzy, no longer with the commercial eyes of Bright and Cobden. Young Hogg did not crow over his father; he too fell under the personal spell of Chamber-lain, who was the most charming of men in private life. Father and son were soon devoted to this quiet and affectionate statesman, under whose courteous and subdued manner burned the fire of really great political enthusiasm.

From that moment entirely devoted to Mr. Chamberlain, father and son sought to make the Polytechnic useful to the great moral ends of Empire. To both of them it seemed that this vast confederation of free peoples, all speaking the same language, all cherishing the same moral ideas, all acknowledging one sovereign law, and all conscious of a kinship sublimely indifferent to the geographical distances which divide them, could not have come into existence for any trumpery purpose, whether industrial or political, and could not be meant to perish before it had served some high purpose in the evolution of mankind.

The father may have put this sentiment into more evangelical language, but at the back of the son's mind was also a religious impulse, however guardedly he might have expressed his imperial sentiments. They were both of them men who believed in God, believed, too, in an over-ruling providence of the universe, and believed strongly in the moral responsibility of each individual soul.

When the war came in South Africa, Douglas Hogg threw aside wig and gown, and volunteered for foreign service. He was rejected. Someone told him that the medical authorities in Scotland were less exigent, and off he went to Edinburgh. By good fortune he encountered a kindly old sergeant who beamed on him, understood him, and passed him fit for active service. He entered the Scottish Horse, and sailed for South Africa.

Whatever he may think of War as a moral question, he thoroughly enjoyed fighting on the veldt, and of those fierce years in his life he has now only two complaints to make—the difficulty of getting a bath, and the unpleasantly dirty conditions of campaigning.

He suggests in his appearance that he would like fighting and dislike dirt. There is something military in his carriage and something pugilistic in his precise and vigorous face. He is also one of those men on whose clear and fine skin soap and water seem to produce a sheen or a glow, such as the manufacturers of a boot polish assure the world is a pedal consequence of using their particular cream. He stands very upright and square-shouldered, with a rather commanding tilt to his head, and a look in his eyes, when he is opposed, which is quick with challenge. He can be the kindest and friendliest of men, as he is certainly one of the most modest; but provoke him to a fight and he will hit you, if the matter involves a great principle, as hard as any man at the Bar or in the House of Commons.

He was Attorney-General before he was a member of Parliament. A seat had to be found for him after he had accepted office. He entered Parliament only in 1922. In spite of possessing no previous experience of the House of Commons, he at once established a reputation as a powerful leader and a keen debater. It is doubtful, indeed, whether there is any man now in the Conservative Party who can address the House with more power or with greater effect. Two years ago no one had thought of him as a politician.

The opportunities for his intervention are just now few and far between. He seems to take, I think, too modest a view of his place in the House. Great questions arise on which he feels deeply, and on which, no doubt, he could speak with weight and sometimes with fire; but so many other members of Parliament desire to speak, and the law is regarded as his particular province, and besides—is he not one of the new members? He has gone back to the Bar, and enormously added to his income. It will be a pity if he is not encouraged to take a far more leading part in Conservative politics.

If he had the genius for public life which so distinguishes Mr. Churchill and Mr. Lloyd George, he would of course make his opportunities in the House of Commons, and fill his engagement-book with "political fixtures" up and down the country. He would nag at ministers on every possible occasion, interrupt whenever the chance occurred to score a point, cultivate, perhaps, the acquaintance of newspaper proprietors, and certainly form a little group of disciples in the House who would regard him as their leader.

I do not think he is altogether to be admired for doing none of these things. One might almost say that it is now the first duty of any man capable of serving his country to cultivate the rough and uncongenial art of self-advertisement. Democracy will not look up from its pleasures or its sorrows unless a bugle is blown in its ear. How the country is to learn that Sir Douglas Hogg might render it valuable service unless his name is repeated as often as the Derby favourite and his personal tastes as constantly advertised as the face-creams and lip-pastes of the latest film-queen, I really do not know. If Colman's mustard has still to be pushed down the public throat as a suitable accompaniment to roast beef, I do not see how modest and retiring men can hope to acquaint democracy with their virtues by an occasional speech in the House of Commons.

Perhaps the Conservative organisation is not so good in seeking for talent as the Labour organisation. I do not know, for I judge these things from the outside; but clearly if any commercial undertaking in the country had a man like Sir Douglas Hogg on its staff it would not be satisfied by asking him to dictate a letter once a month or to cast his eyes over the petty cash account when he had nothing better to do. The genius of the great industrialist lies in finding first-rate men, and making the best possible use of them.

Sir Douglas Hogg holds the faith that Conservatism is the kindliest and most humane form of politics. He says that the Liberal believes, like the Tory, in the value of individualism, but that his individualism is unconditional. The Liberal sees with a certain amount of compassion the weak going to the wall, and with a stir of sorrowful emotion he may observe the devil taking the hindmost; but so long as the statistics of the Board of Trade are satisfactory, and so long as he can compose without absurdity a peroration on the general progress of the human race, he is not greatly concerned by these individual casualties of the evolutionary battlefield.

On the other hand, the Conservative lays it down that just as there is no absolute freedom, and that just as every man's freedom is conditioned by its effect on the freedom of other men, so there is no absolute individualism. His individualism is strong and challenging, but it is conditional. He says that no success in foreign markets can justify inhumanity in our workshops. He keeps his eye on the manufacturer. He claims the right to interfere in the management and conditions of the factory. He has a certain sympathy with the bottom-dog, and is always ready to lend a hand to the hindmost before the devil takes them.

Liberalism, as he sees it, is the philosophy of Nietzsche and the gospel of Bernhardi applied to the trade and commerce of a nation. He hates it deeply.

As for Labour, he hates it with the real disgust of a nature to which all slavery is abhorrent. He cannot understand how any Englishman is able to contemplate the mere hypothesis of a servile State. Personal liberty, he says, is clearly incompatible with Socialism; the one condition which renders the socialistic theory workable is the condition of mass slavery; every man must be the unquestioning and soulless servant of a tyrannical government. Against such an idea he rigorously sets his face. Economically absurd, Socialism is morally destructive.

He said to me once: "Rule out Divine Love and individual moral responsibility, and Liberalism is justified. Rule out the whole history of the human race and the most insistent fact of man's consciousness, and Labour is justified." He told me that he does not see how man is to justify his place in the universe, and so fulfil the ultimate purpose of the Creator, unless he acknowledges the great sanctions of religion, marries his personal liberty to sure unselfishness, and develops his faculties with a high sense of his responsibility both to God and man.

He deplores with the whole force of his moral nature that dreadful speech of an ex-Lord Chancellor of England which seemed to glorify selfishness and to assert in the face of all civilisation and religion that no nation is unselfish. What could be the effect of such a statement in the United States of America? Are not the idealists in both countries striving to destroy that very delusion and to create a partnership between the two great English-speaking nations on the common ground of their moral idealism? What hope is there for the peace of the world and for the higher life of the human race if men of high authority proclaim the exploded philosophical fallacies of the eighteenth century as a new-found working faith for the future of mankind?

There is another matter, a more serious one, which causes Sir Douglas Hogg grave anxiety. He does not see what power in the country can withstand the domination of a commercialised Press. If newspapers with a great circulation, chiefly among people who have never been trained to think and whose opinions are for ever at the sport of mere suggestion, repeat day after day something which they want that public to believe, repeat it in a dozen forms and ever with some new and striking attraction, he does not see how democracy will be able to save itself from such perilous suggestion.

A newspaper proprietor has only to give orders for his journalists to announce and to go on announcing that the Government, whatever party it may represent, is stupid and inept, for that Government, sooner or later, to fall. The newspaper proprietor may be right, and he may be moved by the highest patriotism; but he may also be wrong, and he may also be actuated either by the basest of motives or by the mere pique of hurt vanity. How does the country propose to guard itself against this domination at the hands of two or three men who have turned to journalism, not as a man turns to schoolmastering or to preaching, but for the sake of money or for their own personal aggrandisement?

What is the effect of the worst of these newspapers on English character? Do they steady the national judgment? Do they stimulate the reason, or incite the passions? Do they enlighten the mind, or vulgarise the heart? We see the screaming headlines in the public streets and dismiss them without a thought, merely with a feeling of disgust or contempt; but what work are they doing in the minds and characters of the multitude—good work or bad work? Every newspaper is either helping or hindering civilisation. We make a mistake in dismissing them as things of no account. They count enormously. Day after day they are at work on the mind and in the character of the vast masses of this country, and no other influence is to be compared with theirs in the matter of shaping the moral destinies of our nation.

It seems to me that Sir Douglas Hogg sees as clearly as any man what is wrong with us, but knows as little as the rest of us how to put things right. For example, I doubt if any man in politics more frequently feels the cruel conditions of our industrial slums; at any rate, he and Mr. Neville Chamberlain have spent many days and nights attempting to work out a practical

scheme for their abolition; but he will tell you that
every notion which he has turned over in his brain to
make it safe and sound was defeated by the mere difficulty of not knowing where to place the people whose
homes are to be swept away in the process. The
practical difficulties of reform oppress him, and
sometimes make him sceptical about the power of
politics.

He was amused by the righteous indignation of the
Labour Party in opposition; he is rather grimly satisfied
by its pathetic incompetence in power.

All great questions which press upon Governments
for solution, and some of which must certainly be
solved before long if civilisation is not to weaken and
perhaps perish, require, in his judgment, not so much
a creative genius in Parliament as a new temper in the
people. This temper must be much more conscious of
moral responsibility than the temper of the present
time. It must be moved by a deep tide of human
sympathy. It must be governed by faith in Divine
Love. A nation which is sunk in materialism, cannot be
rescued by the wand of a political wizard.

Perhaps this is why Sir Douglas Hogg is devoted
to Mr. Baldwin. He is convinced, however many
tactical mistakes his leader may make, that no man in
Parliament is more powerfully moved by moral considerations, or more earnestly determined to lift up the
soul of the nation, than the Worcestershire squire who

has said that faith and love are essential to the salvation of England.

I remember Sir Douglas describing to me many months ago the effect made upon him by Mr. Baldwin's speeches in the House of Commons. "He sometimes makes me hold my breath. He speaks in his great moments like a man who is struggling to keep back his feelings, and you can almost see the spiritual effort with which his big thoughts are dragged up from the depths of his soul in a kind of agony."

CAPTAIN ALGERNON FITZROY

CAPTAIN HON. EDWARD ALGERNON FITZROY, J.P., D.L.

Born 1869. Educ.: Eton, Sandhurst. Late Lt. 1st Life Guards. Captain of the Reserve Regiment, 1st Life Guards. Wounded first battle of Ypres. M.P. for South Northamptonshire, 1906 and 1910-. Deputy Chairman of Committee H. C., 1922-24. Club: Carlton.

CAPT. THE RT. HON. E. A. FITZROY, M.P.

VIII

CAPTAIN ALGERNON FITZROY

I find the Englishman to be him of all men who stands firmest in his shoes.—EMERSON.

The proper leaders of the people are the gentlemen of England. If they are not the leaders of the people, I do not see why they should be gentlemen. Yes—it is because the gentlemen of England have been negligent of their duties, and unmindful of their situation, that the system of professional agitation, so ruinous to the best interests of the country, has arisen in England.—DISRAELI.

FEW men in the present House of Commons less resemble a professional agitator than Captain FitzRoy. If his friend and neighbour, the late Bobby Spencer, of Althorp, could convulse a Victorian Parliament by explaining that he was not an agricultural labourer, Captain FitzRoy, I think, could set the Georgian Labour benches on the roar by disclaiming any pretensions to the virtues of a tub-thumper.

A man standing firmer in his shoes it would be hard to find. Six feet three inches in height, holding himself with a marked stiffness, and seldom wearing on

his face any other expression than that of an unsmiling
attention to the business in hand, the Deputy-Chairman
of Ways and Means in the late Unionist Government
does not readily suggest that a battering ram would
disturb his balance, or that he would turn his head for
an explosion of dynamite immediately behind him.
There is about him something immovable and enduring.
I am quite certain that he has never been flustered.   I
am almost sure that his temper, even at its hottest,
never rippled his self-control.   If, as Mr. Baldwin says,
the Englishman is the man for an emergency, here in a
supreme degree stands the authentic Englishman.

He is the second son of the late Lord Southampton,
and while at Eton became a page to Queen Victoria, who
was devoted to his mother.   He entered the First Life
Guards, and was a striking figure in that famous regiment of tall men till his own personal tastes and marriage with a delightful woman took him into the
country.   But there was bred in him such a strong
sense of public duty, that even the pleasures of sport,
the daily interest of his pedigree cattle, and the satisfaction of a most happy and refined family life, could
not hold him from the field of national and imperial
politics.   He stood for Parliament in the division where
he lives, won a difficult election, and has never since
been beaten.   Six victories for Conservatism stand to
his credit; and on the only occasion when he did not
stand, 1906, the seat went to the Liberals.

In the House of Commons he is respected by men of all parties, including Labour men. Too reserved for popularity, and too unemotional to create affection, he is known to the House as a man whose mind is just, whose character is strong, whose life is pure, and whose services are given to his country with no thought whatever of personal reward.

After the debate in which Labour refused to have Captain FitzRoy as the Deputy-Chairman, a body of Labour members sent him a message explaining that no man in their party was moved in this matter by personal feelings against him, but purely by principle. Even in that stormiest of debates under the last Government, when Labour saw red, and the whole House was like a bear-garden, Labour never quarrelled with Captain FitzRoy for the sternness with which he quelled the disorder.

So little does he speak about himself that even some of his friends in the House of Commons are quite unaware of certain qualities in his mind which make him the pleasantest of men in his home life. He is a lover of good music, and has played the piano from boyhood, cultivating in particular the music of Beethoven and Chopin. He has been all his life a judicious collector of old furniture, and there is scarcely a thing in his house, from the silver on the table to the prints on the wall, from the china in the cabinets to the mantelpieces he has collected and installed, which is not both beautiful and good. His knowledge of painting is above the average, and to go with him to Althorp is to learn something as well as to see a great number of things. Add to these tastes a quiet pleasure in borders of old English flowers, a friendly affection for field spaniels, a readiness to sacrifice one of his beautiful lawns to the mashie and the niblick, and another to the cooped chickens of his daughter, and those who know the man only a little will see that the stern exterior conceals, rather than reveals, the soul within.

I set him in this place as a good sample of the quiet, cultivated country gentleman who represents in a democratic Parliament the best traditions of our English aristocracy. How does such a man see the future of Conservatism, and in what spirit does he confront the increasing legions of Socialism?

He tells me that the value of the quiet man in the House of Commons, and probably in the country too, remains as high as ever, but democracies do not look about for a good leader and are inclined to take the noisiest person who with most assurance promises them the moon. In the same way, the House of Commons fills up for an orator who is sure to deliver a smashing attack, and empties when a man who knows his subject, but is no moonshine-seller, addresses the Chair. How it will end he cannot say. His disposition inclines him to think that humbugs are always found out at last; but his experience of men tells him that some humbugs

take a long time to be found out, especially by a democracy not very distinguished for discernment. On the
whole he shakes his head over the future, but not without a smile of amusement.

It is interesting to hear him speak with real friendliness of some of the Labour members, with an amused
kindliness of others, but with the quietest and calmest
contempt of the policy for which they all stand. This
contempt is inspired by the conviction that the policy
of Labour is fundamentally dishonest.

To Captain FitzRoy, with his calm judging eyes and
his imperturbable good nature the political situation
presents itself as a tangle which will not be straightened
out for some time, and which will leave behind it com-
plications of a disturbing character. He does not say
we are marching to perdition; but he does say that we
are very far from being on the road to sanity and prosperity. Things cannot go better with us, he thinks,
until we push sentimentalism out of our path, give up
wool-gathering, and address ourselves like practical
men to the facts of our situation. At the present
moment we are attempting to let Spenser's nymphs and
shepherds run our agriculture, and encouraging Russian
lunatics to run our industry. There is a sad un-English
touch of Watteau and Robespierre in our present
politics.

He thinks that in some measure the Conservative
Party is to blame for this state of things. The leader-

ship is not definite and determined enough to please him. "After all," he said to me one day, "politics is very like hunting a pack of hounds. If you want hounds to be keen and full of mettle you must give them blood. They get listless and apathetic if you don't. A pack that doesn't kill its fox, soon goes off colour. They must have blood."

The difficulties of leadership at the present time would, in his opinion be nothing like so great if advantage were taken of the opportunities for attack. He would like to see Labour well trounced in the House of Commons, and Socialism chased up and down the country. "The business of the Conservative Party," he says, "is to keep democracy well-informed, and to protect it from the cheapjacks and impostors of bunkum. It's a big job; but it's a clear duty."

When I have discussed with him the difficulties of such a crusade he has always insisted, in his quiet and unexaggerating way, that a man whom democracy trusts can always speak to it about the Empire. "I find in my village meetings," he tells me, "that someone there has relations in Canada, or New Zealand, or Australia, or in South Africa, and that everyone is willing to listen to a reasonable argument based upon the imperial character of our race. I never talk down to an audience. I tell them what I believe to be the facts of the British Empire, and I endeavour to make them think what the future of such an Empire may become.

As for social reform, there is nothing you cannot bring into a speech on Imperialism."

He regards the whole matter of Free Trade as a business question. He sees that there are considerable dangers in a general tariff. Each particular trade or industry should be judged, in his opinion, entirely on its own merits, with no reference whatever to a general principle supposed to govern the whole field of our commercial activity. "Act like men of business, not pedants," he says, and goes on to speak of Imperial Preference as a thing essential to the growth and development of our industry. "That's a thing we've got to preach up hill and down dale. It's our highroad to the future."

Agriculture is a matter on which he speaks with authority. "I don't answer for the figures," he said to me only the other day, "but according to an under-secretary in the present Government there are now only eight people in every hundred of our population who are engaged in agriculture. Cotton is King indeed! We have sacrificed the unequalled peasantry of this country in order to supply the pale and stunted population of Lancashire with white flour from over the seas. Well, I don't complain of free trade in grain; I accept it; I don't like it but I accept it; but I do say that if free trade in corn diminishes and weakens our rural population, it must be sound policy to subsidise agriculture, to increase small-holdings, and to lighten the monstrous rate now levied on land, so that the science may revive.   Surely the congestion in towns has reached a point to satisfy the most exigent of free traders; isn't it time we turned to re-populating the countryside?   I should have thought so."

You might discuss politics with this man for six weeks and never hear from him one word that betrayed his sympathy with the working-classes.   He does not talk in that vein.   But he does not advertise to the world his affection for his wife or his devotion to his children.   It is a part of the character of such a man not to play the mountebank to his deepest feelings.   He may admire the platform skill of Mr. Lloyd George, or the amusing energy of Pachmann at the piano; but he himself could no more bring himself even to attempt an imitation of the methods of these famous people, than he could talk noisily at his own table or behave showily in the public streets.

But one day, quite by chance, I discovered in him a depth of sympathy with the English people which, I confess, surprised me—as it also delighted me—for it was charged with admiration for their noblest qualities.

In September, 1914, he rejoined the Life Guards as a subaltern.   Two of his sons were fighting.   A third, destined too soon to give a young and most beautiful life for his country, was then at Oxford.   On November 6th, FitzRoy was with a composite regiment of cavalry reservists in Sanctuary Wood. The thunders of the first great Battle of Ypres filled the air and shook the earth. News came that the French troops had broken and run. The regiment in Sanctuary Wood mounted their horses and galloped forward a mile. Then they dismounted, lined out, and advanced in skirmishing order on foot. They advanced through the haggard and retreating French. Not one of them was shaken by that panic streaming past them to safety. On they went, to restore the line, to fill the gap left by the French between British troops and British troops.

They came to a small clearing between two battered woods, and halted. The line was restored. But just in front of them, not much more than a hundred yards away, were German machine-gunners, raking that whole front with a ceaseless fire.

"I don't believe anyone gave an order," FitzRoy told me. "It was one of those strange moments in a battle when bodies of men seem to be moved by a common impulse. The men went forward, straight at the Germans. I shall never forget them. Ever since then the British soldier has seemed to me the most wonderful fellow in the world. Nothing's too good for him—nothing! They went forward because they knew they had got to go forward. They'd have gone into hell; they would really. You never saw such calm; you never saw such determination. Men were falling like rabbits at every moment, rolling over and lying still, one after another, quick as lightning. You kept on saying to yourself—'Of course, this can't go on; I'm bound to go down. And soon; any minute; perhaps now.' But the line went on—on and on. I got a smack from a bullet; but it didn't hurt at the time; I was thinking of the men. Oh, wonderful fellows! the most wonderful fellows in the world! Something in their advance, something inexorable, something inevitable, seemed to get on the Germans' nerves. All of a sudden, Fritz jumped up and ran for his life. The Briton had beaten him."

I asked about his wound. "Oh, it was really nothing," he answered; "the only bother was lying in bloody sheets for a couple of days"; and once more he began to speak of the British soldier, of his unbreakable courage, his terrible determination, his bitter anger, his gay spirits, and his mordant wit—all learned in England, all learned in English homes.

"The Higher Command left much to be desired; but for the British soldier my admiration is boundless. He is not only a great hero, he has got an utter disregard of self, and at his best he is something that searches the heart of anyone who has served with him. The finest thing I can say of the British soldier is this, nothing in the world puts him out."

That conversation has haunted me for many days. It makes me wonder whether there has not been in the

Conservatism of late years something of the ineffi-
ciency of our Higher Command in the War, and too
little of the close comradeship between officer and man
in the trenches.

What might not the British nation accomplish in
the field of its imperial destinies if the straight and
upright gentlemen of England put their education, their
leisure, and their traditions at the disposal of democracy,
and, through the retreating and reactionary hordes of
an alien and class-hating Communism, advanced to fill
up the gaps, made by these recent troubled years, in the
great far-stretching line of our British unity?

Would that these words of Emerson could sink into
the mind and consciousness of every Englishman of
every class.

"The difference in rank does not divide the national
heart. . . . Each of them could at a pinch stand in
the shoes of the other; and they are more bound in
character than differenced in ability or rank. The
labourer is a possible lord. The lord is a possible
basket maker. Every man carries the English system
in his brain, knows what is confided to him and does
the best therein he can. The chancellor carries England
on his mace, the midshipman on the point of his dirk,
the smith on his hammer, the cook in the bowl of his
spoon; the postillion cracks his whip for England, and
the sailor times his oars to 'God Save the King!'
The very felons have their pride in each other's English

staunchness.　In politics and in war, they hold together as by hooks of steel.　The charm in Nelson's history is, the unselfish greatness; the assurance of being supported to the uttermost by those whom he supports to the uttermost.　Whilst they are some ages ahead of the rest of the world in the art of living; whilst in some directions they do not represent the modern spirit, but constitute it—this vanguard of civility and power they coldly hold, marching in phalanx, lock-step, foot after foot, file after file of heroes ten thousand deep."

SIR WILLIAM JOYNSON-HICKS

THE RT. HON. SIR WILLIAM JOYNSON-HICKS.
BART. (cr. 1919)

Born 1865. Son of Henry Hicks of Plaistow Hall, Kent. Assumed surname of Joynson on marriage, in 1895, to Grace Lynn, d. of the late Richard Hampson Joynson. Head of the Solicitors' firm of Joynson-Hicks, Hunt, Cardew and McDonald. M.P. for Brentford, 1911–18, for Twickenham, 1918–. Secretary Overseas Trade Department, 1922–23. Postmaster General and Paymaster General (in the Baldwin Cabinet), 1923–24. Financial Secretary to the Treasury, with Seat in Cabinet, 1923–24. Chairman Parliamentary Air Committee; Chairman of Parliamentary Road Transport Committee; Member Select Committee on Indian Affairs; and the Advisory Committee of the Ministry of Transport; Chairman of the Motor Legislation Committee; Member of the National Church Assembly; Honorary Treasurer of the Red Cross County of Middlesex; Member of the Finance Committee of the Y. W. C. A., and of the Zanana Bible and Medical Mission; president of the National Church League; Late Chairman of the Automobile Association; Chairman of the Belgian Field Ambulance Service; President of the Lancashire Commercial Motor Users Association; Vice President of the Roads Improvement Ass'n.; President of the National Threshing Owners Association; President of the National Traction Engine Ass'n.; Raised for the war in France the 17th and the 23rd Service Battalion of the Middlesex Regiment; Vice President of Safety First Council; First Chairman of the London Safety First Council; Vice President Institute of Transport. Clubs: Carlton, Bath, Constitutional.

© Vandyk

RT. HON. SIR WILLIAM JOYNSON-HICS, P.C.

IX

SIR WILLIAM JOYNSON-HICKS

Despatch is the soul of business.—CHESTERFIELD.

So the bruisers of England are come to be present at the grand fight speedily coming off. . . . There is Belcher, the younger, not the mighty one, who is gone to his place, but the Teucer Belcher, the most scientific pugilist that ever entered a ring, only wanting strength to be, I won't say what.—GEORGE BORROW.

A land may be covered with historic trophies, with museums of science and galleries of art, with universities and libraries; the people may be civilised and ingenious; the country may be even famous in the annals and action of the world, but, gentlemen, if the population every ten years decreases, and the stature of the race every ten years diminishes, the history of that country will soon be the history of the past.—DISRAELI.

AN interesting chapter might be written on solicitors. Their mental differences are as great but more subtle than their temperamental differences. They all change with the manners of the time but remain the same thing. In every generation they have their out-and-out rogues, their sly hypocrites, their down-at-heel failures whose

153

only office is a tavern or a stationer's shop, and their hard-swearing men of the world, who specialise in getting women out of scrapes and keeping the names of distinguished people out of the newspapers. On the whole, however, they are just and upright men, rendering civilisation an essential service, and may roughly be divided into two useful classes, the confidential friend of the family, and the powerful adviser of public companies.

It is to the latter class that Sir William Joynson-Hicks must be assigned, and in that honourable class he occupies an eminent position. With an infinite capacity for taking pains he is no genius, and probably entertains a supreme distrust for geniuses of every order. He is himself a practical man, and he likes to deal with practical men. Work is his passion, and he works magnificently. He does not believe in hair-splitting; but as regards head-hitting he is an enthusiast. Give him something to punch and he is the happiest man on earth. Offer him something to love and he might inquire if you were impertinently attempting to pull his leg. He is a Protestant of Protestants, and among the disciples of cold water he would always take the head of the table.

His biography largely consists of public service. He motors, shoots, and plays golf, but his heart and brain are absorbed in work. He has been, and still is, the chairman, the honorary treasurer, or a member of I know

not how many societies, institutions, and committees.
Look for him in the Threshing Owners' Association,
and he is there; in the Young Women's Christian Association, and he is there too. Seek him in the Zenana
Bible and Medical Mission, in the Motor Traction Committee, in the National Church Association, and in anything to do with roads and air, and, as sure as God's
in Gloucestershire, there you will find this steam-engine
of a man, puffing away like anything, and ready to pull
the whole movement to a practical terminus.

He learned his oratory as a boy on temperance plat-
forms, and still there clings to it the fervent character
of a moral enthusiasm. He does not so much abstain
from alcohol as hate it, and he hates it as a destroyer
of domestic happiness, an insidious enemy of health.
He wants men to be strong and happy, alert and energetic, free from all slaveries, and never in a condition
of spiritual fugginess or moral decrepitude. Whenever
he is speaking of these things one has the feeling that
he is about to take his coat off and go for the head
of a distiller or the stomach of a brewer. And it is the
same thing with his politics. Liberalism is the enemy.
Socialism is a liar and a traitor. Up, guards, and at 'em!

On occasion he can adopt a fatherly attitude even to
opponents, and there is a story on this head which is
worth the telling. It is said that he was one night
addressing an audience of working-men on the matter
of taxation, and laid himself out to explain to them

the fallacious character of socialistic economics. "Now you have all heard," he said, or so the story goes, "a great deal about unearned increment. It is a favourite phrase with Socialists. But what does it mean? What is unearned increment? Does any man in this audience know what it means?" "Yuss, I do!" replied a voice. "Come along then; tell us what it is; what is unearned increment?" "It's the 'yphen between the Joynson and the 'Icks."

But as a rule Sir William does not indulge in paternal kindliness. His whole nature is corded together by that vigorous form of Protestantism which Matthew Arnold described as the dissidence of dissent. He might be tempted in a leisure moment to develop "a system of unsectarian religion from the Life of Mr. Pickwick," but in his working hours he is fighting with all his force those enemies of Puritan England who, in his judgment, would reduce her to spiritual flabbiness and mental parasitism.

His Conservatism has all the moral qualities of Bright's Liberalism, and a good deal of the Puritan enthusiasm which once inspired the youthful minds of Mr. Asquith and Mr. Lloyd George. He looks, as Dizzy looked, but with an altogether different vision, for the strength of England "in what is more powerful than laws and institutions, and without which the best laws and the most skilful institutions may be a dead letter or the very means of tyranny, in 'the national character. It is not in the increased feebleness of its institutions," said Dizzy, "that I see the peril of England: it is in the decline of its character as a community."

Sir William Joynson-Hicks, "Jix," as he is compendiously called in the House of Commons, holds the opinion that Socialism is a form of alcohol, and that its poisonous and subversive doctrines are everywhere intoxicating the brain and sapping the moral fibres of the nation. Burke's magnificent tribute to "the ancient and inbred integrity, piety, good nature, and good humour of the people of England," can no longer be uttered with a whole heart by any man who knows the country. A large body of the people has adopted the deliberately dishonest policy of ca'canny, has ranged itself on the side of impiety and the grossest materialism, has exchanged its good nature for hatred, and its good humour for a cynical bitterness. "The various classes of this country," as Dizzy foretold, "are arrayed against each other." We live in a condition of civil war. The sense of unity is lost. The feeling of brotherhood is gone. We are not marching to a destiny; we are shambling and slipping into anarchy.

For this state of things in England, Liberalism was first responsible, and now Socialism. The crime of both parties, in his opinion, is the unforgivable crime of deceiving the people. They have taught the multitude to believe that the Conservative is the champion of vested interests, tied hand and foot to the brewer, the landowner, and the parson; and they have encouraged the masses to believe that political materialism can give them spiritual happiness, and that they, these dishonest politicians for ever moulding the hypocrisies of sentimentalism and the saliva of demagogic rabies, are the only men in the State who sympathise with human suffering.

"Out upon such rascals!" is the cry of Joynson-Hicks, and he refuses to listen to those who would give the Labour Government more rope to hang themselves withal. He himself would do the hanging, and now at once; and gladly would he exhibit the dangling corpse to the multitude whom it so basely tricked and deceived at the last election, and whose sufferings it intends to use only for its own sordid communistic plots. Not one scrap of sympathy will he give the Labour Government, not one allowance will he make for its difficulties. In his eyes, Labour is a canting hypocrite of the worst possible kind, and the most deadly enemy of the people of England.

Take the case of housing. The domestic happiness of the nation depends upon a plentiful supply of cheap good houses. Cheap good houses are essential to the moral character of the rising generation. The middle-classes, the lower middle-classes, and the working-classes, are suffering very dreadful things, suffering physically and morally, from this dearth of cheap good

houses. Why cannot they be built? No landowner
is holding up sites. No builder is unwilling to take
a contract. Materials are not withheld by any ring.
They cannot be built because the Building Operatives
Union—the bricklayers, the slaters, the carpenters, the
painters, and the plumbers—refuse to take more men
into their union. Old men who never raised one finger
to help this country in the war have banged, barred,
and bolted the door of their union against young men
who fought, and suffered, and were wounded in order
that their country might be free.

The Conservative Government strove in vain to bring
this union to reason, and it was against the stubborn
opposition of the building operatives to dilution that
they built thousands of working-class houses. But the
Labour Government, which preaches working-class
solidarity, and got into power largely by abuse of the
Conservatives for their housing policy, and which has
the means of bringing this recalcitrant, anti-social, and
most selfish union to a sense of its public duty, has done
nothing in that direction, nothing strong and nothing
effective.

Moreover, as a practical man who orders his life
by the principles of what is called horse-sense, Joynson-
Hicks is outraged by the thought that this great country
should be governed for a day by men who fear trade
prosperity lest it should strengthen Capitalism, and who
are opposed to strengthening the unity of the Empire

lest it should delay a World Republic. How is he to believe in the good sense of the English people when they can tolerate for an hour such traitors as these at the head of their affairs?

His mind is as different as anything one can imagine from the mind of Mr. Edward Wood or the mind of Mr. Baldwin. In him one catches glimpses of a Conservatism which is at once old-fashioned—of the stern unbending order—and extremely modern. He is as go-ahead a person as one could meet, ready to undertake at a moment's notice any social reform that is practical and of general service to the community, but a man so set to hold no truck with the enemy, so pugilistic in his manner of clearing obstacles out of his way, that he does not, I think, clearly see the causes of our present discontents, and so does not give to democracy the feeling that he knows the way to a better order.

It is no bad thing to have in the counsels of Conservatism a man who is apt, perhaps, to regard the British Empire as a capable company-promoter regards a valuable commercial undertaking. Such a man may not inspire, but he may well prevent the man of imagination from entering upon hazardous courses. So long as he is morally strong, and so long as personal ambition does not render him suspicious to friends and foes, such a man may render great service to his party and some service to the higher life of the human race.

MR. OLIVER STANLEY

THE HON. OLIVER STANLEY

Born 1896. Second son of the 17th Earl of Derby and Lady Alice Maude Olivia Montague, d. of the 7th Duke of Manchester. Had service in France during the late War. Conservative Candidate for the Kendal Division of Westmoreland. Married, 1922, Lady Helen Vane-Tempest Stewart.

THE HON. OLIVER STANLEY

X

MR. OLIVER STANLEY

Come, give us a taste of your quality.—SHAKESPEARE.

Neither in the name of the Multitude do I only include the base and minor sort of people; there is a Rabble even amongst the Gentry, a sort of Plebian heads, whose fancy moves with the same wheel as these; men in the same level with Mechanicks, though their fortunes do somewhat guild their infirmities, and their purses compound for their follies.—SIR THOMAS BROWNE.

Although it is humiliating to confess, yet I do confess that cleanliness and order are not matters of instinct; they are matters of education, and like most great things—mathematics and classics—you must cultivate a taste for them.—DISRAELI.

IT is thought by many good judges that Mr. Oliver Stanley, the second son of Lord Derby, is the most promising of our politicians among the younger Conservatives. His mind is certainly interesting. He has qualities which are singularly attractive. Moreover, he is only eight-and-twenty, and in spite of having fought in the War, keeps much of his boyishness. His

163

contemporaries will see what time makes of him, and what he makes of time. For myself, I am disposed to feel that his personality lacks that irresistible strength and that furious drive of a consuming ambition which make the great leader in modern times.

His interest for me lies in the philosophical character of his Conservatism. He is above all things a thinker. One feels in talking to him that he is a very young don who has recently won the blue ribbon of scholarship, and is so modest about it that he blushes whenever he utters even an ordinary opinion. Never once does he startle or electrify. Stridency is not in his mind, nor violence of any kind in his soul. Quietly he looks upon life, quietly he reflects upon it, quietly he tells you where he thinks it might be bettered.

He is well over six-feet in height, three or more inches above that noble altitude; but he carries himself as if he wishes he were five-feet eight. The same spirit of wishing to escape notice appears in his face, which is handsome enough to please a Victorian male novelist, but lacks that aquiline fierceness and cave-man brutality so dear to the Georgian lady novelist. It is the face of a boy. The skin has all the freshness and smoothness of youth; the round eyes, in spite of a certain mischievousness, are rather shy and self-conscious. The smiling mouth appears to be at present a little uncertain of its own character, while the chin would rather recede lamentably than have any "punch" in it. Thick brown hair, disposed to cluster into curls, gives to this round and boyish face, with its prominent eyes and its radiant skin, the look of Byron in his teens—

> Before Decay's effacing fingers
> Have swept the lines where beauty lingers.

It is difficult to realise that Mr. Stanley is a married man devoted to the middle-aged satisfactions of domestic life; or to understand that he has inherited in full measure his family's affection for horses, and loves to find himself well-mounted in full chase of a fox. Always the impression he makes in serious conversation is that of a shy and reticent scholar who has found all that he asks of life in some cool corner of a beautiful Oxford college.

That such a man should have made already some mark in the world is a hopeful sign. It encourages a faint hope that democracy may one day lose patience with the moonshine-seller, and give its thoughtful attention to men who, inspired by true humaneness have set their reasons to solve the political problems of our complex and industrialised society. The cave-man of politics is not, I think, quite so great a force in the national life as he was before the advent of a Labour Government; but it must, one supposes, be many years before the true and earnest thinker is regarded as a heaven-sent leader by the rabble of all classes. At the moment a thinker in politics is respected rather than followed, tolerated rather than taken seriously.

Mr. Stanley was at school in 1914. He went straight from the cloister and chapel to the trenches in France. Up to this time he had been interested in politics, but in France he found himself thinking things out with an unusual determination to find a straight road to social betterment. He hated war, and began to think how so foul and atrocious a barbarism might be expelled from the earth. He still dreams of the Great War, or rather that another Great War has come, and that he cannot bring himself to face it. From the time he went out to France till the day on which he was wounded, he never actually shook in his boots or felt that the strain of horror was more than he could endure; but now, long afterwards, in these occasional dreams of his, he is conscious of a physical and spiritual inability to face again the dreadful beastliness of those direful days.

Few men, I think, have more patiently examined the idea of a league of nations. If he could see hope of peace in such a league he would certainly give himself up to work for its establishment. But he has come to the conclusion, he tells me, that such a league must remain ineffective for this great purpose until the democracy of the world is solidly and enthusiastically behind it.

I told him what Edward Wood had said to me on

this matter, viz., that since Europe had shown no desire for peace when it was animated by affection for one common centre of loyalty, the Church, it is difficult to see how men can now find in the present revival of nationalism, and all the fierce clashes of competitive commerce, a common consecration for a league of peace.

Mr. Stanley replied, "But the Church did not attempt to get democracy on its side, did it? It was an autocracy. It dictated to the peoples of Europe what they must think and how they must act. I do not think that any body of men can give orders in these matters. Don't you think that democracy must want things before it can get them?"

He told me that the result of his hard thinking in France was to convince him of one most pressing need in the affairs of men—the need of education. It is not, he thinks, class distinction, or even difference in fortune, which keeps people apart, but intellectual inequality. He has arrived at this remarkable conclusion that while there may be comradeship between the educated man and the ignorant man, there cannot be any real and effective comradeship between the educated man and the half-educated man.

Almost all our problems, he thinks, have their rise in this purely spiritual region. Society has said to the child of the ignorant man, "We will teach you to read and to write; and as soon as we have dragged you out of the ignorance in which your parents live, we will abandon you to the struggle for existence.   You will be neither ignorant nor educated.   Your contact with nature will be broken, but no contact will be established for you with culture.   You will lose your father's peace and your mother's contentment; you will no longer be able to find satisfaction in the simple things which gave them pleasure.   On the contrary, your mind will be filled with unrest, discontent, and cynicism; you will go through life unconscious of the beauty of the earth, the majesty of the heavens, and the glory of art; you will discover that nothing is worth your while; you will look upon culture as an affectation, upon religion as a form of hypocrisy, and upon patriotism as a political dodge.   And in these delusions you will give yourself either to the vulgar imitations of snobbery or to the excitements of political agitation.   So living, you will pass through life in a daze, and die without peace in your mind or gratitude in your heart."

Let me quote Disraeli, who has exercised a powerful influence on Oliver Stanley's mind:—

A man who knows nothing but the history of the passing hour, who knows nothing of the history of the past, but that a certain person whose brain was as vacant as his own occupied the same house as himself, who in a moment of despondency or of gloom has no hope in the morrow because he has read nothing that has taught him that the morrow has any changes—that man, compared with him who has read the most ordinary abridgment of history, or the most common philosophical speculation, is as distinct and different an animal as if he had fallen from some other planet, was influenced by a different organisation, working for a different end, and hoping for a different result. It is knowledge that equalises the social condition of man—that gives to all, however different their political position, passions which are in common, and enjoyments which are universal.

Over and over again Disraeli sounded this note, and warned the Conservatives of his day that they had no greater enemy in the State than ignorance. He said he looked for power in "the invigorating energies of an educated and enfranchised people." He did not fear "public opinion," but "public passion." "I, for one," he says, "have no faith in the remedial qualities of a government carried on by a neglected democracy, who for three centuries have received no education."

Again: "Europe is not happy. Amid its false excitement, its bustling invention, and its endless toil, a profound melancholy broods over its spirit and gnaws at its heart. In vain they baptise their tumult by the name of Progress; the whisper of a demon is ever asking them, 'Progress from whence, and to what?'"

And finally: "It has been my lot to have found myself in many distant lands. I have never been in one without finding a Scotsman, and I never found a Scotsman who was not at the head of the poll—he was prosperous; he was thriving; often the confidential adviser of persons of the highest position, even of rulers of States; and although I myself am inclined to attribute much to organisation and race, I am bound to say I never met a Scotsman, even if he were the confidential adviser of a pasha, who did not tell me he owed his rise to his parish school."

Mr. Stanley is now the honorary secretary and treasurer of the British Institute of Adult Education, founded by Dr. Albert Mansbridge. He has edited a book called *The Way Out*, to which Lord Haldane, Lord Grey of Fallodon, Professor Zimmern, and Lord Eustace Percy have contributed; a volume worthy of every serious politician's notice. He is convinced that there is no greater matter to which statesmen can now give their attention than this matter of facilitating in every possible and attractive way the adult education of the people.

Ignorance, in the beautiful atmosphere of nature, acquires a wisdom and a serenity of spirit which keep the heart sweet and the mind sensible: but ignorance in the depressing and demoralising atmosphere of a manufacturing town can never find in a broken and incomplete education either wisdom or serenity. The mind of an office-boy or a lift-girl, is not the mind of a great nation.

Mr. Stanley's political principles can also be expressed in a Disraelian phrase. He tells me that he is a Conservative because he believes in strengthening our institutions, increasing the liberty of the subject, and furthering the social welfare of the people. He says that these three things are co-relatives. Socialism seeks the last of them, but it is indifferent to the first, antagonistic to the second. "I do not see that it is possible," he says, "for a man to be happy without personal freedom, nor how it is possible to have personal freedom without Parliamentary institutions. Russia has discovered that personal freedom must be sacrificed, and slavery brought back to earth, if the principles of Communism are to operate; she freely acknowledges that fact, and the extreme Labour men in this country are never tired of abusing our institutions, because those institutions protect the people against the despotism they long to exercise. Therefore it is not immodest for the Conservative to say that he is on the side of human liberty against the forces of State slavery."

In the matter of social reform, he is, first of all, enthusiastic about education. Then comes housing— the rebuilding of the homes of the people, the destruction of all that is ugly and sordid and squalid in our towns and cities. Then comes Insurance; he is converted to the virtues of what is called the All-In Insurance which is a popular topic in the north. Finally he claims it as the right and duty of a Conservative to keep a watchful eye on the use the manufacturers are making of their power, and to interfere as often as the circumstances justify between the employer and employed. He feels strongly that the Conservative Party is responsible for the humaneness of English life.

He holds the interesting idea that Conservatism is something much more than a principle in politics. He regards it as the religion of social life. It is a spirit drawing men together into a sensible comradeship and uniting them for great and noble purposes. He thinks that this view of Conservatism would be more general, and better comprehended by democracy, if men who call themselves Conservatives practised Conservatism in their relations with other men. He would like to see the Conservative manufacturer practising the humaneness and the comradeship of Conservatism towards his employed people, and every qualified man of leisure lending a hand to improve the education and the social conditions of the poor. Every Conservative should make his Conservatism tell in all the relations of his social life. It ought to be a social expression of his patriotism.

There are no Die-Hards in the north, he tells me. Up there Conservatism is represented by an active, enthusiastic, and forward-looking body of men and women who believe that with strong leadership and a disciplined and educated party, Conservatism can do far more than the other parties for the good of the whole people. What the serious and responsible person is now asking for is confidence. He wants to feel that life is not in the melting pot. No party is so likely as the Conservative Party to bring back to the nation a sense of that well-founded security and that abiding order which gave confidence to the creative energies of the Victorians.

"In one thing," he said to me, "I think our party lags behind the Labour organisation. I find that a local secretary in the Labour movement regards himself as a potential member of Parliament, and is always straining forward to justify this promotion. He reads, he discusses, he thinks, and he works hard. But our local secretaries are not encouraged to nurse so ambitious a dream. They are a somewhat depressed body of men. I think that if our headquarters people were looking out for first-rate men, and were always ready to encourage talent and to promote genius, we should more readily convert democracy to the truth that we are essentially a people's party. I should like to see more enthusiasm and more intelligence in our propaganda."

But he comes back to education for his final word: "The basis of Conservatism is helping a man to help himself. The whole idea of our party is based upon the notion that self-reliance is essential to the moral character of a man, and that it is the business of the State to help men to become self-reliant. In what better way can this need be reached than by education? A man who is educated can not only help himself to get on in the world, but can find pleasures and consolations which have no existence at all for the half-educated man. I believe in better education for children, and in every possible extension of adult education. Dizzy emphasised this point so often. He said that the three objects sought by Conservatism are the maintenance of our institutions, the preservation of our Empire, and the improvement of the condition of the people; and he said that we could only hope for the first two by seeking in education the road to the third. The more I study the works of Dizzy the more do I feel how far he was ahead of all the Liberals and Conservatives of his day. He saw far, and he saw deeply."

I find in him no disposition to adopt Sir Robert Horne's attitude towards Liberalism. This was his comment on the views expressed in my second chapter: "No doubt there is an historical basis for what Sir Robert says; but I think it is wiser to acknowledge that Liberalism has contributed many great and noble ideas to the life of humanity; and certainly, as a Conservative who follows Dizzy, I would do nothing to hinder any approach towards co-operation on the part of sincere and honourable Liberals. The future seems to me as if it would have no room for any parties except Constitutionalists and Socialists. It would be very stupid, I think, to split the forces of Constitutionalism, and to spend time, that ought to be devoted to strengthening our discipline and discharging our duties, in quarrelling over the origins of Toryism and Whiggery. I don't think scoring points gets us any further. I feel that our first task is to enlighten the electorate on the great differences which separate Constitutionalism from Revolutionism, to awaken them to the danger that threatens us all, to gain their confidence, and then to work steadily and wholeheartedly for a better order of things, a higher order of citizens."

It seems to me that the headquarters of the Unionist Party might be well-advised to get a body of educated young men from the public schools and the universities to go round the industrial centres explaining the principles of Conservatism to the working-classes. At the head of such an order of preaching friars, Oliver Stanley, with his sympathetic nature, his moderation, and his penetrating intelligence, would do much to destroy the dangerous propaganda of Socialism.

He will soon be coming to Westminster from Westmorland, and though modesty may keep him from the notice of his countrymen for some years, I do not think much water will flow under the bridges before his moral and intellectual influence is felt among the younger men of the Conservative Party.

Some men who strike one as little likely to take Socialism by the throat may perhaps do more than others to persuade and convert the most honest of its deluded disciples. I am quite sure that Oliver Stanley will antagonise nobody, and will win the respect and affection of good men in all parties. He will go slowly, but I think he will go far.

CONCLUSION

ENGLAND

I see her not dispirited, not weak, but well remembering that she has seen dark days before; indeed, with a kind of instinct that she sees a little better in a cloudy day, and that in storm of battle and calamity she has a secret vigour and a pulse like cannon. I see her in her old age, not decrepit, but young, and still daring to believe in her power of endurance and expansion . . . with strength still equal to the time, still wise to entertain and swift to execute the policy which the mind and heart of mankind require at the present time.—EMERSON in 1856.

Physically and morally it is a very healthy country.—PRINCE VON BÜLOW in 1899.

. . . bring up our children with reverence for English history and in the awe of English literature. This is the only job now in the world worth the whole zeal and energy of all first-class, thoroughbred English-speaking men.—WALTER H. PAGE in 1916.

CONCLUSION

From these glimpses of various minds the reader who has not hitherto taken any particular interest in political differences may be able, I hope, to form a useful idea of modern Conservatism. He will see that certain definite principles govern the Conservative thesis of social development, and that however the temperaments of individual Conservatives may vary, and however their opinions may clash, those principles are common to all.

Between Mr. Edward Wood and the Duke of Northumberland there exists a close likeness in physical circumstances, but no intellectual likeness at all; between the Duke and Sir William Joynson-Hicks, on the other hand, there is no resemblance in heredity and tradition, but a notable intellectual resemblance; Mr. Stanley Baldwin's early circumstances, training, and traditions are very unlike the early circumstances, training, and traditions of Sir Robert Horne, and their intellectual and temperamental differences remain to this day extremely dissimilar; yet these two men, and the others I have just mentioned, and all the men whose opinions are expressed in this book, find in their political thinking that a distinct body of principles unites them together and enables them to act as a single political force in the national life.

We may say that at the centre of Conservative thinking is the idea of unity, and that the impulse of Conservative action is to promote unity in every sphere of the national life, extending it steadily and naturally until it includes the entire commonwealth of free people which we call the British Empire.

This spirit of unity, it is believed, can strengthen and develop all those minor and sectional loyalties which play so useful a part in the social life of the nation. Conservatism declares its faith in an ideal which is comprehensible to the simplest intelligence and by no means beyond the reach of human accomplishment; it is the ideal of a united people consciously, deliberately, and peacefully extending its power in the world—extending that power in the region of trade, in the region of science, in the region of art, and in the region of character; seeking to impress upon the civilisation of mankind the stamp of its historic genius for good government, good humour, good sense, and good nature, until the whole world is of one mind on the fundamental things of human life.

Conservatism pursues this ideal on the high road of history. It refuses to take any short-cuts to millennium, or to waste any of its time in vain speculations concerning abstract questions. It is of all the schools of political thought in the world the most practical. It has no liking for pedants; it is contemptuous of cranks; and it will have no truck with political emotionalists. It believes that the road to the future is clearly marked, and that it is no smooth and pleasant road, but intentionally and usefully a road full of hardship and difficulty, not a track for sheep, but a road that calls out of a man all that is best and strongest in human nature.

The attitude of Conservatism towards change and progress is governed by the conviction that self-reliance, personal liberty, and as free a field as possible for the exercise of exceptional qualities, are essential to the moral and intellectual life of the whole nation. It believes that the State should help men to be self-reliant, should fit them to develop within themselves those powers of mind and soul which alone can render them free and independent; but it also believes that the State should interfere to prevent any individual from using either his gifts or his financial power to the detriment of others.

By reminding men of the greatness of their forefathers and by calling upon them to realise the glory and the blessing of their heritage, it seeks to lift up the soul of man from all forms of selfishness, from all narrowing and sordid economic obsessions, and to give it something to live for which is worthy of a man's love and which provides him with a rational thesis for human existence.

The great word on its lips is the word Duty. It does not stoop to flatter, it does not wish to deceive, it does not seek to infuriate and excite the passions of the ignorant and the half-educated. It appeals to what is best in man's nature—to his moral strength, to his spiritual self-respect, to his human kindness—and it bids men rise to a level of self-forgetfulness from which they can see the path of their duty stretching to the land of their children's glory.

Disraeli has defined the spirit of Conservatism in these words: "To build up a community, not upon Liberal opinions, which any man may fashion to his fancy, but upon popular principles, which assert equal rights, civil and religious; to uphold the institutions of the country because they are the embodiment of the wants and wishes of the nation and protect us alike from individual tyranny and popular outrage; . . . to be vigilant to guard, and prompt to vindicate the honour of the country, but to hold aloof from that turbulent diplomacy which only distracts the mind of a people from internal improvement; to lighten taxation; frugally, but wisely, to administer the public treasure; to favour public education, because it is the best guarantee for public order; to defend local government, and to be as jealous of the rights of the working-man as of the prerogatives of the crown and the

privileges of the senate—these were once the principles which regulated Tory statesmen, and I, for one,
have no wish that the Tory Party should ever be in
power unless they practice them."

Conservatism seeks to establish security, confidence,
and peace; to create, that is, the only atmosphere in
which men can do fruitful work; and it seeks the
prosperity of British trade and the union of the British
Empire because it desires to increase the independence,
the self-respect, the security, and the domestic happiness of the working-classes, and to possess revenues
sufficient for the three great branches of its social
policy—better houses, better health, and better education.

Now the Socialist mind, even at its best, is the
very antipodes of the Conservative mind. It may
express itself in language not unlike the language of
Conservatism, and it may profess a faith which has
certain points of resemblance with the faith of Conservatism; but penetrate to the principles which inspire
it, track down its pious utterances to the source of all
its thinking, and one discovers that the Socialist is no
ally of the Conservative, marching side by side with
him to a common goal, but rather an enemy standing
directly in the path of the nation, not merely obstruct-
ing its way but actually plotting its destruction.

"It is a matter of infinite difficulty, but fortunately
of comparative indifference," says Coleridge, "to deter-

mine what a man's motive may have been for this or that particular action. Rather seek to learn what his objects in general are—what does he habitually wish, habitually pursue?—and thence deduce his impulses, which are commonly the true, efficient causes of men's conduct, and without which the motive itself would not have become a motive."

Fundamental to the thinking of the Socialist, I find three principles: fear of greatness, distrust of human nature, faith in political machinery. He inherits the thinking of the old Liberals. He has no feeling for the Empire, no love of individual men; all his actions are governed by a pedantic enthusiasm for academic ideas. The Liberals would not interfere with the management of factories, and ridiculed Disraeli's health legislation as "a policy of sewage"; their enthusiasm was given to the disestablishment of churches, the immediate granting of self-government to any people whose agitators asked for it, and the continued extension of the franchise. With this statesmanship went a propaganda of abuse. The Conservatives were held up to the contempt of uninformed people as the champions of vested interests.

Socialists have continued this line of thought. They say that both Liberals and Conservatives have a vested interest in darkness, both are damnably *bourgeois*, and if there is anything to choose between the two of them, the Liberal is the greater enemy of the proletariat than the Conservative. They do not bother their heads about advocating the abolition of the House of Lords or the disestablishment of the Church, but declare their intention to get rid of all Parliamentary institutions, which, they say, have outlived their day, and to sweep the present solid economic basis of human society into the limbo of exploded theories and decayed superstitions.

They do not seek to make men happy, but to invent an entirely new form of political machinery. They regard enterprise in the individual as a crime, self-reliance as a form of priggishness, and thrift as a piece of selfishness. Their idea is to crush all these natural springs of human action out of the mind, and to set up on the earth a great wheel of monotony and mediocrity to which the bodies of men may be bound from the cradle to the grave. Their Garden of Eden is a place where there is no serpent of ambition; but where nothing grows, nothing changes, nothing happens; all the flowers are made of paper and all the vegetables of plasticene. Their Marathon Race has its goal at its starting point, and there the emotions of the human heart and the ambitions of the human mind are to be pegged down for ever more. Evolution is to cease. The dictatorship of the proletariat is to supplant the Will of God.

But these aims of Socialism are not clear to the multitude. The issue is confused by the complexities of the present situation.

The Labour Party, having spent many years in denouncing the other political parties for refusing to do this, that, and the other thing, suddenly finds itself unexpectedly in power, and utterly unable to do any of those very things for not doing which it denounced its opponents with such outrageous vehemence. It has now discovered that its opponents did not refuse to do things which they might have done, but that they were unable to do things which cannot be done without ruin to the State. Disillusioned and timid, bewildered by the facts of economic law, appalled and unnerved by the practical conditions of human life, these visionaries and agitators of Labour have swung completely round from the fiery position they so recently occupied as champions of the oppressed proletariat, and, expressing a pained surprise that the world should expect them to practice what they have preached, conduct themselves as the capitalistic trustees and the bourgeois guardians of a State founded upon the principles of individualism and private enterprise.

For the nonce the Labour Party is a party of moderation, and some of its members are now genuinely converted to moderation; but the more vigorous minds, and the intelligences most thoroughly besotted with the pedantry of socialistic economics, are only wearing moderation as a mask. I have taken great pains to ascertain the truth in this matter, and in my opinion it is beyond dispute that the moderation of Labour is only an exhibition of tactics, masking a policy which is directed to the complete destruction of the present individualistic basis of human society.

I put entirely on one side the utterances and the actions of extremists. I am not speaking of the Irishmen in Glasgow who are drilling for a revolution of physical violence, nor of those feverish enthusiasts of atheism who are corrupting the minds of children in Socialistic Sunday Schools, nor of such Communists as those who publish prurient books exalting free love and degrading marriage; dangerous as these people are, and fatal as they would like to be to the greatness of this country, their violent opinions are not necessary to my argument.

The point I desire to establish is this: no influence now at work in our midst is more perilous to the welfare of the nation, that is to say, to the physical and moral welfare of all classes in the community, but in particular the wage-earning classes, than the influence of moderate and respectable Labour. For, however reasonable or merely stupid their proposals may seem to be, the whole spirit and energy of Labour is directed to the inflaming of sectional passion and the fomenting of class hatred. At a time when it is essential to the national welfare that employers and employed should be of one mind, and that complete confidence should take the place of brooding and poisonous suspicion between them: at a time, too, when everyone who loves his country and feels the greatness of England in his blood, and sees how long a time must elapse before Europe recovers from her ruin, should be working with all his heart and with all his soul for the unity of the Empire, Labour, if it is not actually doing everything in its power to keep employers and employed apart, and everything in its power to drive our Dominions into the arms of our market-hunting enemies, is at least doing nothing whatever to bring employers and employed together, and nothing whatever to consummate the unity of the Empire.

The spirit of Labour makes for, and is intended to make for, unrest, discontent, suspicion, and disunion. It derives its strength at the present time from the failure of the capitalist to solve, at a single stroke, the post-war economic problems arising from the dishonest currencies of many principal nations. It does not wish the capitalist system to succeed. It is the capitalist system which it is set to destroy. It is necessary to the success of its propaganda that unemployment should continue, that the cost of living should be high, that wages should fall, that strikes should recur, and that the foremost organising brains in the nation should be disheartened. Among the noblest spirits in its ranks are men whose books and pamphlets tell the workers that there is no sin, but, on the contrary, great virtue in slowing down production and giving the employers a dishonest day's work for an honest day's pay. Among ministers of the Crown are men whose published writings and public speeches are crammed with incitements to the workers to destroy the works of capitalism. The Prime Minister himself, a religious man and a real statesman of tactical moderation, has published a book on Socialism in which condemnation of the present individualistic system of society is expressed without compromise of any kind.

How can we expect the nation to prosper if a Party actuated by such motives is in charge of its future? Moderation is not in the minds of these men; it is merely a mask worn on their faces. They are deceiving the nation while they are establishing a grip on the machinery of its government. They have deliberately decided to lull the electorate into a doze of unsuspecting good-will; and while they protest in secret to their extremists that they are only biding their time, they are counting on a majority at the next election which will enable them to begin gradually the constructive work of establishing a slave State.

I am one of those who think that no great harm could come to the nation from the first five or ten years of socialistic legislation. I mean that society could continue to support the present population of these islands, and to pay its way, albeit with increasing difficulty, while the Socialist Government was nationalising the mines, the railways, and perhaps even the land. But

I am convinced that while such legislation as this could not greatly, or at any rate fatally, injure the national prosperity, the very fact that a Socialist Government was in power with a working majority, and a Socialist Government doing nothing to establish confidence between Capital and Labour, nothing to increase the unity of the Empire, and showing more boldly every day that its axe was laid at the root of individualism, would shatter the greatness of this country at the very outset.

It is not the first doings of Socialism that will break us, but its spirit; and that spirit is at work in our midst at the present moment, fettered, it is true, and functioning with difficulty, but at work in the nation. Let it grow in strength and we shall fall into ruin. These islands will become a Russian bear-garden. Trade will cease; the population will starve; armed violence will rend the nation from top to bottom, and the statesmen of Socialism will be crossing the Atlantic Ocean to beg the help of American capitalists to save their economics from destruction.

Further, the Labour Party encourages the working-classes to brood upon the devitalising idea that they are wage-slaves, encourages them always to be mindful of their wrongs, teaches them a form of auto-suggestion which is fatal to mental health and physical energy. The anger and bitterness of our working-classes, their suspiciousness and their lack of all heartiness and good-

will, are much more the result of political auto-
suggestion than the infliction of an economic system.
If medical science teaches us that dark and unhappy
thoughts are injurious to health, how can the Labour
Party hope to improve the welfare of the wage-earners
by encouraging them always to look upon the black side
of things and always to think of themselves as the ex-
ploited victims of another class? Is it possible for any
man, day after day, week after week, deliberately to
practise ca' canny without suffering both in mind and
body? Is it not true that the Labour Party, in taking
the joy out of every man's work and breeding mistrust
between employer and employed, is lowering the national vitality and creating a spirit of discord and disunion in our midst which is as bad for the workers as it
is for the employers? Must we not say that men who
spend their lives in teaching their fellows to entertain
gloomy and bitter thoughts are either very ignorant or
shamefully dishonest?

The fallacy of the Socialist is the fallacy of Mr.
H. G. Wells and all other men who have fallen under
the mechanistic theories of materialistic science. The
soul of man does not interest the Socialist. He is
unaware of personality. He can see nothing, this
pedant, but the bodies of men and women, bodies that
can be moved here and there like the cannon-fodder
of Prussian militarism. He believes, in his madness,
that by subjecting these mechanical bodies to the disci-

pline of a theorising bureaucracy he can not only provide sufficient and increasing wealth for the needs of our huge population, but can destroy in the human mind its desire for self-expression, and its immemorial passion for freedom and for growth.

He is a hater of genius, and the champion of pliant mediocrity. He is out to degrade the highest, and to enchain the strongest, not to strengthen the inefficient. For the humble and meek he has the ferocious contempt of all violent minds. His desire is to put down the noble from their seats, and to exalt the incompetent and the weak.

To this end he goes up and down the country looking for misery and searching for wrong. To this end, and only to this end, he sympathises with suffering and expresses indignation against oppression. To this end, the setting up of a bureaucratic despotism, he inflames the anger of the depressed and organises the cupidity of the incompetent.

With such a spirit as this in England, how can the nation expect its commerce to revive, its art to flourish, its virtue to develop, and its place at the head of civilisation to go unchallenged by lesser peoples? We are not marching towards our destiny, but tossing on a bed in a fever hospital. The frankness and candour of our nation, its outspoken honesty, its strong good sense, its kindly good-humour, and even its intrepid courage, are deserting us in the hour of our crisis. We are becoming an Ireland, and Socialism's purpose is to make us a Russia.

Unless all that is strong, self-reliant, moral, and kindly in the nation soon exerts itself with renewed energy and a fully-awakened intelligence to destroy this spirit of class-hatred, suspicion, and atheistical materialism, our trade will leave us, our population will become impoverished, and we shall fall into such disunion and decay as that which opened the gates of Rome to Alaric, and enabled Lenin to compass the destruction of Russia with German gold. No nation divided against itself can long stand in such an economic storm as is now ravaging the world.

Sad will it be for us and for many peoples,. and for many great causes, if it can ever truly be said of England, the weary Titan, staggering under the too vast orb of her fate, that she—

> Scarce comprehending the voice
> Of her greatest golden-mouthed sons
> Of a former age any more,
> Stupidly travels her round
> Of mechanic business, and lets
> Slow die out of her life
> Glory, and genius, and joy.